Smells

Smells

A Cultural History of Odours in Early Modern Times

Robert Muchembled

Translated by Susan Pickford

polity

First published in French as *La civilisation des odeurs (XVIe – début XIXe siècle)* © 2017, Société d'édition Les Belles Lettres, 95, Boulevard Raspail, 75006 Paris
This English edition © Polity Press, 2020

Polity Press
65 Bridge Street
Cambridge CB2 1UR, UK

Polity Press
101 Station Landing
Suite 300
Medford, MA 02155, USA

ISBN-13: 978–1–5095–3677–1
ISBN-13: 978–1–5095–3678–8 (paperback)

A catalogue record for this book is available from the British Library.

Library of Congress Cataloging-in-Publication Data

Names: Muchembled, Robert, 1944- author. I Pickford, Susan, translator.
Title: Smells : a cultural history of odours in early modern times / Robert
   Muchembled ; translated by Susan Pickford.
Other titles: Civilisation des odeurs (XVIe-début XIXe siècle). English
Description: Cambridge, UK ; Medford, MA : Polity, 2020. I Includes
   bibliographical references and index. I Summary: "A rich cultural
   history of smells that sheds new light on an under-appreciated sense"--
   Provided by publisher.
Identifiers: LCCN 2019045567 (print) I LCCN 2019045568 (ebook) I ISBN
   9781509536771 (hardback) I ISBN 9781509536788 (paperback) I ISBN
   9781509536795 (epub)
Subjects: LCSH: Odors--Social aspects--Europe--History. I Smell--Social
   aspects--Europe--History. I Civilization, Modern. I
   Europe--Civilization.
Classification: LCC GT2847 .M8313 2020 (print) I LCC GT2847 (ebook) I DDC
   612.8/6094--dc23
LC record available at https://lccn.loc.gov/2019045567
LC ebook record available at https://lccn.loc.gov/2019045568

Typeset in 10.5 on 12 Sabon by
Servis Filmsetting Ltd, Stockport, Cheshire
Printed and bound in Great Britain by TJ International Limited

The publisher has used its best endeavours to ensure that the URLs for external websites referred to in this book are correct and active at the time of going to press. However, the publisher has no responsibility for the websites and can make no guarantee that a site will remain live or that the content is or will remain appropriate.

Every effort has been made to trace all copyright holders, but if any have been overlooked the publisher will be pleased to include any necessary credits in any subsequent reprint or edition.

For further information on Polity, visit our website: politybooks.com

For Jane, who loves French perfumes

Contents

Contents

Illustrations

Introduction

In *The Civilizing Process*, Norbert Elias put forward an overarching vision of the progress of Western civilization based on the slow domestication of affectivity, increasingly leading the subject to develop self-control.[1] He explained how coarse emotionality gradually came to be driven out of its central position in the public sphere, giving way to highly codified attitudes of politeness that defined decency. His deeply optimistic, Eurocentric theory has given rise to much debate, at times heated, and has remained highly influential. It drew on a long-standing and diverse school of humanist thought, whose proponents believed in the capacity of their fellow humans to improve over time, following Erasmus – much quoted by Elias – who dreamed of a golden age in the near future, and Condorcet, who held that 'the human race [is] advancing with a firm and sure step along the path of *truth, virtue* and *happiness*'.[2]

When it was first published in 1939, Elias's work offered a valuable intellectual antidote to the looming threat of Nazism; however, its approach to sensory phenomena does not reflect the latest in scientific research. It takes as its main example the court of Louis XIV, seeing the restriction of bodily functions in public and the increasing disapproval of excessive or indecent reactions in the presence of others as part of a broad civilizing process. Elias argued that these new models of behaviour became ingrained in childhood among the upper classes, leading to increasing suppression of aggressive tendencies at an individual level that were then slowly adopted by other social groups.

This valuable basic framework can be used to underpin new directions in research. Smells, the focus of this book, were a key point in innovative conduct manuals such as Erasmus's *De civilitate morum puerilium* [*On civility in boys*], published in 1530 for a select readership. Recent scientific research has shown that smells are vital gateways for emotions and their recall. As the first chapter will demonstrate, smell is arguably the only one of our senses to be acquired from experience, rather than being innate. As it is binary in nature, it can easily be inflected by affective messages towards pleasure or, alternatively, fear and disgust. This opens the door to a sort of experimental history, drawing on the vast body of information left by people long since dead. This means trying to understand how their world worked, how they saw it and thought about it, rather than projecting our own presuppositions onto them. This is the path historical method must take to achieve a degree of objectivity, whatever claims may be made for other methodologies. Disgust at smells is a fundamental sensation in humans, but not one that is biologically programmed. It takes four or five years at least for European children, for instance, to construct disgust at their own excrement. Few people nowadays are willing to acknowledge this, preferring to believe that such disgust is as natural as it is universal; in fact, it is the result of several centuries of cultural pressure. Stubbornly maintained from generation to generation, this pressure has given rise to individual reactions of shame and disgust at anal excreta. The slightest suggestion of a whiff of excrement makes us literally nauseous. We can also feel the same uncontrollable repugnance at the mere sight or mention of it, even in a scatological joke; once the smell has become categorized as negative, all our senses seek to keep it at arm's length and communicate this to our consciousness. This was by no means the case in the sixteenth and seventeenth centuries, with the exception of a tiny minority who stood apart not only from the masses, materially mired in stench, but also from the majority of intellectuals, including storytellers, who took pleasure in spreading a lively scatological culture.[3]

While *Smells: A Cultural History of Odours in Early Modern Times* draws admiringly on Norbert Elias's pioneering work, it adopts a far less linear perspective. The significant shifts in our sense of smell from the Renaissance to the Napoleonic Empire cannot be framed in terms of inevitable human progress. Rather, they are approached here as first and foremost a reflection of the daily concerns of our ancestors. The aim is by no means to conjure up an image of the 'good old days'. The stench in centuries past was dreadful and omnipresent, the air saturated with nauseating emissions and dangerous pollution, particularly in urban areas hemmed in by city walls. The air in towns and cities became even harder to breathe in the eighteenth century as the population swelled, reaching noxious new heights with the advent of industrialization, until mains drainage systems were installed from the late nineteenth century on (see chapter 2). The constancy of the situation makes it impossible to believe that developments in the sense of smell under the *Ancien Régime* were essentially driven by material progress, symptomatic of the broader struggle against the stench of widespread putrefaction. People simply lived with it as best they could. Having no choice but to see and smell what Rabelais called 'joyous matter' on a daily basis, they showed little disgust at faeces and urine, whether human or animal; indeed, both were widely used in medicine and beauty treatments. Until the 1620s, literature and poetry both delighted in excreta which now disgust us. The smells of excrement and body odours were both formative aspects of eroticism and sexuality, for the social elite and the popular classes alike (see chapter 3). The minority opposed to such practices grew following the devastating wars of religion. After 1620, the bands of Catholics and Calvinists preaching intolerance grew and fought hard against man's animality. Making unwitting use of the simplifying binarity of smell, they taught increasing numbers of students and followers that the Devil lay nestled in the lower body, couched in excrement and urine, laying the distant foundations for the anal repression that underpins much modern psychoanalysis. Their most virulent discourse was aimed at women. Doctors relayed their opinions, believing women to be disgusting by their very nature, particularly when on their period. Older women were even a target for extraordinary hatred from men, as shown by numerous works of literature. They were accused of being close to the putrid Devil, and some were even burned as witches in the most misogynistic periods of our past (see chapter 4).

At the same period, medicine explained terrifying recurrent out-breaks of plague by Satan's poisonous breath corrupting the air. Ambergris, musk and civet came to be seen as vital bulwarks against the Devil's breath, a metaphor for sin, which was held to cause dread-ful epidemics. Scents were worn like armour against the plague, and doctors explained that harmful forms of pestilence were dispelled by even worse fetid stenches. Plague was thereby correlated with terrible stenches of all sorts in countless scholarly treatises, while pleasant scents such as those emanating from the bodies of saints were thought to open the gates of paradise (see chapter 5). The finest scents were therefore initially used as repellents and prophylactics as well as to increase the wearer's desirability. This ambiguous role embodied negative and positive aspects: the scents were in many cases obtained from the sex glands of ruthlessly hunted exotic animals, transmitting a message on what death meant to people in the past, yet they were also closely bound up with the vital human impulses of eroticism and love. Their detractors may have promised eternal hellfire for those who used perfumes for pleasure, but all classes of society came to use them as a matter of course as their sole protection against the plague, and the only way of masking body odours that proved particularly rank in two centuries that took against water and bathing. Their popularity earned a fortune for the closely allied professions of glove-making and perfumery, as clothing and leather, whatever its intended use, had to be steeped in perfume to protect the wearer against contagion. Fashion did the rest to trigger the first revolution in smells and smelling of the modern age, from the Renaissance to the age of Louis XIV (see chapter 6). The second such revolution, over the course of the eighteenth century, saw a thoroughgoing rejection of musk-based fragrances in favour of fruity, floral and spice-based scents. In the absence of any decisive advances in the control of fetid stenches, this shift was essentially driven by social and cultural factors: it may be seen as a way of escaping the worsening stench of faeces which spared neither the rich nor the powerful. It was also rooted in increasing disgust at the somewhat ghoulish nature of perfumes and leather, both derived from animal carcasses. Collective sensitivities were undergoing a deep-rooted shift. The disappearance of the plague after 1720 and sharp decline in fear of the Devil meant there was no longer any point in using perfumes to fight the forces of evil. A less misogynistic society also meant that it was no longer fashionable for men to wear virile, powerful perfumes to conquer women. Softer, sweeter perfumes came into fashion, heralding the triumphant return of femininity, rooted in a gentler vision of nature. This was particularly true of aristocratic culture and Enlightenment salons. Between 1789 and 1815, years of war and conquest, musk-based perfumes became relatively fashionable once more, though floral and fruity perfumes still reigned supreme (see chapter 7).

The women's perfume sector is still dominated by fruity and floral scents. Contrary to some claims, the present day is by no means devoid of smells. Such claims merely reflect a striking shift in our attitudes to pain and mortality, now kept out of sight and out of smell. Western society has certainly not lost the use of a sense as vital as smell. Though science long paid our noses little attention, recent research has shown that they are in fact home to the sharpest of all our senses, capable of distinguishing between huge numbers of smells. This book sets out to explore this sudden return to favour, starting with an overview of the current state of scholarly research on this fascinating topic (see chapter 1).

1

Our unique sense of smell

Prior to 2014, our sense of smell was significantly devalued, even derided. It was held to be too animalistic, an encumbrance in the human quest for exceptional status in an age of dazzling technology and scientific discovery. As a superfluous, vestigial remnant of our pre-human past, it came to be powerfully repressed in our deodorant-addled civilization. It barely raised a flicker of interest among scientists, who had never bothered to test the hypothesis commonly held by earlier generations of scholars that even the keenest human noses could only distinguish some ten thousand smells at best, making our sense of smell a distant runner-up to our eyes, able to detect several million different shades of colour, and ears, which can distinguish nearly five hundred thousand sounds. Smell seemed to be a biological dead end, doomed to gradual extinction.

Is science always objective?

Then 2014 brought a scientific bombshell. A team at Rockefeller University in New York claimed that humans are capable of discriminating over a trillion smells.[1] Did the nose's spectacular rise from also-ran to top dog, the sharpest of all the senses, prove the point of those who argue this is an age of dazzling progress? Alas, like the fleeting beauty of Ronsard's poetic rose, the fabulous discovery soon lost its bloom. Two articles published soon after pitilessly skewered the flawed mathematical model used to scale up the team's experiments on twenty-six volunteers.[2] It could almost have been the episode of *The Big Bang Theory* in which Sheldon Cooper is thrilled when Stephen Hawking compliments him on his brilliant demonstration of a new theory, then crestfallen on hearing a moment later that the only problem is an error in arithmetic on page 2.

This is all very confusing for the historian. The science goes right over his head; he cannot work out which side is right and can only wonder what can justify such diametrically opposing views. After all, aren't the critics of the 'soft' humanities always banging the drum of 'hard' science and its objectivity?

Experimental research on the human sense of smell has been gaining ground for some twenty-five years. The discovery of nearly four hundred olfactory receptors in humans has led to limited progress in molecular biology and physiology but has proved of major interest to neurobiologists.[3] Scientists seeking to understand how cells recognize specific signals consider our sense of smell as an ideal subject for study because of the number and diversity of receptors. Furthermore, every individual has a practically unique set of olfactory receptor genes, creating a sort of personal 'noseprint' linked to our immune system, among other things.[4]

Yet it would be naive to think that science is driven solely by disinterested curiosity. The recent surge of interest in the human sense of smell is part of a vast cultural phenomenon whose underlying causes are deep-rooted, yet readily identifiable. You just have to follow the money. First and foremost are perfume companies, which come up with thousands of new products; in recent decades they have inclined to natural scents, which were considered beyond the pale until about 1990 by detractors of bad smells both physical and moral.[5] Such companies, eager for information, are commissioning ever more studies. Other major sectors of the modern economy are also on the hunt for information – those that pollute our planet and their opposite numbers, the hygiene and health sectors, not to mention the vast food flavouring industry. Considerable amounts of money are at stake. Many promising young scientists are turning to potentially lucrative research projects in a highly profitable, fast-developing market. Some are hard at work identifying human pheromones. These are chemical substances supposed to attract the opposite sex: their very existence is questioned by some experts, though one 2009 experiment did conduct tests that suggested the existence of 'putative human pheromones', secreted by the glands of Montgomery in the breasts of lactating women. The as yet unidentified volatile compounds are thought to play a vital role in helping the newborn infant learn to suckle and in developing the bond between the mother and her baby.[6]

The food industry also greedily latches onto discoveries that align with its own interests. Teams of taste scientists work hard on studies such as the aforementioned project on the 'smellscape' of lactating women's areolas, conducted at Dijon University Hospital. The stakes are high indeed, as, unlike the perfume market, this has every man, woman and child on the planet as a potential customer. Our fate is in the hands of laboratories that decide what is, or is not, good for us. For example, in 2008, the European Union took the precaution of banning a number of ingredients added to foodstuffs to give them a particular aroma (i.e. taste and/or smell) or to modify their own natural aroma. The list includes various flavourings naturally present in foodstuffs, found in plants such as chilli peppers, cinnamon, tarragon, St John's wort, mint, nutmeg and sage.[7]

In this context, it is easy to understand why there is so much competition among research teams to come up with new data on smells, tastes and flavours, covering the whole range of sensations detected by our mouths. Even though the claim that humans can detect one trillion smells has been debunked, the article is still regularly quoted, commented on and referenced in popular science material, unlike the two articles that pointed out the flaws in the claim.

My own intuitive, highly subjective reading of all this is that science without consciousness of the past is but the ruin of the soul. At the very least, the recent deluge of studies on smell points to a new interest in a sense that is often underrated and underestimated. While the major causes of this spectacular shift may be the market economy and the drive for maximum profit, they have at least brought the nose to the fore after several centuries of neglect. When I first began researching the topic in the early 1990s, I asked a particularly promising student to join me in the project,[8] but I eventually had to drop the idea for a full-length book because no publishers showed any interest. Things have changed, and now the time seems ripe for a historian to play his own little tune in the great orchestral concert of Smell Studies. Indeed, it has become a pressing necessity to prove that the humanities and human sciences are neither dead nor passé; rather, they are what give life its meaning in a world run by robots, a dictatorship of aloof multinationals where what matters is the bottom line. In 2015, the Japanese government requested the country's eighty-six public universities to close their humanities and social sciences departments, or at least downsize and reduce enrolments, to focus on 'more practical, vocational education that better anticipates the needs of society'. In September 2015, twenty-six of them complied.[9] Despite a considerable public outcry, seventeen immediately stopped enrolments in the humanities and social sciences for the academic year 2015–16. The ministry proved it was playing the long game by staggering the reform over several years, until 2022. Other countries have carried out similar measures, albeit more discreetly, leading in the long term to a genuine threat to the culture of the humanities. I hope to demonstrate in this book that history and her sister disciplines are vital to our understanding of the modern world.

A sense of danger, emotions and delight

The human sense of smell is remarkable and unique. The team of scientists who first discovered the role of molecules produced by the areolas of lactating mothers concluded that their role was to help the individual, and therefore the species, to survive. This is true for all mammals. The widely held idea that the human sense of smell is weak and residual is merely a myth with no real basis: in fact, our sense of smell fell prey to cultural repression with the triumph of the bourgeoisie in the nineteenth and twentieth centuries.

While the fourth of Descartes' *Méditations métaphysiques* ranked olfaction the third of all our senses, it was later scorned by philosophers and thinkers alike. Kant rejected it out of hand, considering it and its close relative taste to be the only subjective senses; Freud explained its supposed decline by 'organic repression', generated by the march of Western civilization. In around 1750, 'aerist' hygienists condemned smell for bringing people into contact with 'putrid dangers'. Fast-paced urbanization in the industrial area saw smell become a major factor in class discrimination.[10] The long period when our sense of smell was unloved and unsung is now coming to an end before our very eyes, and it is recovering some of the long-lost glory the great historian Robert Mandrou intuited it must once have had. Way back in 1961, Mandrou argued that in the sixteenth century, when hearing and touch ranked higher than sight, people were 'highly sensitive to smells and perfumes' and delicious food. Ronsard's poetry, for instance, associates kissing with the 'sweet-smelling breath' of his beloved.[11]

Our sense of smell has a number of highly original features. It develops in the foetus at twelve weeks. Learning about tastes and smells begins in the womb with amniotic fluid, which absorbs chemical traces of everything the mother eats. Some babies are born with a taste for garlic, for instance. It then takes another few years for the sense of smell to mature fully. The American experimental psychologist Rachel Herz is 'convinced that our aroma preferences are all *learned*', whereas the five basic tastes – salty, sweet, acid, bitter and umami (savoury) – are innate and therefore codify how we experience food and drink.[12] My years of experience with American cuisine make me question her second argument somewhat, as the American love of combining sweet and salty foods is quite alien to the French palate and umami has a very different tone in the two countries. I do, however, agree fully with her former point, however subjective it may be, because it maps perfectly onto my own purpose in writing this book: demonstrating that smell is the most flexible and manipulable of the senses, making it a rich seam for any historian interested in the forces driving long-term cultural and social change.

A further characteristic specific to smell is its direct link to the oldest part of the human brain, as olfactory information is decoded in the prefrontal cortex. The 'limbic system', to use a familiar expression now out of favour among specialists, is also the site where memories are formed and emotions such as pleasure, aggression and fear are managed. Like smell, aggression and fear are controlled by the amygdala. In simple terms, our sense of smell is the primary seat of our emotions. It reacts in a flash to alert us to potential threats, before sight and the other senses validate the message. The initial warning is of necessity simple and binary: good or bad. For newborns to survive, they must latch on to the breasts of an unfamiliar woman who smells good before she tastes good. Conversely, children coming across a chopped onion for the first time cry when it triggers their trigeminal nerve; the pain becomes indelibly associated with a smell that is recorded as highly unpleasant. Things do not smell good or bad in and of themselves: our brains categorize them and then record the memory. Humans adapt perfectly to strong smells: after about fifteen minutes, we stop smelling even the worst stench or most delightful fragrance. Nor can we detect our own odour, which floats around us like an invisible bubble about a metre in diameter, protecting our personal space, on the model of the hero of Patrick Süskind's novel *Perfume*.[13] The brain must learn to create an association, negative or positive, with smells that are impermanent and trigger an initial, fleeting danger signal. Even things that now disgust us deeply require a process of social conditioning that can, in some cases, be very lengthy indeed. In the United States, world-beaters when it comes to masking smells, Rachel Herz reports that children like the smell of their own excrement until the age of about eight. It takes them the same amount of time to come to appreciate the taste of bananas or to reject the 'stinky' cheeses that adults are so disgusted by. To my knowledge, no French researchers have explored the reverse mechanism by which French cuisine has come to be dominated by strong-smelling foodstuffs that disgust people across the Atlantic. This is a missed opportunity, because a well-thought-out marketing campaign targeting very young children, associating such products with pleasure rather than pain, could boost international sales considerably. A French anthropologist has studied the lack of disgust at faeces and urine in children up to the age of four or five; yet the sixteenth-century essayist Montaigne wrote that everyone likes the smell of their own excrement, while Erasmus said the same of farts.[14] These monuments of sixteenth-century culture did not learn anal repression, as we will see in chapter 3.

Smell is useful in allowing us to swiftly identify and decide whether to approach or avoid everything from food and sexual partners to predators and toxins, promoting the survival of individuals and hence the human race.[15] This multifaceted sense shapes our instinct for contact or revulsion, helping forge solid social bonds, training our taste buds, and encouraging procreation to keep the species alive. Far from casting us back to the animality of our earliest ancestors, such intertwined olfactory fields are part of the rich tapestry of what it means to be human. The earliest olfactory exchanges between mother and foetus in the womb from the twelfth week of pregnancy are followed in the first days of life by a powerful bond generated by the irresistible lure of the mother's nipple. This is in turn followed by a long period of preferential attachment, as children can identify their mothers by smell alone, starting from between two to five, until they are around sixteen.[16] This vigorously contradicts the old dogma of the deodorized society some argue we now live in. It also has potential long-term consequences for the dominant note of womanhood it foregrounds. Our experiences as infants 'could be a sort of imprint that leaves its mark on us for the rest of our lives'.[17] Recent experiments have demonstrated that women can detect, identify and memorize smells better than men. There seems to be some mysterious link, as yet unexplained, between our sense of smell and human reproduction.[18] Research in this area could shed light on our understanding of the widespread terror caused by the power of women's bodies in the sixteenth and seventeenth centuries, with numerous broadsides against their stench, as chapter 4 will show. Are the sudoriferous glands, which begin producing sweat in puberty, mainly around the nipples, anus, genitalia, groin and armpits, more active in women than in men? The current norm is to deodorize these body parts. This is relatively straightforward, as the substances emitted have no smell of their own. They are, however, very rich in proteins that are ingested by bacteria that then release foul-smelling gases.[19] Five centuries ago, it was a very different matter: it was impossible to rid the body of such smells, since water and bathing were considered dangerous. At best, they could be masked by powerful scents.

The eighteenth-century philosopher Diderot held smell to be the 'most voluptuous' of the senses. Other Enlightenment philosophers such as Rousseau and Cabanis were of the same opinion.[20] Freud's theories led the ethnologist Yvonne Verdier to research the role of excremental odours in male erotic sensibility. The sociologist Marcel Mauss posited the existence of a relationship between armpit sweat and the notion of personality, with bodily odours offering excellent clues to a potential sexual partner's suitability.[21] The exact mechanisms at work remain a mystery, since no formal scientific proof of the existence of human pheromones has been found. The most commonly accepted theories posit that such mechanisms are necessary to the survival of the species. Pleasant smells suggest excellent health rooted in a strong immune system that puts up a powerful fight against parasites and microbes, making the potential partner – male or female – a good bet. Unpleasant smells, on the other hand, are signs of disease, and therefore of danger and failure to reproduce successfully.[22] Binary olfactory signals are connected to our emotions, as we have seen. The neurobiologist Antonio R. Damasio has identified six such 'primary' or 'universal' emotions: fear, anger, sadness, disgust, surprise and joy. Our emotional range is completed by secondary emotions reflecting well-being or discomfort, calm or stress. In the end, he considers biological regulation to be based on pleasure, connected to the notion of reward, and pain, aligned with punishment.[23] Our first olfactory impression is absolutely fundamental, particularly when it comes to falling in love.

Finding the perfect life partner should not be seen as a bolt from the blue, but rather as a brief instant of olfactory ecstasy. The romantic quest for a Prince Charming or Sleeping Beauty takes on a surprising new dimension. We all have our own unique smell, described by scientists as our 'olfactory fingerprint'. There are currently over seven billion such signature smells on earth. And though we are unaware of it, it is our noses that lead us to the man or woman of our dreams, the Romeo or Juliet who will help us perpetuate our genes and thus protect the future of the species. It is no surprise that all sorts of myths have sprung up to explain the mystery. Plato's concept of androgyny, taken up centuries later with lasting influence by the humanist philosophers and poets of the Renaissance, explains our constant quest for our twin soul: humans were originally dual beings with two sexes, before being split into two separate entities, both dissatisfied with their lot.

The roots of this myth may well lie somewhere in the biological quest for the ideal partner. Men and women are literally led by the nose to the one bubble of scent that suits them best, by a process of trial and error, illustrated by a series like *Sex and the City*. The flood of positive emotions that washes over us when we discover someone who smells right is automatically memorized along with their pleasant scent. Coming across the same scent again spontaneously triggers the whole bundle of affective memories in a sort of chain reaction that could be called the 'madeleine effect', after the famous scene in Proust's *Remembrance of Things Past*. Clever investors have doubtless seen this as a potential money-spinner, which explains why 'natural' scents have made such a comeback in perfumes and body-care products for men and women alike. Systematically stripping away our natural odour upsets human sexuality by removing the signals that instinctively guide it. It is an insidious cultural mechanism for controlling sexuality and setting humans apart from the animal kingdom – which can only be done by turning us all into robots or denying the obvious truth that we have a highly developed sense of smell, albeit downplayed by dubious legends. There are a number of other smell-related facts about animals. Did you know, for instance, that the mammal with the keenest sense of smell is not the dog, but the cat? It might have been awkward to admit before science stuck its nose in, because household cats, the most sensuous of all the animals tamed by man, make no attempt to hide their torrid sexuality. That is, when their owners have not had them neutered, supposedly for their own good, but actually in line with an unspoken moral vision of castration that deprives children of a once common erotic apprenticeship.

Smell is also a profoundly social sense, producing binary reactions of bonding or rejection. Each human grouping has its own preferred aromatic field arising in particular from the local cuisine and collective management of smells. Lucienne Roubin's ethnological fieldwork in the Haut-Verdon region in the south-eastern French Alps in around 1980 provides one example. The local cuisine was dominated by pairings of garlic with onion and thyme with bay leaf for protection against disease and witchcraft. Onion was also associated with virility and parsley with lactation. In the first case, the painful sensation overcome by little boys first encountering the taste of onion was given a positive slant towards the expression of masculinity, indicating how infinitely flexible our sense of smell really is. The ideal life partner has the base note shared by the wider community, the note of their gender, and their own personal 'smellprint'. Their smell will also vary from season to season. In the summer it is sweatier, in autumn more animal, after cleaning manure from the stables. Every stage of life is saturated with scented messages. The merry month of May is when young swains court their beloved by wearing hawthorn blossom and basil, and break up with them with cypress and thistles. Rosemary expresses the joy of shared attachment. Unpleasant smells are associated with social disapproval: the custom of *charivari*, or ritual public heckling, at the nuptials of ill-matched couples came with the stench of a donkey carcase being burned. As everywhere, wafts of foul smells heralded the arrival of elements likely to challenge the local social order, particularly strangers, who naturally smell unpleasant.[24] There is no need for words to see danger coming: it is inherent in anyone from other parts who eats other things and smells different. In Asia, Westerners are reputed to stink of butter.

In all cultures, smells are of major significance in the relationship between men and the supernatural, the gods, or God. Some three thousand years ago, the ancient Greeks laid the foundations for the Western concept of smells, which in their understanding could not be neutral. Either they were pleasant, like the delicious perfumes of Olympia, or unpleasant, like the fetid stench of the Harpies who would swarm in and devour everything, then fly off again leaving only their droppings. In the Greek world, pleasant smells were associated with the divine, as in Plutarch's description of Alexander the Great's delightfully fragrant mouth and body. Even after death, his body did not smell of decay and his tomb gave off a sweet fragrance: this was later picked up by the Christians, who invented the sweet 'odour of sanctity' for dead saints. Ordinary mortals were less fortunate. According to the medical theory of humours, men were warm and dry, and therefore supposedly smelled better than women, who were cold and damp, but there was no denying some individuals still smelled terrible. The worst insult the sixteenth century inherited from ancient medicine was to accuse someone of stinking like a billy goat: 'A fearsome goat lodges in the hollow of thine armpits', wrote one poet. Another wrote of a 'pestilential stench' more terrible than 'a billy goat that has just made love'. Human beings were not to behave, or smell, like animals. Body odour, bad breath, faeces, urine and burping were stigmatized, sometimes humorously. In all cases it was doubtless a way of exorcising the inevitable slide towards death, hinted at by noxious whiffs. In the Greek myths, such smells were constantly bound up with death and sacrilege.[25]

Perceiving a fetid smell was an immediate trigger for the fear of death in ancient Greece. In our own culture, lengthy exposure to a relatively smell-free environment suggests that our deodorized world now offers a kind of antidote to existential anguish, as olfactory 'silence' has developed in parallel with the silence surrounding disease and death, dating from around the same time. In France, the custom of burying the dead in and around churches in the centre of towns and villages, often in very shallow graves, was outlawed in 1776 by a royal decree that forced the transfer of graveyards far away from centres of population on grounds of public hygiene. Keenly opposed at first, the new norm gradually came to be accepted over the centuries. In parallel, the sick and dying were taken ever further out of the social sphere and isolated from the public gaze in hospitals. The recent positive reappraisal of our sense of smell doubtless reflects shifts in the deep-rooted bond linking it with our fear of ageing and death, though it is impossible to pinpoint their scope and cause.

One final aspect of this fascinating question is how extremely difficult it is to express olfactory experience verbally, whatever language you speak. Those in professions that deal regularly with smells, such as chefs, forensic pathologists and perfumers, encounter this problem on a daily basis. Perfumers have solved it by developing their own metaphorical jargon to differentiate 'green' and 'pink' fragrances, 'spicy' and 'grassy' perfumes, fruity and floral scents, dissonant, balsamic, fresh and amber notes.[26] The explanation for this mystery stems from the direct correlation between scents, emotions and memory, wholly unconnected to the parts of the brain that handle verbalization. The binary system warning of danger is triggered initially in a flash, with no need for language processing. The memory that remains has no link to the rest of memory function and cannot be conjured up at will. As a result, many scholars have sought to draw up typologies of smells with their own naming system, including the great Linnaeus in 1756. The results, however, have always been disappointingly subjective. In 1624, the doctor Jean de Renou took a great interest in smells, defined as 'a vaporous substance emanating from odourable matter', identifying a close analogy with flavours detectable by taste. The concept fills some hundred pages of his book, recording nine varieties of smell categorized according to the theory of humours. Acrid (or mordicant), bitter and salty smells were caused by heat; acid, austere and astringent smells by excessive cold, while soft, fatty and insipid smells were triggered by moderate heat. Jean de Renou further argued that our weak sense of smell explains why an infinite number of scents have no name of their own.[27]

Scientists are still hard at work drawing up a universally accepted inventory of smells. In 2013, a factorial survey conducted in the United States identified 144 combinations of smells divided into ten related basic families perceptible by humans: fragrant, woody-resinous, fruity non-citrus, sickening, chemical, minty-peppermint, sweet, popcorn, lemon and pungent.[28] It is by no means clear that this represents significant progress over the past four centuries, or that such progress is indeed possible. 'Salty' has been replaced by 'sweet', which dominates American food and drink, now available globally. Both salty and sweet, however, refer to tastes rather than smells. 'Fragrant' and 'chemical' are somewhat perplexing, as their meaning is so broad and unspecific that it is hard to imagine noses all over the world agreeing on them. The same is true of 'popcorn', granted universal pride of place even though the sickly-sweet smell is not familiar in every urban jungle or remote rainforest. Might it be the case that the scientific categories were 'contaminated', as it were, by the taste preferences of the scientists themselves? When the lead author Jason Castro was asked why the 'popcorn' category also included 'woody-resinous' elements, his answer was that there was not enough vocabulary to describe the incredible complexity of smells. He also conceded that classification was still an open question, explaining that the team might have come up with nine or eleven groups, but that they found ten was the smallest number to capture the interesting features of smell.[29] In other words, the subjectivity of the so-called 'soft' sciences has found its way into the conclusions of what is at first glance a highly scientific factorial analysis. Was the project's main objective to catch the eye of financial backers, particularly in the food and perfume industries, who might be interested in a set of labels for identifying smells without actually having to smell them? It might even be imagined that the correlations identified between types of base might generate business opportunities, for instance by encouraging popcorn-buying cinema audiences to consume closely related 'woody-resinous' products and perfumes. Who could have predicted that Proust's literary madeleine might one day become a powerful vector for scientific and economic innovation?

2

A pervasive stench

The good old days are a myth. The towns and villages of Europe stank terribly in days of yore. Since even the most dreadful smells were not necessarily as great a threat to health as the pollution that chokes us today, it is tempting to downplay the impact such foul stenches had on people's lives. However, we should not overlook the fact that the noxious smells generated by a number of trades had the potential to harm the broader population. The dearth of research on this topic is not due to a lack of evidence, which is plentiful. Nor can it be attributed to our ancestors' lack of sensitivity to such smells, as is often lazily suggested to dismiss the topic. We have long been coached into silencing our sense of smell, as required by a clean, orderly society, and we react against such disturbing olfactory phenomena. Only a few daring voices have dared touch on the unmentionable subject. 'All smells are primordially the smell of shit', one writes.[1] This claim requires further substantiation: is the message received by an individual nose deemed good or bad? The answer really depends on the historical period. Nowadays it takes children a long while to learn to feel disgust for their own excrement. No such conditioning existed in the Renaissance. Yet in every culture, negative signals received by the brain are associated with death, warning the body of the risk of harm, while positive signals are associated with life and pleasure.

No human society is indifferent to smells. They are often thought of as tools mediating magical interactions. Various rites were thought to protect our ancestors against the foulest of smells, while sweet fragrances were used to earn the favour of the gods.[2] Even before the advent of mains drainage, Europeans were perfectly aware of the terrible fug of smells that surrounded them. The Swedish scholar Carl Linnaeus proved a man of his time in 1756, when he drew up a subjective list of seven categories of natural smells, the majority of which were unpleasant: *aromaticos* (carnation and bay leaf), *fragrantes* (lily, saffron and jasmine), *ambrosiacos* (amber or animal musk), *alliaceos* (garlic and asafoetida, also known as Persian ferula), *hircinos* or 'goat-like' (goat, valerian), *tetros* or 'foul' (French marigold, some solanaceous plants) and *nauseos* (cucurbitaceous plants).[3] Bad smells could now be labelled, but not eradicated: ways had to be found to deal with them, particularly in large urban areas where the air was thick with all sorts of stenches. As seen in chapter 1, we stop noticing even the most powerful smells after about fifteen minutes of exposure. However, such offensive odours were still a major risk to public health, as noted as early as 1700 by Bernardino Ramazzini, the father of occupational medicine.

The foul air of medieval towns

It is fruitless trying to pinpoint when humans first started getting rid of their rubbish.[4] Men have always tried to identify and limit such health hazards. The Middle Ages had a wide range of expressive terms for the principal causes of foul smells: shit, dung, mire, ordure, filth, muck, turds. When the air became too grim to breathe, the populace turned to the authorities to sort it out. In 1363, professors and students at the University of Paris complained to the king that the local butchers

> kill their animals in their homes, and the blood and waste from the animals is thrown day and night into the Rue Sainte-Geneviève, and on several occasions the waste and blood of the animals was kept in pits and latrines in their houses until it was corrupted and rotten and then thrown into that same street day and night, until the street, Place Maubert and all the surrounding air was corrupted, foul, and reeking.

Three years later (the wheels of justice turned slowly, then as now), the Paris parliament ordered the butchers to slaughter their animals outside the city on the river before bringing them back into the capital for sale, or face fines if they refused.[5]

Odour pollution was often caused by animals, as towns and villages were full of horses needed for travel and transport, as well as poultry, pigs and goats, left to forage the streets for food, even in Paris. Then there were the strays, mainly dogs, which proliferated though men were employed to catch and kill them: these men were paid by the head, particularly in urban areas under Burgundian control. Only when epidemics seriously threatened did the authorities make temporary attempts to limit the number of animals, whose excrement was a regular feature of urban life. The same was true of humans, who 'made water', defecated or spat wherever the need took them.

Certain trades were a major source of noxious emissions for their immediate neighbourhood, including butchers, tripe makers, fishmongers, potters (who deliberately left their clay to sour in cellars in Paris and elsewhere), and painters who used pigments made from metal oxides. The worst were tanners, glove- and purse-makers, and fullers, who made abundant use of toxic plant and animal substances as mordants, like alum, tartar and soda, urine (often collected from humans), chicken droppings and dog excrement, which accelerated the process of fermenting and rotting the fibres they worked with. Attempts were made to force the smelliest and most harmful trades away from the overcrowded centres of towns and villages to the outskirts and downstream on rivers to keep the water at least vaguely drinkable. However, the growth of urban centres in the late medieval period only made the toxic pollution worse. More and more complaints were made about 'fetor', or foul smells, fetid water and unhealthy air, particularly in the warm summer months, when the atmosphere was simply impossible to breathe. Growing awareness of the problem led to progress in a number of areas, including the establishment of 'privies' and latrine pits shared by men and women, often placed at the back of a yard or giving onto a river. Efforts were also made to instil greater discipline in those living in such urban centres and to force the local authorities to take action to limit the accumulation of rubbish, combat dangerous emissions from latrines and graveyards, and prevent the pollution of streets, canals and rivers. While financial penalties played their part, the most significant steps were the installation of public latrines, sewers and gutters, and paving the main streets. However, real improvements were several centuries in the making.

Urban cesspits

From the fifteenth century on, the increasing number of regulations issued by local authorities seeking to police antisocial practices that caused odour pollution reflected not so much increased awareness of the problem as the severe and ongoing worsening of the situation, driven largely by urban expansion. In France, the urban population reached 10 per cent by around 1515 and 20 per cent in 1789; by the Second Empire, one in two French people lived in a town or city. Overcrowded urban centres, hemmed in by their city walls, almost literally choked to death during the dreadful outbreaks of plague that were an all too regular occurrence prior to 1720.

The noisy, dirty, crowded streets were home to more and more polluting trades, well before the Industrial Revolution. The 'aerist' movement of the 1750s was merely a flash in the pan, sparked by the concerns of a forward-thinking minority. The vast majority of the urban population took little notice of the aerists' philosophical theories, preferring to put up with the stench rather than pay the significant costs of the works required by the authorities, particularly as several major instances of odour pollution arose from deeply ingrained habits that in some cases were a source of unspoken pride and pleasure. Nineteenth-century hygienists wrote despairingly that the size of the dung heap outside a peasant's door was a visible sign of wealth that its owner refused to move. The same was true in urban areas, including in the Paris of François I.

In Grenoble, 'masters of the street' were responsible for the upkeep and cleanliness of public spaces. However, there was little they could do when their fellow citizens simply refused to cooperate: locals were ordered to clear away the heaps of dung from outside their homes in 1526, but by 1531 they were back again.[6] Grenoble, a small town of some 12,000 inhabitants under Louis XIII, faced significant odour pollution, judging from evidence from regulations that were simply ignored and travel accounts: one visitor described its streets in 1643 as 'very ugly and very dirty'. Yet the apocalyptic stench described by historians nonetheless formed the olfactory backdrop to many people's lives. Their sense of smell was no less sensitive than that of outsiders; rather, they had become accustomed to the smell and simply no longer noticed it.

Despite its delightful setting, Grenoble shared all the unpleasant characteristics typical of urban areas of the time. Rubbish lay piled up everywhere, including human and animal excrement, which befouled the streets and ramparts. They mixed with rain and waste water and streamed down the streets, which were built with a slight downward incline towards a central gutter. The hoi polloi were expected to let their betters walk on the higher side away from the gutter, giving rise to the expression *tenir le haut du pavé*, literally 'to keep to the upper paving stone', meaning to have the upper hand. Walking on the higher side of the street meant avoiding being splashed with foul, stinking water or stepping in stagnant, fetid puddles. Dogs and pigs

acted as walking rubbish disposal units, rooting around in the waste
for food. Perhaps they appreciated the smell of human excrement,
though a belief passed down by the medical theory of Antiquity
held that it smelled much worse than animal droppings.[7] The local
population's sense of smell, long accustomed to the urban fug, was
triggered afresh by unusual events such as unexpected flooding from
the Isère or Drac rivers, which left behind a tide of 'stinking mud,
a mix of latrines and graves', as one observer wrote in 1733. The
perhaps surprising evocation of graves came from the practice of
burying bodies in very shallow soil. Just as in the medieval period,
the stench arising from certain trades was also particularly off-
putting. Butchers, skinners and tripe makers were among the worst
offenders, along with candle makers, as pig tallow (or lard) smelled
famously revolting. The seventeenth century saw the development of
textile and leather workshops that generated foul-smelling emissions,
though the urine and excrement used as raw materials in these trades
did not trigger displays of disgust. Stored in abundance outside the
workshop, they pointed to the owner's prosperity just as dung heaps
did, attracting customers. Until as late as 1901, barrels were left
at major crossroads to 'harvest' urine from passers-by and local
workmen. Tanners, leather curriers, dyers and fullers would share
the contents out between them. Workers in the leather trade, including many glovers, used animal urine and dog excrement to prepare
the hides. Fabric workshops were an equally unpleasant source of
smells. Putrefied urine was mixed with vinegar to fix colours on
fabrics and leather. Fullers soaked cloth in a blend of urine and warm
soapy water to clean it before working it with their bare feet. Starch
makers left ears of wheat to rot in water, generating stinking, acidic
fumes. Lime and plaster kilns had to be built outside the town walls,
though emissions of smoke and carbonic acid were still a nuisance
if the wind blew the wrong way. Ironically, lime is excellent for
neutralizing bad smells: it was used for whitewashing houses and
bleaching canvas, readying latrines for emptying, and in burials, particularly in common graves following epidemics. It was also believed
to protect against the plague: one author advised readers in 1597 'to
whiten household linen often and to perfume clothes, as nothing else
disinfects so well as air, water, fire, and earth, adding perfumes'. In
Grenoble and towns and cities all over France, huge fires of sweet-
smelling wood were lit morning and evening in each neighbourhood,
sometimes sprinkled with violet or sorrel water.

   Paris was on another scale altogether. Home to around 200,000
individuals by the dawn of the sixteenth century, it was the biggest
city in Europe. It remained so until the late seventeenth century,

when the population reached over half a million. It rose by at least 100,000 by the Revolution, but by this time it had been outpaced by London.

A royal edict issued on 25 November 1539 should be read with this population boom in mind. Paris was then nearing 300,000 inhabitants, a milestone reached in 1560.[8] The edict criticized the 'mud, dung, rubble and other rubbish' piled up outside people's doors and blocking the streets, despite earlier royal decrees. The filth also caused 'great horror and very great displeasure to all people of decency and honour' due to the 'foulness and stench' that they generated. Locals were ordered to remove the rubbish or face fines that would be increased if they persisted. They also had to pave the area outside their own home and maintain the road surface and were banned from throwing rubbish or waste water into the streets and squares. Orders were given to keep urine and stagnant water at home before emptying them into a stream and making sure they flowed away properly. Further bans were placed on burning straw, manure and other rubbish in the streets; rather, they were to be tipped outside the city and its faubourgs. Pigs and other livestock could no longer be slaughtered in public. Anyone owning housing without a latrine had to have one installed immediately or face having their home confiscated by the king or being banned from letting it for ten years, in the case of church property. Breeding pigs, goslings, pigeons and rabbits was now outlawed for all inhabitants, including butchers, cured and roast meat sellers, bakers and poultry sellers. Anyone who owned such animals had to send them out of town or face confiscation and corporal punishment. The latter directive, usually intended to avoid contagion, suggests that plague was either present or in the offing and therefore that the edict was reacting to specific circumstances. Whatever the case, its long-term impact was no greater than the numerous other urban regulations on the same theme laid down earlier or indeed subsequently. Way back in 1374, a royal decree had already required owners of housing in Paris to 'have sufficient latrines and privies in their houses', to little avail.

The lack of records of such facilities in estate inventories drawn up by notaries makes researching their development a challenge. However, one study of twenty-seven such documents from the Marais district of Paris from 1502 to 1552 has shown that commodes and/ or chamber-vessels were available in eighteen homes, while nine had neither, including five after the edict of 1539.[9] It is unlikely that the poorer sections of the population all had access to collective latrines. Rather, the conditions of the time suggest that they simply relieved themselves outside, possibly on dung heaps, like those living in the countryside. Those fortunate enough to have home facilities were unlikely to trouble themselves with taking their waste to a stream to be washed away. Housing in Paris was typically built on several storeys: the higher the floor, the poorer the occupants, and most would simply have dumped their waste out of the nearest window. 'Gare à l'eau!' or 'Watch out, water!' was a cry to be heeded in the streets of Paris throughout the *Ancien Régime* to avoid an unpleasant dousing. Owners of sensitive noses and curmudgeons would sometimes complain, but the few traces of cases in the legal record by no means suggest a shift in collective sensibilities. In around 1570, the neighbours of a certain André Bruneau of Nantes complained that they had to avoid his windows in the town centre at around seven or eight every night, or else risk a sudden and very smelly shower. Some of his fellow residents of Nantes shared his bad habits even if they had a latrine at home. One such was Pierre Gaultier, who not only persistently threw 'full pots and basins [. . .] of foul, stinking matter' out of the window, but also sent his children out to relieve themselves in the street.[10] The stench emitted by latrines was hardly pleasant, as recorded by the poet Gilles Corrozet's 1539 ode to the 'secret room or privy':

> A retreat one dares not discover
> Nor the top of the seat uncover
> For fear (let me not lie)
> That the powerful perfume rise high.[11]

The stench of Paris rivalled its vast size. A report by the faculty of medicine, drawn up after a dreadful outbreak of plague in the early summer of 1580, clearly identified the lack of adequate sewerage as the leading cause. It proposed widening the network by paving streets to slope down to a site a quarter of a league outside the city, like the one already in place outside Porte Barbette. A further suggestion was to dig deep, sloping canals to carry refuse down to the city's great moats, where it would be swept away by the current. The city's dumps also had to be moved further away, 'due to the noxious vapours they emit, swept into the city by the wind, which grow thicker at night, creating a dangerous fog that causes a thousand ills at all times'.[12] Montaigne complained about the filthy sludge in Paris, as did many other writers and travellers over the following century. The seventeenth-century historian Henri Sauval (1623–76) described it as 'black, foul-smelling, its stench unbearable for those from elsewhere; it stings the nostrils from three or four leagues distant'. The mud clung to everything it touched, giving rise to the proverb *tenir comme boue de Paris*, 'to stick like Paris mud'. The libertine poet

Claude le Petit, publicly burned at the stake in 1662 for slandering the royal family and Mazarin, associated the sludge with the Devil in what was to become a common trope, as will be seen below:

> Elixir of rotten excrement,
> Cursed turds of Paris,
> Shit of the abominable damned,
> Faecal black of Hell,
> Black dreg of the Devil,
> May the Devil choke you.[13]

The smell of profit

A stroll through eighteenth-century Paris was an attack on all the senses. The city was a vast building site, under construction to meet the insatiable needs of a population that was growing at prodigious speed, generating hellish problems. Unlike in smaller towns and rural areas, private latrines were becoming common, but old habits died hard, as demonstrated by a 1777 police decree that repeated former regulations on 'the most frequent offences'. One of the articles banned all private citizens, whatever their social status, from 'throwing faecal matter and other rubbish of whatsoever kind out of the window into the streets, by day or by night'.[14] The same habit was shared in Versailles, where the first *lieu à l'anglaise*, as English-style toilets were euphemistically known, was installed rather late in the day, for Louis XV. The writer Louis-Sébastien Mercier shed some possible light on why such habits proved so long-lived in his denunciation of the 'putrid miasma' and 'poisonous fumes' emitted by latrines, the 'dangerous seats' that as a child he took for 'the road to Hell'. He advised his readers against them, preferring the great outdoors.[15] Such negative olfactory experiences in their formative years may have discouraged many eighteenth-century men and women from installing something that was not yet a convenience in any real sense. Not even those at the highest level of the state were keen on the idea, as indicated by a letter written on 9 October 1694 by the Princess Palatine, Louis XIV's sister-in-law, to her godmother. Describing a court visit to Fontainebleau, where her house was not equipped with a latrine, she crudely wrote of being upset 'at going and shitting outside, which annoys me because I enjoy shitting in comfort and I cannot shit in comfort if my arse is not resting on something. *Item*, everyone can see us shitting; women, men, girls, boys, abbots, and Swiss visitors pass by.'[16]

As money smells sweeter than shit, faecal matter became an increasing source of economic growth in the modern era. Like urine, which was vital for certain trades and medical treatments, excrement became a source of income. The doctor Jean de Renou wrote in 1624 that his colleagues were using rat droppings to treat kidney stones, dog dirt for throat infections, and peacock droppings for 'falling sickness' (epilepsy), while human excrement was 'marvellously suppurative'.[17] Human and animal excrement fill sixteen pages of remedies and beauty treatments in a 1689 book by Nicolas de Blégny.[18] Another twenty-seven recipes involved urine, particularly distilled in cosmetics for women to hide wrinkles and lighten the skin, as tanning was considered vulgar and rustic. In 1666, Marie Meurdrac published a recipe to treat dry, scaly skin and improve the complexion that included 'urine from a young person who drinks nothing but wine'.[19] Madame de Sévigné used spirit of urine against rheumatism and the vapours. On 15 December 1684, she advised her daughter to rub her sides with ten or twelve hot droplets of it; some months later, on 13 June 1685, she wrote of having taken eight drops by mouth to cure the vapours. She could likewise have used a preparation by the deceptively poetic name of *eau de millefleurs* ('water of a thousand flowers': English distillers kept the French name). This was made using not only spring flowers, as the name suggests, but also fresh cow pat (four pounds, according to one author) gathered alongside them for distillation. There are numerous variants on the basic recipe, one of which simply involved crushing cow pat and snails in their shells together in white wine, then distilling the result. Some people were content simply with a morning purge of two or three glasses of cow urine for ten days every spring and autumn.[20] Meat, milk, dung and urine – cows really are man's best friend! In 1755, Polycarpe Poncelet, a Recollet monk and keen agronomist, published a recipe for a cheap and excellent liqueur that simply required distilling a ripe cow pat in brandy. It is unlikely that the smell and taste would go down well with modern consumers . . . yet Poncelet was by no means joking: he was very keen to prove the health-giving properties of such liqueurs and the harmony of their flavours. Unfortunately, he neglected to mention where his delightful cow-pat-based drink came in his own theory of a correspondence between the 'delicious music' of the seven full notes and the 'seven primitive flavours': acid, piquant, insipid, sweet, bitter, bittersweet and austere.[21]

Like any raw material, urine and excrement were grist to the mill of rapidly expanding trade capitalism. They gave rise to surprising new black markets, as enterprising individuals spotted gaps for niche products, as they have always done. A royal decree of 1667 records the criminal activities of numerous market gardeners in La Villette, now in northern Paris, who fed their dogs and pigs on human excrement 'harvested' with the help of a corrupt night soil man.[22] It is no exaggeration that the raw material was worth its weight in gold to the farmers working the land around Paris, furnishing vital fertilizer for vegetable fields, fruit orchards and vineyards outside the city. Without it, the lucrative market for intensively farmed produce destined for Paris would not have flourished. However, the regulations on such fertilizers were cautious, banning their use unless they had been kept in a dump for three years and reduced to powder. Even so, some specialists complained that the practice only yielded 'poor seed and vegetables that are harmful to health'. There is no way of knowing whether the taste of such produce worked like Proust's madeleine on the consumers who produced the organic fertilizer that grew the food. At least it can be said that the persistent ring of fug around the capital was the result of active and ongoing collaboration between Parisians and their more rural cousins.

It was even relatively common practice for farmers to sneak in overnight and steal night soil from the dumps where it was left to dry out, despite warnings from agronomists who were of the firm belief that using fresh excrement as fertilizer gave fruit and vegetables a foul smell. However, the rural population resisted pressure and obstinately refused to use the stinking sludge from various sources stocked in separate dumps, though the source was ten times larger than the city's holdings of excrement in three permanent dumps that survived until 1779. These were estimated to have taken in 27,000 cubic metres of sewage in 1775 alone. The sewage dumps in Faubourg Saint-Germain and Faubourg Saint-Marceau had been moved some four kilometres out of town back in 1760, the aim being to avoid 'foul air' contaminating the foodstuffs transported through the vicinity, including fresh bread baked in Gonesse, north-east of the city. A further aim was to avoid visitors arriving in Paris from being assailed by a terrible stench. The third such dump, in Montfaucon near Buttes-Chaumont (now a park in north-east Paris), was the only one still in service in 1781. It had had a terrible reputation since the days of the late medieval poet François Villon, who wrote of the rows of hanged bodies dangling from the gallows there. Its ten hectares of cesspits full of fermenting sewage and its slaughterhouse piled high with rotting carcasses could almost have been something out of Dante's *Inferno*.

Even the heart of Paris was an unpleasant experience for the sensitive of nose. Sewage was removed from the Île de la Cité and Notre Dame neighbourhoods by boat, leading to complaints from local residents that they were forced to keep their windows closed and noxious emissions from the boats were tarnishing and bleaching their silverware, gilding and mirrors. The black, nauseating, corrosive sludge was a nightmare for people walking the streets of a city where pavements were few and far between. Over the course of the eighteenth century, work to remove the sludge, overseen by the lieutenant of police, had limited success. First, rag-and-bone men would go through the streets picking up anything of any value, including dead dogs and cats, to sell on. Then came the rubbish carts. To meet the needs of the swelling population, they doubled in capacity in around 1748 to reach 1.5 cubic metres. By 1780, 500 such carts were doing the rounds of the Paris streets every day. At the same time, the city's seventy sewers, in dire need of maintenance, frequently overflowed, flooding the surrounding streets with sludge whenever there was a storm. Urban sprawl spread out to absorb the dumps that had lain outside the city since the days of Louis XIII, so that an unbearable stench drifted over the surrounding neighbourhoods whenever the wind blew in a westerly or south-westerly direction. The Vaugirard dump stank out Chaillot and Passy. The situation became so untenable by 1758 that the Royal Council ordered new dumps to be created well beyond the faubourgs. The lieutenant of police Henri Bertin (a favourite of Madame de Pompadour) estimated the annual cost of cleaning the city streets at 56,000 livres, given the distances covered: cleaning the sludge may have been one source of his considerable wealth.[23]

Sewage was big business. When fines and corporal punishment were brought in for anyone caught relieving themselves outdoors, in around 1771, the lieutenant of police Antoine de Sartine had barrels set up on street corners for anyone caught short. Some ten years later, one enterprising Parisian came up with a folding portable privy, charging four *sous* a go. He soon had competition. The Tuileries terraces were so filthy and stank so badly that Louis XVI's Director of the King's Buildings had the yew trees lining the walk cut down. Rather than hiding beneath them to defecate discreetly, visitors could now use the latrines installed there at a cost of two *sous*. Finding the cost too high, many people simply crossed the river to Palais-Royal. The police had no control over the Palais, which was the property of the Duc d'Orléans. To stem the tide of urine, he had twelve privies built, earning him 12,000 livres in income in 1798, spinning filth into gold like something out of a fairy tale. A three-act tragedy published in 1777 by Pierre-Jean-Baptiste Nougaret and Jean-Henri Marchand, *Le Vidangeur sensible* [*The Sensitive Night Soil Man*], foreshadowed Freudian psychoanalysis in drawing a clear link between excrement and money. It starts with an argument between a wastrel son and his tormented father, William Sentfort [Smellstrong], who refuses to let his son and heir's intemperate excesses dishonour his family and eventually poisons him. Early in the play, one of the son's friends tries to persuade him of the value of his humble trade: 'The disgusting mines you together dig shall one day become mines of gold.' The wastrel son's reply: 'It is true he converts foul change into fine silver. I often let him work with his boys while I go and play.'

Pollutant trades

Bernardino Ramazzini (1633–1714), professor of medicine at the Universities of Modena and later Padua, published *De Morbis Artificum Diatriba* [*On the Diseases of Workers*] in 1700.[24] Reprinted with additional material in 1713, the book proved a major success, being translated into numerous languages; Ramazzini's role as the founder of modern occupational health is a subject of some debate in specialist circles.

He explained that the idea for the book first came to him while watching night soil men at work in his home, basing his research on direct observation and theoretical inquiry. He noted that all trades were associated with specific ailments, studying over fifty trades and their health issues. Some diseases had physical causes such as heat, cold or damp, for instance in glass workers, bakers and brick makers. Others stemmed from lengthy, violent or irregular efforts or repetitive postures affecting the body. Polluted workspaces could also have a deleterious effect on the health of those working there. The colours and substances used by painters, such as red lead, cinnabar, Venice lead, varnishes, walnut and linseed oil and so on, caused a 'foul, latrinal smell' in their studios, eventually killing off their sense of smell altogether – though they may have sought consolation in their superior eyesight. Those making wines and spirits became drunk on the fumes of their produce. Apothecaries also suffered from the harmful effects of the preparations they handled. Ramazzini advised them to drink vinegar for the good of their health when making laudanum. Other doctors made considerable use of vinegar during outbreaks of plague, as it was thought to neutralize the corrupt air causing contagion. Pleasant smells could also have harmful effects: apothecaries making springtime rose infusions often complained of headaches.

Many such trades were also a source of odour pollution for the surrounding area. The fumes from lime kilns were so harmful that

Ramazzini professed himself astonished they were allowed in urban centres at all. He also expressed great sympathy for night soil men, who risked losing their sight, though he did believe that the fetid air they breathed in protected them from the plague, and the same for leather curriers. Like Ramazzini, some doctors believed that one cure for airborne contagion was breathing in an even fouler smell, advising readers to protect their health by sniffing at a latrine every morning. This was a serious medical opinion, not folk wisdom; its popularity among the poorest sections of society was doubtless due to the fact that it was free. In 1777, the book's young French translator added a long note on the extreme dangers faced by night soil men in Paris.[25] Fatal suffocation was a real risk on opening a latrine, particularly if it was to be scraped down, which meant disturbing the thick crust of solid matter that settled at the bottom beneath the liquid. The rotting excrement released a dangerous, fetid sewer gas called 'mofette' (English has adopted the French term) or 'plomb' (the French term for lead, as the symptoms were thought to be similar to those of lead poisoning). The gas sometimes caught fire, as in Lyon in July 1749. The night soil men took vital precautions, including rubbing their hands and faces with vinegar. If a worker fell unconscious after breathing the fumes, he was rubbed down with vinegar, which was also held under his nose, and tobacco smoke was blown over him. He then took a dose of theriac. The 22-year-old translator, the son of an Enlightenment apothecary and himself later to become a well-respected physician and chemist, was still bound up in medical superstition. Cases of fatal sewer gas poisoning among night soil men remained a cause for medical research throughout the nineteenth century.[26]

Human urine had both helpful and harmful properties. It was widely used as a remedy, as shown by Madame de Sévigné. Doctors advised drinking it to cure hydropsy, and Ramazzini describes nuns drinking it to bring on a menstrual period. The doctors in Molière's comedy *Le Malade imaginaire* gravely study their patients' urine for clues to their state of health, in line with the theory of humours. Other less salubrious practices were a legacy of Antiquity. The Romans dyed wool red by soaking it in urine twice: the poet Martial recorded that the imperial purple gave off an extremely fetid smell. Might this have been a practical demonstration of the famous Roman expression *Arx tarpeia Capitoli proxima*, 'The Tarpeian Rock is close to the Capitol', a reminder that it was but a short step from the site of ultimate power to the site of execution? The technique was still in use in fulling, stripping the lanolin from wool, and dyeing as late as 1700. When Ramazzini visited such workshops, he recorded the presence of 'barrels where all the workers urinate and where the urine is left to rot, to be used in that state' to bleach cloth so the dyes took better hold. He also wrote of being struck by the powerful, unpleasant stench emanating from such workshops.

He seems to have found them less offensive to visit, however, than those of oil producers, leather curriers, catgut string makers, butchers, fishmongers, cheesemongers and candle makers. Such places, he wrote, turned his stomach and gave him headaches and nausea. He thought it right that tanners and curriers should be relegated to the fringes of towns and cities, for fear that their odour might befoul the air breathed by people living nearby. The same was true of candle makers, whose workshops he described as 'noisome'; their boiling cauldrons full of tallow from goats, pigs and cattle 'throw out a nauseous foul stench that spreads to all the surrounding area'. As the demand for bleached thread and collars and wig powder grew, particularly over the course of the eighteenth century, starch production became a growth industry. Ears of corn were left to soak in water until they germinated, then fulled, generating an unbearable stench that left him feeling unwell.

Graveyards were also a cause of disease, not only for grave diggers. Ramazzini's French translator must have handed his work in to the publisher shortly before the 1776 order to relocate France's graveyards out of urban centres, as he complains that it has not yet been done and lists the harmful consequences of their presence, pointing out that keeping the dead cheek by jowl with the living is a dangerous practice, with doctors blaming outbreaks of disease on it. On a more positive note, however, he records that over the past two decades Europe has woken up to the risks of 'mephitic vapours'.

Much of Ramazzini's moral censure was reserved for the peasantry, though even then his scholarly superiority and scorn for the rustic masses remained moderate in expression. He simply expressed disapproval of their 'slothful carelessness in heaping up the dung intended to improve their grounds, right outside their cow byres and pigsties, and just by the door of their dwellings, and keeping it there all summer as a nosegay'. At that rate, he concluded, 'the air they live in must be polluted with the foul vapours that rise constantly'.

Countryside smells

Nineteenth-century hygienists, appalled at the filth and stink of the villages they visited, bequeathed later generations a very negative image of rural life. Yet in insisting on the need to control odour pollution in the countryside, they were merely projecting their own standards of decency onto country folk. The civilized noses of today, even that of the careless historian, experience the countryside as 'a concentration of bad smells: sweaty livestock, poultry droppings, rotting rat carcases, bodies living together in a single room, rubbish hidden in dark corners, and combustible fumes steaming from the dung heap outside the door'.[27] The country folk themselves had a very different point of view, using the height of dung heaps as a measure of wealth, as has been seen. They were also practical, as the locals used them to relieve themselves. One villager in Flers, near Douai in northern France, was accidentally shot in the buttock at dusk on 17 December 1651 as he 'did his easement on a mound outside his house'.[28] Nor were powerful smells of human or animal origin considered repulsive, particularly as they fulfilled significant social and cultural functions for the community as a whole.[29] It is more than likely that for such villagers, their city visitors were the ones who smelled unpleasant.

The myth of the terrible stench polluting the country air spread along with the 'civilizing process' from the seventeenth century on, when life in urban centres and at court was increasingly shaped by refined codes of civility that rejected animality and gave rise to new expectations of modest behaviour. Previously, bodily functions were openly carried out in public. Even the king gave audiences from his commode, a practice that proved fatal to Henri III of France, stabbed to death while on the 'throne' by the monk Jacques Clément. People would relieve themselves wherever convenient. The seventeenth-century scholar Antoine Furetière recounted an anecdote from the court of Louis XIII in which the queen's gentleman usher let go of her hand to go and urinate on a wall hanging. The great puddle that formed at the feet of Mademoiselle de Lafayette on another occasion simply made the king laugh. It was common to urinate in corners, on staircases and particularly in fireplaces.[30] While such behaviour met with increasing disapproval among the upper classes, it remained common practice lower down the social scale, feeding into elite attitudes of scorn for the masses.

The county of Artois, a province of the Spanish Netherlands before it was conquered by Louis XIII's troops, offered a rich documentary record of the lives of the rural population. Drinkers at country inns would 'make water' outside, in the garden or outbuildings, on the walls of the inn itself or the nearest church or graveyard wall. Some even simply urinated out of the nearest window, like one young man in 1602 who found it highly amusing to soak anyone unfortunate enough to be standing outside. Some documents record the existence of channels in the floor at the foot of each table. Apparently the smell was not a problem. One constant practice was urinating in the fireplace, even when it was lit. One evening in around 1550–1, in Éperlecques, near Saint-Omer in northern France, the innkeeper's wife was sitting by the hearth when two drunken young bachelors came in to urinate on the fire. One of them turned and splashed her, perhaps as a joke. The other criticized his ungentlemanly behaviour. A quarrel broke out, and the splasher ended up dying from a stab wound. The rural population was aware of the new codes of decency, as the second man's disapproval in this case indicates. However, his comment on the wrong done to the innkeeper's wife was intended mainly as an appeal to clemency from the judges at his own trial for murder. After all, he had himself shamelessly urinated in the fireplace in front of her. Such behaviour was commonplace. On 25 June 1638, a man and two women, spotting a man urinating on a tree, began to laugh and called out to him waggishly, 'there goes a devilishly odd fellow!'[31]

Bodily waste was also used in dares, particularly by young men, who 'jokingly' sprayed urine over their victims or slipped some into their beer at the tavern. This often provoked angry confrontations that ended badly, not so much due to the soiling itself but because of the feeling of humiliation. Such tricks were also a source of much anxiety at a time when witches were still being burned, as all bodily waste was liable to be used in magic, for good or ill. It seems such aggressions were considered worse if they involved excrement. In the village of Montigny-en-Ostrevent in northern France, in around 1594, some young men of marriageable age accused a fellow drinker of disrespecting them in the courtyard of an inn where they were urinating by dropping his britches and defecating in front of them. Others at a wedding in nearby Gonnehem on 1 September 1612 professed themselves shocked at the sight of an 'idler' defecating in plain sight, five feet away from the table laden with food, an action which was 'abominated by several'. The document is not explicit on this point, but the distaste of the witnesses would have arisen not only from the sight, but also from the smell wafting over the food as it was served. The closeness to the table suggests that the nearby guests found the experience most unpleasant. During a quarrel in Annœullin on 6 May 1644, again involving two young men of marriageable age, one dropped his hose, turned to the other, and shouted, 'Here's my arse for you. I will get the best of you.'[32] He bested his opponent by symbolically equating him with his own excrement. This may also be the meaning behind an insult commonly proffered by women. In 1529, a peasant woman quarrelling with a man shouted in exasperation that she was not afraid of him: 'I'd boldly show you my arse if it wasn't all shitty!'[33] The washerwomen on the banks of the Seine often jeered and mooned at passengers on passing boats, as did the women of Paris at their windows.

While country areas undoubtedly smelled ripe and unpleasant for visitors, they were by no means as foul-smelling or polluted as urban areas in the *Ancien Régime*, for the simple reason that villages were home to a few hundred people at most and housed few of the trades that generated much of the odour pollution typical of urban centres and their immediate surroundings. The urban population, hemmed in by the city walls that let epidemics wreak their deadly havoc, did not wait for the Enlightenment to set out for the countryside to breathe fresh air. Anyone who could afford to leave the Paris fug behind for the summer did so, moving to their country homes, which became increasingly common in the sixteenth and seventeenth centuries. The trend became a major fashion in Rousseau's day, partly due to his descriptions of enchanting, virtuous nature where the air bore the scent of simple happiness, but also largely due to the vital urge to flee the putrid, stifling air of the monstrously sprawling, expanding capital. The urban population also sought to leave behind the sheer noise, the crowded streets, the hordes of beggars and prostitutes, the dangerous, grumbling, threatening underclass whose ranks were swelling at a steady clip. The eighteenth century saw hosts of well-heeled, well-connected Parisians leave for the surrounding countryside to live in 'rustic' homes, bourgeois follies devoted to delights of the table and bedroom, or aristocratic manor houses. The richest built their own, or remodelled their family home in the modern style à la Versailles, creating luxurious family châteaux set in vast grounds ringed by walls and fences to keep the locals at a distance. This trend, a forerunner of today's galloping rurbanization, was a way for many Parisian notables to return to their roots. Many had spent their early years with a country wet nurse, which might explain why they felt such sensory kinship with the rural sphere.

Life in the villages around Paris underwent profound changes as a result. To give just one example, Boulogne was a village of around 800 people in 1717. Its soil was not suited to cereal crops and was mostly given over to vines. It did a flourishing trade in laundry for the wealthy inhabitants of the nearby châteaux of Madrid and Bagatelle. By around 1789, its population had grown to 2,000. Nobles and wealthy bourgeois Parisians owned country residences there, set in vast grounds. Such residences were also popular in the Montmorency valley, half a day's walk north of the city. Wet nurses living in the parishes where fruit orchards, particularly cherries, were the main source of income were much sought after for the babies of Paris.[34]

The urge for a rustic lifestyle was expressed in powerful terms by eighteenth-century philosophers and physiocrats. The Duc de La Rochefoucauld, descended from the Louvois family on his mother's side, had a vast garden *à la française* laid out at his château in La Roche-Guyon, to the north-west of Paris towards Normandy, its crowning glory an experimental orchard planted with a hundred or so fruit trees. Following the illustrious example of Louis XIV and his kitchen garden in Versailles, the duke was part of a trend making the simple pleasures of country living fashionable once more. Cultivating one's garden was not merely a philosophical metaphor popularized by Voltaire. It was the only way of healing a sense of smell constantly assailed by unpleasant odours in city and at court. Well before she became the king's mistress, Madame de Pompadour, a Parisienne through and through, left the city and its foul air every summer for the delights of the château d'Étiolles, near the forest of Sénart, north of the city. She later owned, or rented, many other châteaux to give free rein to her passion for the produce from her own lands. She looked after her own dairies and loved plants, exotic or native to France, greenhouses, and growing her own food and flowers. She is said to have ordered beautiful porcelain imitation flowers doused in artificial perfumes to please the king on one of his visits to Meudon, just south of the city. Marie-Antoinette's love of playing shepherdess is also well known. Louis XVI built her a play farm at the Hameau de la Reine in the grounds at Versailles. The prettily beribboned lambs may have smelled slightly of mutton, one of the most reviled of smells in ancient Greece, but the place must have been an olfactory paradise of fresh country air compared to the hellish pestilence of one of Europe's two biggest cities.

3

Joyous matter

'[T]he human being in early childhood learns to consider one or the other aspect of bodily function as evil, shameful, or unsafe. There is not a culture which does not use a combination of these devils to develop, by way of counterpoint, its own style of faith, pride, certainty, and initiative', wrote a famous mid-twentieth-century psychoanalyst.[1] The civilization of sixteenth-century France seems to offer a counter-example to this claim. This chapter sets out to demonstrate that sixteenth-century French adults, whatever their social class, showed no signs of anal or sexual repression. Rather, a robust scatological and erotic culture dominated both rural societies and more learned spheres. Might this be due to the widespread practice of swaddling newborns? Wrapped up like tiny mummies with only their heads left free, they lay in their own excrement and urine until they were changed. Doctors, parents and nursemaids by no means demonized children's excreta, especially as the culture set little store by cleanliness, water being considered dangerous.[2] Only a handful of moralists followed Erasmus's example by seeking to repress man's animal nature. Not until the early seventeenth century did a wave of repression demonizing the lower half of the human body sweep across French society, as chapter 4 will show.

A scholarly culture of scatology

Neurobiologists have argued that the smells we find unpleasant are those 'of strong intensity with a connotation of faeces, urine, or decomposing biological matter'. As a result, they argue, most cultures see bodily secretions and excretions in a negative light; any slight degree of tolerance of such smells can only be attributed to a lack of mains drainage, the use of organic residues in farming, and the existence of scatological rituals.[3]

These three criteria are not the sole preserve of the exotic societies studied by ethnologists. As chapter 2 showed, sixteenth-century Europe met the same definition, with urban centres saturated with the smell of excrement, human fertilizer preferred to any other, and health and beauty treatments making much use of excrement and urine.

A 1557 engraving based on a work by Pieter Bruegel the elder reflects the importance of scholarly formulas giving rise to a whole set of cultural rituals that used bodily waste. The engraving offers a study of the sin of pride. The right-hand side depicts a barber-surgeon's shop, for basic surgical procedures and body care. Perched on a wall overhanging the little awning at the entrance, a pair of naked buttocks can be seen defecating into a round dish. The overspill is leaking down between the awning and the wall, just above the barber-surgeon's head, as he is busy giving a seated client a facial treatment. Behind him, an assistant is pouring a jug out of a narrow window onto a woman's long hair, held over a large basin by a wolf-headed monster. The barber's licence, which also allows him to sell nostrums, is posted on a low wall alongside a pestle and mortar as a message for illiterate customers. Both are very close to the dish overflowing with excrement. The moral of the artist's teaching is clearly that beauty treatments are literally shit. As a moralist, he speaks out against such practices not because they smell bad, but because they are sinful; a peacock and a coquette to the left of the shop represent the results of what were extremely widespread medical and social rituals.[4]

There's more. Human secretions and excretions were a source of humour, at least until medieval farces and Rabelaisian scatology fell out of fashion with the triumph of flowery language, polite society and the *précieuses*, whose pretentious airs and graces were roundly mocked by Molière. The cultural shift can be dated to the 1620s. It marked not just the increasing rejection of vulgarity, with the new breed of foppish coxcombs declaring themselves scandalized by the conduct of the lower orders. Mikhail Bakhtin was wrong to claim that Rabelaisian celebration of excrement as 'joyous' matter was a purely folk tradition. He argued that it arose from the medieval carnival, playing into the symbolic reversal of values and hierarchies in times of festival. In his argument, laughter and the grotesque were an antidote to the dominant 'seriousness'.[5] The closely argued theory, developed prior to 1940 when Bakhtin was being persecuted in the USSR for anti-Soviet activity, posits an equivalence between power and repression on the one hand, and the people and resistance on the other, which is understandable in the context he was writing in. But Rabelais, the priest of Meudon and humanist doctor, had a very narrow audience of cultivated readers.[6] Furthermore, his approach was shared by other great intellectuals of the period and dominated until 1616 and the work of Béroalde de Verville, when it gave way to a vigorously moralizing understanding of human existence that sought to suppress every trace of man's animal nature.

From that point on, men and women of breeding felt increasingly ill at ease with Rabelaisian crudeness. The practice of censoring rude or vulgar words in new editions of bawdy literature reflects a sense of shame quite unfamiliar to the original authors. It was common practice for nineteenth-century editors to cast a veil over risqué content by only printing the first letter of the rude word, followed by an ellipsis. The same anachronistic mechanism of projection explains why the lewdest and most scatological passages were often attributed to folk tradition by writers and thinkers who refused to countenance that men like them could have penned such obscenities in times past. Yet their sources were often purely scholarly in nature. One such is the message on the smell of faeces in a 1562 engraving after Bruegel (figure 4). A monkey is shown grimacing in disgust, holding his nose after sniffing the naked backside of an itinerant haberdasher as he lies asleep. Yet the creature is not bothered by the smell wafting from another nearby monkey shown defecating in the traveller's hat. The scene illustrates the ancient Greek idea, shared by many Renaissance medical practitioners, that human excrement smells worse than that of animals.[7] Similarly, some doctors advised people to breathe in the nauseating air emitted by latrines as a protection against plague, as seen in chapter 2. They were simply following the advice of their forerunners in Antiquity on combatting pestilential air with even fouler stenches. The famous surgeon Ambroise Paré explained that 'one foul smell drives out another', citing the practice of bringing a billy goat into houses to keep the plague at bay. Paré did, however, carefully distance himself from such 'vulgar opinion'.[8] The belief eventually fell out of favour in some medical circles, who looked down on it as common superstition. Yet the long-standing negative symbolism of goats did not stop there. In ancient Greece their smell was seen as one of the worst possible, a sort of distillation of all the stenches of death; their ill fame now scaled new heights as they came to embody Satan in Sabbaths in the days when witches were burned at the stake, particularly after 1580. Even in the closing decades of the twentieth century, goats were commonly put in Provençal cowsheds to keep the plague away[9] – something Hippocrates and his heirs would certainly have nodded at.

Aromatic blazons

Sixteenth-century love poetry turned the female beloved into a sweet-smelling dream. Ronsard was just twenty-six when he published the first of his great works, the *Amours*, a set of odes inspired by Petrarch, in 1550. He had a keen eye for very young beauties, praising their heady scent, a captivating blend of musky, ambrosial and fruity perfumes.[10] 'With ambergris and musk her mouth is filled', he wrote, comparing the beloved with a lovely early spring garden that exudes its own new fragrance. Her tresses 'smell like little flowers'; he feels the desire to 'perfume them with musk, ambergris and balm', in keeping with the customs of the time. Once he achieves almost personal contact within the young lady's olfactory bubble, he faints, 'for your scent fills all my senses with fragrance'. Hoping to be granted permission to explore her even more intimately with his sense of touch, he tactically claims his nose has given him a pleasure as subtle as it is socially approved, contemplating a bee producing nectar on young Marie's lips. Elsewhere, he eagerly drinks in the scent of a rose she wore, the fragrance washing over her face. A kiss from the cruel beloved makes him 'overcome with passion, so pleasurably does my heart beat'. He gives a detailed description of the 'sweet scent' streaming from her mouth, 'which surpasses in sweetness thyme, jasmine, carnation, raspberry and strawberry'.

Banal platitudes? Maybe. But it is clear that the prince of poets made clever use of the sense of smell, combined with taste, to approach his prey and steal kisses that tasted as sweet as they smelled. Yet there is another side to Ronsard's poetry: he can also be bawdy and lusty, as in *Les Folastries* [*Frolics*], published in 1553, then burned on the orders of parliament. As a court poet, he prudently decided not to risk the wrath of the authorities again. Yet he remained a man of his day, penning erotic pieces that were much less tender with the gentler sex than his love poetry. One poem pours scorn on a prostitute whose work

> Pleased her so much that in moving, panting, sweating
> Such a stink of goat rose from her armpits
> and such perfume from her nipples

That Mount Lebanon swathed in saffron
Would have smelled soiled in shit.[11]

In 1535, Clément Marot published an epigram on 'the beautiful
breast'. He was soon copied by other poets keen to engage in literary
sparring on the topic. The year 1543 saw the publication of a collection of verse under Marot's name, entitled *Les Blasons anatomiques
du corps féminin* [*Anatomical blazons of the female body*],[12] containing counter-blazons that were considerably less flattering than
the idealist poetry dedicated to the essence of young womanhood.
Marot himself imagined an old woman's dug hanging limp, so ugly
the sight made him sick:

Begone, great ugly stinking teat
Your sweat would indeed furnish
Civets and perfumes
For a hundred thousand dead.

The *Blason of the Nose*, by Marot's great admirer Eustorg de
Beaulieu, closes with the words:

Nose smelling a hundred times sweeter than balm
Whose scent (when I am with my beloved)
Arouses my five natural senses
More than incense ever did in church.
Nose whose breath is so perfumed
That ambergris and musk are but dung in comparison.

The nose is a very particular appendage, with a direct connection
to the brain, according to modern science. Renaissance intellectuals
believed it was intimately bound up with sexuality. Rabelais was
not joking when he wrote that the length of the nose was a match
for the owner's phallus, though he did also use the comparison to
comic effect.[13] Giambattista della Porta, an Italian scholar, admirer
of Aristotle and specialist in physics and optics, gave a more serious
explanation in a Latin work published in 1586, which proved a
major international success. It pointed out 'a certain proportion
between the parts of the nose and parts of the body'. Men with
long, large noses had genitals in proportion, with the size of the
nostrils indicating the size of the testicles. Such men were known
in French as *nazards*, or nasals, no doubt to the delight of Cyrano
de Bergerac. A large penis adorned with an abundance of curly hair
further proclaimed that its owner was a man of lust. The upshot was
that a man's sexuality was as plain as the nose on his face. Owners
of snub, short or flat noses were not reputed for their prowess in

the bedroom. They were also commonly accused of having foul-smelling nasal cavities: these days we would say that their smell triggered a danger signal in potential female partners, confirmed by the sight of their nose. Female lewdness, on the other hand, needed no visible evidence in the sixteenth century, as all women were reputed to be naturally lascivious. Conveniently, however, della Porta pointed out to his male readers that 'the opening and slit of the mouth and largeness or smallness of the lips denote the opening and slit of a woman's shameful parts and the largeness or smallness of their lips'.

Having started with the nose, Eustorg de Beaulieu – later a Protestant minister – skipped down to the 'netherlands'. He boldly sang of the universal merits of farts, which reign 'without excepting pope, king, duke, or prince', and the 'silent fart warming the small of my mistress's back'. Nothing seems to have been off limits, except for the irritatingly pretentious *précieuses* 'who squeeze their arse tight':

But a bold, round fart that knows no fear
Not a feinted, powdered, forced fart.
A silent gas scented like a shepherdess's fart.
A fart perfuming a laundry-maid's twat
Windy gas, and you, violent fart
That many ladies laugh as they let fly beneath the nose
Stiff, impetuous gas that blows
Sometimes watery, sometimes muddy.
Fart bouncing high and clear without discord
Always joyous, singing until death
You are both immutable in will
And unassailable in power and force.

He took even greater delight in listing the merits of the arse, which 'lords it' over the rest of the body, since many doctors 'take its opinion' to establish the nature of a disease and often seek its collaboration for cures 'by giving it plenty of suppositories / Powders, perfumes, sweet oils and clysters'. He dwelt in loving detail on the delights of a beautiful round female posterior, particularly if on the larger side, 'Paris style'; its sway as its owner walked was full of powerful erotic appeal. He also playfully revealed a little-known privilege enjoyed by women, since

In church, you can
(If you need) sigh and fart
Though the nose might take umbrage
And others call that sacrilege
Which for you is a very fine privilege.

Getting to the bottom of things in the conclusion, he evokes natural bodily functions and 'joyous matter' with a Rabelaisian verve that is as erudite as it is epicurean.

And to strengthen your praise
Say you hold dominion over all the limbs
So that you can dispose of their beauties
Or leave them, or make them lost.
When you are prompt and bold
In natural works, or when you are vexed with them.
And on you depend their joy or sorrows.
Oh valiant arse, full of prowess,
How happy are all the limbs
As long as you shit, fart, and cough.
For meanwhile they know not the bite of fear
Of being bitten by death while shitting.
Thus they confess that without your benefits
They know not beauty, complexion, pleasures, or delights.

An anonymous author wrote a similar blazon for the arse. He made it the lord of all the senses and source of healing for the whole body, adding 'You are the fundament of beauty.' The pun is more profound than it appears. The text expands on the first, literal interpretation:

If betimes you close your door
The eye loses sight, the mouth seems dead
The nose pales, the breast withers.
Your neighbour the twat professes itself amazed
All calling on you to open again
Else they fall into ugliness.

The deeper meaning of the joke lies in the use of human excrement and urine in beauty treatments recommended by Renaissance doctors. The authors of blazons on the twat show less verve, but are equally uninhibited, as the following example by Bochetel demonstrates:

O kind twat, sweet twat, pretty twat,
Round twat, clean twat, well-polished twat.
Twat in the shade of a wisp of wild hair.
Twat where nothing is deformed or ugly.
Little twat, twat whose ruby mouth
Has made many a large virile member prick up its ears. [. . .]
Twat making good the damage of death.
Twat, the end which crowns love.

The humanists of Rabelais and Ronsard's day were no killjoys. They had a lusty appetite for life and called a spade a spade. Their writings are redolent with all the smells in nature, including bodily excreta and uninhibited sex. Painters of the Flemish and Dutch schools were equally at ease with 'joyous matter'. Playful descriptions of excrement became a sort of code enabling writers to communicate with the social and cultural elite, excluding the lower classes who formed the majority of the population. The people buying bawdy, Rabelaisian books were never peasants or the 90 per cent of the population who could not read. Nor were paintings or prints within reach of the more modest social classes, who had neither the financial wherewithal to acquire them nor the cultural knowledge to understand them. Rabelais was therefore not the last intellectual to take a stand for popular culture. Rather, he belonged to a dominant strand of encyclopaedic humanism, powerfully influenced by the beliefs of Antiquity and the resulting resurgence of pagan gods. Christian censors may have been at pains to expurgate his works alongside those of Marot and to ban a book by the young Ronsard. They could not, however, suppress the century-long expression of a philosophy of life that made the case for physical pleasure and dismissed erotic, obscene and scatological taboos.

Only the defeat of this school, close to Erasmus's optimistic brand of humanism, explains why such surviving works were locked away in private cases in libraries until recently. The victors mostly expurgated or hid, and in some cases even destroyed, material they considered indecent, particularly in terms of imagery. As early as 1563, the Council of Trent launched a crusade against nudity, led by armies of *braghettoni* or 'breeches makers', the forerunners of Molière's Tartuffe, hired to cover up the genitals on display in works of art. Later, other forms of lewdness were similarly censored, as the right-thinking bourgeoisie of the day took umbrage at the sight of the many characters shown shitting and pissing in the works of Bruegel and others in the same vein. Artists were often paid to paint such details out. Two paintings by the Dutch master Isaac van Ostade suffered this fate (figures 1, 2 and 3). One scene of a village fair outside a church, painted in 1643, included in the lower right-hand corner a man slightly away from the crowd, crouching and defecating in front of a dog. The painting, which belonged to the British crown, was discreetly altered with the addition of a bush in around 1903, at the start of Edward VII's reign. The work was recently cleaned with a view to being included in an exhibition at Buckingham Palace in 2015, when the detail was revealed. The second painting, which dates from 1641, shows peasants outside a farmhouse cutting up a pig carcase hung by its legs by the door. When the painting, purchased in Amsterdam by a wealthy American in 1969, was restored in 2014, a clothed man sitting on a chair in the lower left-hand corner was revealed to have been initially painted crouching with bare buttocks, defecating with his back to the viewer.[14] Like Bruegel before him, van Ostade was by no means a pervert with a taste for scatology. His customers were wealthy city dwellers, many of them aristocrats, who appreciated his witty illustrations of rural life and customs. The paintings are not purely realistic, but rather moral lessons for the upper classes. By the mid-seventeenth century, new norms of modest behaviour had taken firm root in such social groups. In January 1635, a nobleman committed a murder in an unidentified parish of the Spanish Netherlands. He was eventually pardoned on the grounds that he had called out to warn people off from the isolated spot where he was answering a call of nature, not wanting to be 'surprised in his need, which demands solitude',[15] but they took no notice. Decorating the home with amusing genre scenes of the crudeness of village life left the owner feeling much superior to the lower orders depicted in the painting. As an expression of social disapproval it was subtle, but it ran deep. Van Ostade's two works draw a direct link between country folk and animality. The dog watching the crouching man in the first painting and the cut-up pig in the second are the only two animals that will eat human excrement, even in towns and cities, as shown in chapter 2.

Humour in the *conte*

While the wit of many sixteenth-century artists and writers, most notably Bruegel, sometimes showed a degree of warmth for country folk, it bore the same message of social differentiation. Its backdrop was an elite cultural realm, its function to unite disparate groups separated by tiers of scorn: courtiers, court poets, the king's intellectual entourage, nobles high and low, regular and secular religious orders, the well-to-do bourgeoisie and impoverished intellectuals. The social origins of such writers are somewhat varied, from François I's sister Marguerite de Navarre, who wrote bawdy narratives, to humbler representatives of Rabelaisian wit, though none is from the bottom rungs of the social ladder. Furthermore, it is often forgotten that humans are rarely wholly consistent: Ronsard held up the ideal of pure love in his odes, but his *Folastries* revealed a coarser, more brutal side to him.

Then there was Queen Marguerite, aptly dubbed 'dual Marguerite' by Lucien Febvre.[16] She dipped her quill in the finest holy water and in more stomach-turning liquids. She wrote works of great spirituality alongside seventy-two 'joyous' tales, published as the *Heptameron* ten years after her death, in 1559. The tales seem to have originated in a court entertainment where the members of a chosen society conducted verbal jousts to delight their audience. Queen Marguerite and her court seem to have been anything but strait-laced, to say the least. The narrative takes place at the Cauterets baths, where five men and five women take turns to tell stories. The fifth story involves two Franciscan monks who try to sexually assault a ferrywoman, who gets the best of them. The eleventh recounts the misfortunes of a lady of quality who

> was constrained to go in great haste to a certain place, and, not looking to see whether the seats were clean, sat down in a filthy spot and befouled both her person and clothes; whereupon crying out for assistance, in the hope that some woman would come and cleanse her, she was waited on by men, who beheld her in the worst plight in which a woman could be found.

The moral of the story is that the victim ended up laughing about her misadventure along with the others. Future readers are also tipped the wink by one of the women listening to the tale, who enjoys the story, 'filthy' though it is, because she knows who the heroine is. The king's sister clearly acknowledges that a detailed description of 'joyous matter' is on the borderline of what is acceptable in her own social circle, yet she also feels that the pleasure from sharing the tale with an audience makes up for infringing the rules of decency. The fifty-second tale is an account of pungent revenge. An apothecary's valet punishes a lawyer who is plaguing him by 'dropp[ing] from his sleeve a lump of frozen ordure, wrapped in paper like a sugar-loaf'. The lawyer, who has been following him, picks it up and hides it in his bosom. While he is feasting at a tavern, the 'sugar-loaf' thaws in the warmth from the fire. When the stench reaches his nostrils, he castigates the serving woman: 'Either you or your children have strewn all this room with shit.' She replies, 'By Saint Peter! there is no filth here unless you have brought it in yourselves.' He then realizes that his luxurious fox-lined cloak is ruined.

A discussion then follows, revealing an essential difference in vocabulary between the male and female characters. Marguerite uses the male narrator's voice to suggest 'my story is not a very clean one'. While 'words have no stink', a female character suggests that some 'are spoken of as nasty, and [. . .] of such evil odour that they disgust the soul even more than the body'. The debate skirts around the taboo word, 'shit [*merde*]', which in fact only features once in the entire book, spoken by the lawyer. The lower-class tavern keeper prefers to use the word 'filth'. In reality, Marguerite de Navarre knew that she was treading on delicate ground in terms of her own social class. In the first version of the anecdote, it was the lower-class woman who used the more vulgar term. The second version, closer to norms of female behaviour at court, seeks to ward off criticism by explaining that women often like to laugh at such matters due to hypocrisy, as the imperfection of human nature prevents them from maintaining the standards of virtue they should display at all times.[17] Modesty, involving a refusal to mention any lower bodily functions but not to enjoy any pleasures arising from them, was slowly gaining ground among women in the highest social class; under their influence, men at court also began to show more civilized manners. Jacques Tahureau, a gentleman from Le Mans who wrote a set of *Dialogues* some time prior to 1555, hinted at this development in criticizing the Italian manners of Henri II's entourage, who had to sprinkle their conversation partners with 'holy Court water' to get ahead in their own careers.[18] However, deeply crude language and bawdy behaviour remained perfectly acceptable for men throughout the sixteenth century, as Brantôme's *Vies des dames galantes* [*Lives of gallant women*] amply demonstrates.

Marguerite was the only female author of such narratives in her day. The much more numerous male authors expressed a sensibility that was shaped by their gender. Their goal was often to make their readers laugh, and it is no great discovery to point out that they shared the same repertoire of wit: the surprises of love, women, their boundless sexual appetite, lewd and greedy monks and 'joyous matter' were all part of it. Using faeces for comic effect was nothing new: medieval farces had done the same. The main development in the Renaissance was the growing tension between its omnipresence in daily life and the slowly emerging expectation that lower bodily functions should not be mentioned in polite society. For such authors, including Rabelais himself, laughing at bodily functions became ever more important as a way of fighting the progressive decline of the customs that underpinned virility and masculinity. These men sought to defend substances and smells that were intimately bound up with male sexuality. The scatological, bawdy rites they underwent in their youth, whatever their social background, familiarized them with the crude vocabulary they used in their own writings and passed on down to the next generation. However, they were aware of the societal shift then under way, and increasingly placed such indecent language in the mouths of the lower classes living in towns and cities and particularly in the countryside. This gave them the means to keep laughing at the same material without risking the disapproval of strict moralists and modest ladies, as decency now obliged them not to enjoy such comedy too openly.

The earliest such author in the sixteenth century, Philippe de Vigneulles (1471–1528), wrote his tales between 1505 and 1515 in Metz, which at that point was part of the Holy Roman Empire and lay outside French control. Running a business as a draper, he knew the value of money, and most of his characters live in urban settings or the city's rural surroundings. He handles his female characters with a fair degree of respect, as they run their households, work hard, and are a valuable source of advice for their husbands. Yet many of the stories feature wives of easy virtue. Are all husbands of simple-minded women so easy-going and good-humoured? One wife lets the local priest take his tithe of her arse, believing that she had to pay the church in kind even in this private matter. When her husband finds out, he invites the priest home for a meal and gives him his wife's urine to drink: 'It's fine and proper white wine from the vine you took your tithe from', he crows. Philippe de Vigneulles also has a pronounced scatological interest, the subject taking centre stage in some ten or so stories. Metz was indeed a dirty city, where the streets were used as privies once darkness fell. Excrement was a common topic for jokes that nowadays are more cringeworthy than funny. For instance, a peasant takes revenge on a valet by defecating in his helmet. When he puts it on, his comrades show their disgust at the smell: 'Fie, fie! By the very devil, fie! What devil is it that stinks so? I think you have shat in your breeches.' Another take makes comic use of a gentleman's delicate sensibilities to put him in a tricky situation. He is obsessed with cleanliness and demands that glasses should be rinsed and hands washed before touching them. He cannot stand strangers touching his door and has it immediately cleaned when they do. Having had the misfortune of soiling one of his fingers with his own excrement, he wants to have it amputated – but as it hurts, he puts it in his mouth.[19] Two conclusions can be drawn from the story. The first is that the new norms of behaviour and cleanliness were already extant at this early stage, but were seen by the author as unusual and laughable. The second sheds light on the mechanism of soiling and self-contamination: excrement becomes dirty only on leaving the body, as indicated by the gentleman's panicky reaction, deciding his finger was now so disgusting that amputation was the only answer.[20] Excrement could also be used as a weapon to contaminate another organism or to wreak vengeance, as in the case of the valet's helmet. Then there is the ultimate twist of the cuckold scoring a point over the bawdy priest by making him drink his wife's urine. The lover is humiliated by ingesting liquid produced by a woman he has had carnal knowledge of, triggering laughter from his contemporaries.

More such bawdy and scatological tales were published towards the mid-sixteenth century. One such author was Marguerite de Navarre's *valet de chambre* Bonaventure Des Périers, who published his tales in 1558. His humanist, epicurean style reveals a lighter approach to such comic material, with no major references to smells, nauseating or otherwise. At most he points out an amusing lapse in taste when a young widow is kissed 'Italian style' [i.e. French kissing]: which the author points out was then a very new practice in France. When she discovers that in Italy, that style of kissing is reserved for prostitutes, she takes the indelicate kisser to court. Accused of sticking his tongue in her mouth, he exclaims, 'But why did she open her beak, madwoman that she is?', prompting the judges to burst out laughing and dismiss the case. They add mischievously that the next time the widow lets herself be kissed she should keep her jaws squeezed tightly shut.[21]

Other authors mined the scatological seam of smells yet further. In around 1555, the gentleman and landowner Jacques Tahureau wrote his *Dialogues*, which contain numerous references to bad smells: one fat valet is described as 'smelling like a shoulder of mutton', while another inconsiderate character takes off his shoes, wafting those present with 'the suave and precious scent of his feet'. Like Philippe de Vigneulles, Tahureau displays a conventional sense of superiority, widespread among the elite, over the lower classes, 'the foolish and inconstant common herd'. Similarly, the anonymous author of the *Comptes du monde adventureux* [*Tales of the adventurous world*] (1555) pours scorn on the peasant classes for their ignorance, particularly in terms of smells. The thirty-eighth story recounts an unnatural love story between a wealthy young villager and the daughter of a poor country nobleman. The young woman gives her beloved a pair of perfumed gloves. Being used 'to smell[ing] nothing but the perfume of piglets', he wears the gloves all the time, even to muck out the cowshed, and claims to love his fiancée 'as much and more than the best of his cows'.[22]

The final third of the sixteenth century saw a considerable upswing of works of this sort, as if to draw the sting from the tragedy of the terrible wars of religion. Authors included Jacques Yver (1572), Étienne Tabourot, sieur des Accords (1572? and 1588), Antoine du Verdier (1577), Philippe d'Alcrippe (*c.*1579), Bénigne Poissenot (1583, 1586), Nicolas de Cholières (1585, 1587), Noël du Fail (1585), Benoît Du Troncy (1594) and Guillaume Bouchet (1584, 1597, 1598). Such authors embody the ongoing Rabelaisian tradition of the body and joyous matter. The country gentleman, jurist and member of the parliament of Brittany Noël du Fail is one of the best known. His considerable professional responsibilities did not stop him writing the occasionally somewhat noxious *Contes et discours d'Eutrapel* [*Eutrapel's tales and discourses*], published in Rennes in 1585. The tales offer a curious combination of smells: seeing a gallant courting a young lady with a violet, another, less silver-tongued suitor produces a 'pyramid-shaped masterpiece' for her, sticks the violet into it, and tops it off with a hat. Did the author know that violets only have a very fleeting scent, making it one of the hardest flowers to extract perfume from? Of the other aforementioned authors, Étienne Tabourot of Dijon, a judge, likewise scatters his writings with smells for comic effect. One such is the motto of his idiotic hero Gaulard, 'From one to the next', placed over two engravings of a baker's oven and a privy. Another such work is *Le Formulaire fort récréatif de Bredin le Cocu* [*Bredin the cuckold's highly entertaining form*], published in 1594 by Benoît Du Troncy, secretary to the consulate in Lyon. Claiming to be a countryside notary, he writes thirty-five absurd contracts full of sexual jokes and references to excrement, both human and animal.[23] Of the fifty tales in the *Escraignes dijonnoises* [*Dijon spinning parlours*], published pseudonymously by Tabourot in 1588, ten rely for their humour on sex, twelve on farting, eleven on defecation and two on urinating. The forty-first has a dull-witted farmer unknowingly entering an eloquence contest with the clever daughter of a nobleman to win her hand in marriage. When he asks her to cook him some eggs for dinner, she snaps '*C'est bien chié*' [literally: that's well shat, meaning what a cheek]. He then hands her his hat which he had hastily used as an improvised toilet shortly before, saying 'Here you go, my young lady', leaving her speechless and winning her hand.[24]

Such collections reflect major changes in behaviour. Du Fail records a sort of past golden age of nobility from the days of François I, when everyone helped themselves to meat and vegetables from a large dish in the middle of the table. Now, he laments, meals are served in individual dishes, but those who now live on 'smoke, speeches, hand-kissing, and bowing, are but half men'. He has his hero Eutrapel tell the killjoys who have no love of 'filthy' tales that there is nothing ugly in nature, and that such words are even to be found in holy scripture. He shows much forbearance for 'the good person who lets a large fart fly (Froissart would have said "ring a pair of bells" and affected types "a sonnet")'. He remembered the old country customs fondly, with amorous play and petting of an evening, young men dancing round the graveyard, and hiding stones in their clothing in anticipation of the inevitable clash with rivals. For, claimed du Fail, there were no barriers between the common folk and nobility in the countryside.[25] Jacques Yver, a mayor of Niort who died young before his only work, *Le Printemps d'Yver* [*Yver's spring*, with a pun on the author's name, which is a homonym for *hiver*, winter], was published in 1572, similarly regretted the loss of a simpler life for gentleman landowners in the Poitou region. Times have indeed changed, he sighed, as a young man of high birth must now see the world, display good breeding and pretend to be blasé. Yver pours scorn on the affectation of his fellow men influenced by Italian manners, who stupidly call their mothers 'Madame'.

Clearly, the new standards of behaviour created a gulf between the rural nobility and the farming folk they once rubbed shoulders with on a daily basis, particularly in their early years. Bénigne Poissenot, who feigned admiration for Yver while taking the opposite view, shows obvious disdain for rural folk a decade later in his *L'Esté* [*Summer*] (1583). Born in around 1558 in a village near Langres, he was neither a gentleman nor a peasant, but a law student with a wide-ranging humanist education. His ideology was close to that of the Parisian bourgeoisie, who were fervent Catholics and sworn enemies of the Huguenots. His tales, told by a group of students travelling in Languedoc in southern France, are highly scathing about the poverty, coarse manners and filth of the field labourers. He gives a terrifying account of their cruelty towards soldiers and travellers found alone and sees their festivities as drunken debauchery, characterized by dreadful brutality to unmarried young men from neighbouring towns and villages. He writes of constantly wearing his sword, so little does he trust them, and pours considerable contempt on 'these plebeians', 'the rabble', these 'people of such little merit'.[26] But Poissenot differed from his predecessors in one significant respect: he saw the world through a filter of religious intransigence. In 1586, he published his final work, *Les Nouvelles Histoires tragiques* [*The new tragic stories*], and vanished from history without trace. He belonged to a growing culture of intolerance that, under Louis XIII, energetically rejected Rabelaisian, hedonist narratives as being too erotic and scatological to be decent. Nicolas de Cholières has some similarities with this model, though his work still has some profoundly salacious features.

The old taste for comedy was not quite dead yet, however; nor was the relatively indulgent, gently teasing attitude to poor country folk. Even with his urban background, Du Troncy still looked kindly on them in 1594, as did Guillaume Bouchet's three series of *Serées* [*Soirées*], published from 1584 to 1598. Bouchet was the son of a

well-known printer, the well-educated scion of a bourgeois family
from Poitiers, who enjoyed scholarly soirées and good jokes. He
looked down on villagers with an air of benevolent superiority,[27]
delighting in recounting their naivety and their comical mishaps
for the amusement and delight of his social equals, like Bruegel
and other genre painters of the day. His cultivated soirées hosted
widely read people like himself, who, under the sway of the civilizing
process, laughed at risqué themes while adopting a detached attitude
to them. Guests at the soirées, for instance, returned to a subject
much discussed in medical circles since Antiquity: 'The excrement of
dumb beasts does not smell as bad as that of men.' They delighted
in scabrous accounts such as the tale told at the start of one supper
about a monk hoist by his own petard:

> A doctor was consulted by a mocking priest
> On the following point
> Why, when he pissed, did he always fart:
> It is nothing, he said to the farter,
> That is often what donkeys do.

Bouchet adds that the guests greatly appreciated the tale, though 'the
subject was a little dirty'. Another anecdote about a fat monk urinating in the street to the hilarity of women passing by was cut short
when the narrator started to explain that fat men 'are badly hafted'.
The women present threatened to leave if he continued. One of them,
'good and well-taught', held that 'it is neither decent nor proper to
piss in the streets', adding that even Turks find it scandalous and are
embarrassed if they have to do so.

The sense of smell plays a significant role in the work. The best
way to get a dog to love and follow you, it explains, is to give
it some bread you have held in your armpits for a while. Maybe
faithfulness means being led around by the nose? Smells also had a
gender component. Menstruating women were supposed to induce
abortions in mares. The claim, made by Pliny the Elder and shared
by all Renaissance doctors, was that the poisonous air emitted by a
woman's 'flowers' was destructive. The seventeenth *Serée*, wholly
devoted to smells, is a compendium of contemporary scholarly and
folk wisdom on the topic. Smells are stronger from a distance than
close up, it is claimed at the outset, as they are merely 'a vapour
arising from heat'. People suffering from sickness and corrupted
humours give off bad smells. The stronger the smell, the greater the
threat to health. Laughter is health-giving as it leads to farting, as the
diaphragm muscles control breathing and 'also serve to expel excrement'. The discussion then turns to ways to avoid fetid body odour.

The medical answer is that like cancels out like, so that an individual wearing a musky perfume cannot smell the scent on other people. Eating foul-smelling foodstuffs cancels out body odour. One joker then interjects that all it takes to avoid feeling the cold is to sniff a fresh turd in a handkerchief, as that will fill the senses. His sally is met with a burst of laughter, and the group is amused by a discussion of nourishing smells and pleasant effluvia of the sort described by Aristotle as improving health and even encouraging sensuality, as their heat combats the brain's innate chill. Garlic is one such: 'Those who eat it should not be rejected, as they are at this time.' Is this a veiled allusion to Henri IV, reputed to be over-fond of the bulb and to smell less than fragrant? Garlic and onions, Bouchet continues, are food for soldiers, encouraging them to fight. The French used them in generations past but disapproved of perfumes, which masked natural flaws, 'the most perfect scent of a woman being to smell of nothing, as Martial writes'. He dates the decline of the Roman Empire to the first use of perfume, making the Romans effeminate.[28] On the other hand, people brought up surrounded by foul smells cannot breathe in fragrant scents without fainting. A peasant on a visit to the town went into an apothecary's, where he felt so ill he thought he was going to die. One waggish passer-by saved him 'by making him sniff some manure, the smell he was brought up on'. The tale translates the olfactory superiority felt by the urban population, though they, too, were surrounded by vile smells on every side. As far as they were concerned, only common country folk smelled bad. Yet such scorn was also a matter of mere convention, as Bouchet often reveals a degree of fondness, even gruff affection, for country dwellers. He continues with an allusion to a mythical people of Antiquity who drove out 'foreign soldiers or others who wore perfumes and scents'. He does, however, allow that musk, civet and ambergris can be used as remedies against foul, pestilential air. He concludes by highlighting the difference between the nice scents enjoyed by humans and the bad smells we dislike, 'pleasant smells relating to our nature, and all stinking things resulting from a natural discord'. In short, the former are evidence of the harmony of divine creation, while the latter undermine it, as will be further shown in chapter 5.

The Way to Succeed

This is the enigmatic title of the last great flowering of Rabelaisian literature, published in 1616. The author, François Béroalde de Verville, conjures up a mock banquet bringing together characters from across the centuries, often scholars, who engage in idle conversation. The result is an inexhaustible string of apparently unconnected anecdotes. The author, whose real name was François Brouard, was born in 1556 in Paris. His father was a rigid Protestant and a humanist scholar and teacher of Hebrew. François borrowed his father's pseudonym, Béroalde, and added his own, pseudo-noble particle. From his father he learned vast swathes of humanist knowledge alongside two fellow pupils who were later to become famous, Agrippa d'Aubigné, later Henri IV's Calvinist conscience, and Pierre de L'Estoile, a scion of the Parisian grand bourgeoisie who became a high-ranking magistrate and renowned chronicler close to the moderate Catholics who lent their support to Henri IV in 1589. Little is known of François Béroalde de Verville's life. His father remarried when he was eleven. After the Saint Bartholomew's Day massacre he was exiled to Geneva, alone. There, or on the way there, he received a letter from his father exhorting him to conduct himself as befitted his Calvinist faith: 'Yet refrain from joining forces with people of bad morals or who scorn God: the habit of vice would risk corrupting you, and you would draw the wrath of God on yourself.' He seems not to have followed his father's advice religiously: he wore a sword and fought in duels to convince people of his so-called nobility. He studied medicine and defended his thesis in around 1575–6. He seems to have been in Lyon in 1578 before returning to Geneva. He moved back to Paris in 1583, at which point Protestants still enjoyed the freedom of religion granted to them in 1577. This is when he published his first works. He wrote in a wide range of genres, from allegorical novels and poetry to treatises on morality and literary miscellanies, not to mention the *sui generis* work *Le Moyen de Parvenir, Œuvre contenant la raison de ce qui a été, est et sera, avec démonstrations certaines selon la rencontre des effets de la vertu* [*The Way to Succeed: A Work containing the reason of all that was, is and shall be, with certain demonstrations according to the encounter of the effects of virtue*]. By 1589 he had moved to Tours. He forswore Protestantism at some point and left the army for the material comforts offered by a tempting sinecure as a canon at the collegiate church of Saint-Gatien in Tours in 1593. He died in 1626.

Le Moyen de parvenir, published in 1616, is a perfect example of the art of narrative. Béroalde borrows a number of details and devices from Rabelais. Some forty of the stories are taken from the comic narratives of Gian Francesco Poggio Bracciolini, the *Cent Nouvelles Nouvelles*, Des Périers, du Fail and Bouchet. A handful of narratives seem to have their roots in the oral tradition, while thirty or so others probably came from the author's own imagination or

real-life experience.[29] The language is rich and earthy. In defiance of
the very strict norms of purity and decency promoted by Malherbe,
court poet since 1605, Béroalde de Verville obsessively refers to the
nether regions of the body. 'To talk about arses only would be a
beautiful thing', he writes, 'It would be a rather good conversation
topic.' He keeps his word, as the term features no fewer than 154
times in the book. He made it the basis of an entire philosophy: 'Oh!
You poor mortal animal! My friend, you probably haven't grasped
that all corporeal beings have to defecate?' However, his burlesque
theological argument must have drawn the wrath of religious con-
formists: 'My friend, if you want to kill someone without anyone
finding out, blow deep into their rectum, so that the soul escapes
through the mouth.' Yet

> everything on this planet happens only to train monsieur in butts, for
> to fill one without touching (a great miracle!), it's essential to allow
> nothing to get in the mouth. But before I finish off, I would like to
> ask you something, both of you, Frenchmen and Englishmen, because
> you enjoy kissing: which part of a woman's body do you like to kiss
> most – the first vertebra or the funnel of the arse? Ah! Ha-ha! Hey-hey!
> The mouth is the funnel of the arse. And, in fact, all tasty things are
> ultimately designed to be turned into shit by your teeth, and thus to
> bring Master Arse into action. *Id est frater culus*, brother arse, which is
> the body's rudder and the soul's sweetheart. I will prove it you. If the
> butt is out of sorts, not doing so well, things are out of order. And this
> affects the soul.

He also outlined a somewhat unorthodox riddle for telling Turks
from Christians that required both to be naked: 'I'll tell you exactly
how! It is the pong of their arses: if there is a musty scent, it is a
Christian – especially since the Turks don't drink wine.'[30] Bodily
functions are constantly under discussion, with seventy-three references to various vulgar synonyms for excrement, twenty-nine to buttocks, seventy-seven to piss or pissing, and a further five references
to urine. The expression 'turned into shit by the teeth' comes up
twice. The author also reveals a deeply irreverent stance to his former
fellow Calvinists:

> There's a particularly beautiful place in Alsace where women enjoy
> certain liberties. [. . .] those ladies are extremely clever: they pee no
> more than once a week. Each Friday morning, they all come a-flocking.
> [. . .] they go to pee – one after the other – as other people would go
> to the market. [. . .] On the privy, they merrily empty their bladders,
> relieve their kidneys, and thus bring into being an almighty river. The
> Germans, Flemish and English use its water to brew two special types

of beer [. . .] And that's the reason why the women of these nations do not love their men as much as French women do: they think their husbands want to pour their very own urine back into their bodies. In case there are any women around who do not know how to pee properly, please send them to Geneva. Over there, you will find numerous wonderful schools where they teach you how to piss and shit – publicly and in company. This is good news for all those prudes who are taught there how to let go of their silly squeamishness that clogs their intestines.

He likewise poked fun at Parisians, mocking their way of talking about bodily functions:

Our Margot [. . .] was walking through the hall to bring Madame an egg. When she arrived in the middle of the room, she greeted us. And, exactly at this very moment, she felt the great urge to pass wind, in other words the desire or lust to do so came over her. (As they say in Paris: 'I'm hungry for a piss, thirsty for a shit.') For fear of an accident, she tried to squeeze her buttocks, but the opposite happened. She clenched her fists so firmly that she surely could have crushed an egg, but this somehow opened her buttocks even more and a very loud fart escaped her. I asked her, 'What? Did you just fart?' She replied, '*Vere*, Monsieur, it's because I've eaten peas.'

Béroalde also indicates that if no 'piss-pot' is available, Parisians simply urinate in the courtyard or even into the fireplace, 'just as travellers do in the taverns on their way to Paris'.[31] The nose, whose erotic potential has been seen above, features seventy times. 'Check out the nose, and you will know / How well-endowed is he whom women like', he advises. However, unlike della Porta, who argued that a woman's lips indicated the size of her genitals, he draws the reader's attention elsewhere: 'In contrast, look at the foot and you will see / How wide the thing of a woman may be.' Foot fetishists will probably agree. Sex underpins the entire book. Words considered vulgar then and now are to be found on almost every page, such as *con* (twat), *cul* (arse), *vit* (prick) and *foutre* (cum).[32] He delights in using rich verbal imagery or inventing his own new expressions. The frustrations of a canon recalling his own misspent youth give rise to a veritable cornucopia of colourful language, particularly to refer to coitus: *bouter, culbuter, fouailler, ficher sans pic, appointer, faire la belle joie, faire l'office culier, secouer le prunier, faire la bête à deux dos, tuer de la douce mort, affiler le bandage, pigeonner la mignotise d'amour, mettre chair vive en chair vive, avoir accointance mystique, cognebas fesser*, not to mention the enigmatic *faire la pauvreté* and *faire la cause pourquoi*.[33] One entire passage is devoted to a list of terms for coitus, describing a witness's astonishment at

> the spectacle of immortality. The virtue of lustfulness. The process of procreation. Four pieces of ham were hanging from a bolt. Two passionate bipeds created an up and down bobbing quadruped: an animal with two bodies or two heads, a beast with four eyes, the female-male, the male-female, the protype of an anagogic mob, a woman just about to be mutilated, a man ready to be gelded (*décoché*).[34]

What are modestly known as the 'nether parts' come up hundreds of times, sometimes in very coarse terms. The penis is mentioned in some thirty words or expressions: *cela* (that, also used for women) occurs 321 times, *vit* (prick) thirty-five times, alongside *couteau naturel, canon à pisser, manche Priape, chaussepied, outil à faire la belle joie* (natural knife, pissing cannon, Priapus's handle, shoehorn, and tool for making fine joy), and, doubtless for the religiously inclined, *goupillon* (a holy water sprinkler). The testicles are *couillons, billons, pendeloques, caillettes* (belonging to a ram), *cymbales de concupiscence, boulettes de Vénus*; one is arbitrarily isolated and defined as the mother of stories. Women assuredly reign supreme in this sensuous literary realm, though they are not always handled with tact or indulgence. There are in total 913 references, singular and plural, to women, ladies, girls, mothers and beauties. The author displays virtuoso skill in coming up with variations on their *cas* (case, used seventy times to refer to female genitalia), their *cela* (that), their *comment a nom* (what is its name), their *con* (twat, 113 instances). He also refers to their *chose* (thing), *minon* (kitten), *trou*, sometimes described as *de service* (service hole), *fente* (slit) and, once, to the clitoris.[35] Expanding on Aristotle, he explains that 'God creates girls, and men turn them into women.' All women, even nuns, 'think about one thing only, because ultimately this is what the female gender was created for'. Elsewhere, he discourses on the calendar of a woman's life:

> 'Hope is far nicer when yet unrealized. This is mainly because the *connins* (rabbits) of little girls have a much nicer design than those of women. There is also the *connin*: it is a sweetheart's backside, which is wiped near the fire, or exhibited when peeing. The *connaut* belongs to those who hit puberty at a tender age: it may fall into shameful sin, and little pubes start sprouting through the skin. Then there is the *con*: it belongs to adult women who had few or no children at all. The *connasse* is the one of old women: it is a complete shambles.' One of the guests adds, 'And what do you have to say about the *connue* (familiar)?' The reply: 'It is a widow's. It's neither one, nor the other.

And yet, but it may just be that way'. Another guest chimes in, 'I think the *connasses* are vexing. They belong to the lower class'.[36]

Béroalde illustrates female lustfulness by staging himself in his mother's womb. As she was being worked over by a president's two-balled lance, he explains, she farted, frightening him so much that he popped straight out, barely four and a half months after his mother got married. Conversely, he mocked the displays of modesty by the women in his narrative, who echoed the verbal hypocrisy of Marguerite de Navarre's tales, in a rather startling exchange between guests:

> They are rather ashamed when being asked, because their target of desire is near the arse. True, infertile women are much happier than fertile ones, because their butts don't reek. As a matter of fact, the bum of a woman who has given birth always stinks [*est toujours faguenant*].[37] Yet, the butt is not the one to blame.

> – Really and truly, do you think they would be happy if they had no butts? But thinking of the little hole, this wouldn't be a good idea.

> – I don't think they have one. Or, they wish that they didn't have one. Especially since they are so moralistic, or at least they pretend to be to make us believe they don't even take a shit.

> – Exactly! It's true that they more or less play the 'goody-goody' to turn us on so that we give them what they crave for so much.

Such women nonetheless came up with stratagems to achieve their ends, like the insatiable merry wives in medieval farces. A haberdasher's wife 'was yearning for' the barber next door. The two of them came up with a plan. She feigned illness. The barber was called in to see her and warned that she was suffering from a potentially fatal contagious disease. He made a light vinegar poultice, commonly used against the plague, telling the haberdasher, 'My friend, you will have to put it on the tip of your penis and push it into your wife's vagina.' The man cried out, 'What, me? Why don't you do your job, Maître Pierre?' 'But, it's your wife.' 'Do your duty, my friend!' 'Without delay, the barber put the plaster on his cock.' When he reached the bed, he took off his clothes and 'put his penis into her hole. In other words, he put it into the hole of indulgence – as fresh as a daisy and in cheerful spirits. In doing so, he cured Madame, the haberdasher's wife. May the same thing happen to everyone who has a craving!'[38]

Smells are mentioned some fifteen times in various burlesque variants, some powerfully excremental. One husband talks philosophically about the love his wife takes from her own belly for him. For when waking up in a jovial mood, 'she opens her buttocks and lets off a fart from hell. It must have gestated between the fatty coils of her intestines, as it exuded a fragrance of a thousand foul-smelling demons.' Women have an abundance of 'grooves that emit odours that are even stronger than the scent of a musk cat', he sighs. Yet every cloud has a silver lining, as the dreadful stench makes him stick his nose out of bed, open his eyes and decide to get up. 'Voilà, now you know more about the astounding habits of the holy arse', he concludes.

One tale that was to remain highly popular for a very long time, as will be seen below, transformed such rancid whiffs into powerful sex appeal, albeit only in the realm of the great courtesans. It furnishes a brief treatise of contemporary olfactory theory, evoking the irresistible attraction of musky perfumes, extracted from animal sex glands. Which begs the question whether nature really gave the smell of human genitals less power, or whether their so-called stink may not be the result of long-standing cultural repression.

Now, all smells are warm in themselves, for they are but subtle exhalations and vapours released by plants, herbs, gums and trees, that spread in the air by means of heat. Let me tell you what happened to Sieur de Lierne, a French nobleman, when he was having sex with a prostitute in Rome. As a chaste courtesan does, she had a collection of small, delicate pieces of membrane – quite similar to chicken skin. And, as artful as a perfumier, she had filled those pouches with a musky fragrance. Now this beautiful Goddess, who in fact owned quite a lot of these little balls, took the nobleman in her arms and made love to him. The two lovers had been caressing and playing with each other for quite a while, when the lady secretly reached for one of those delicious balls. With one hand, she stuck it between her buttocks and let it burst so that it sounded like a fart in a hurricane. The nobleman naturally wanted to stick his nose out from the sheets to gasp for air, but she called out, 'It is not what you think! [. . .]' Feeling reassured, he let the pleasantly musky fragrance flood his senses. It was quite different to what he had expected at first and gave him so much pleasure that he beseeched her to do it again and again. Curious, he asked the mistress whether it was really she herself giving off such fragrant wind, because normally a French lady who blew a fart would stink to high heaven. Thereupon, she explained in a very philosophical manner that her traditional diet – second nature to Italian ladies – was rich in aromatic fragrant herbs; their quintessence would be released through the behind as through a beaker with spout. 'That's true. Where I come from, the ladies blow farts of a different kind', he asserted. Yet, after having issued such delicate scents, this Roman Goddess happened to slip out a fart that was not only natural but really and truly pongy. Hearing and sensing this bodily emission, the Frenchman, who was now very fond of hunting for trumps with his nose, stuck his head underneath the blanket straight away. [. . .] Wishing only to follow his nose, he wanted to seize the chance to get another whiff of this delicate fragrance. But he was sorely disappointed when his nose picked up far more than it could have done with the fourteen wooden shovels that were used to measure out corn in Orleans. But why did this happen? From a nearby public toilet a putrid stench was streaming out, reeking more than the most foul-smelling fart ever. 'Oh my lady', he cried out, 'What have you done?' The moment he opened his mouth, he sensed an evil-smelling moisture that loaded his palate with a feculent perfume. She replied, 'Seigneur, I merely wanted to match the flavour of your country by my gallant gesture.'[39]

The *Moyen de parvenir* was initially published anonymously. The author's name was first given in a 1757 edition, and the canon of Saint-Gatien seems to have published nothing more in the last ten years of his life. He may not have been keen to be known as the author of a book felt to be obscene and scatological. Books were subject to much more powerful censorship after 1618, when religious minorities were persecuted with fresh vigour as the Catholic Counter-Reformation took strict hold in France. The famous court poet Théophile de Viau, accused of irreligion and indecency, was banned from the kingdom in 1619. On his return to France, he was condemned to be burned at the stake in 1623 after his name was attached to some bawdy poems in a 1622 collection, *Le Parnasse satyrique* [*The satirical Parnassus*]. He was eventually sentenced to lifelong exile. The case caused much debate. Théophile de Viau was the leading figure in a group of young aristocrats much frowned upon for their scholarly libertinism and reputation as atheists, but who were under the protection of powerful patrons such as the Duke of Montmorency, who took de Viau into his household in Chantilly, or indeed such as the king's own brother, who welcomed several other members into his entourage.

Béroalde had no such support and had much to fear. *Le Moyen de parvenir* lay wide open to accusations of impiety. Should the defenders of the faith have counted its reference to religion, they would have found more occurrences of various synonyms of the Devil (165) and the Antichrist (six) than references to God (ninety-six) and Christ (one), not counting a further five to pagan gods. Even without counting, they would have been scandalized by certain passages, particularly the one on blowing up the rectum to make the soul fly out of the mouth. The author, a doctor and member of the Catholic church just like his model Rabelais, responds to such pompous pontification with extraordinary insolence: 'As I see it, the land of idiots is not an island. It is our world itself and not outside of it. And yet, there are people outside this world who are calvish.' As a former Protestant, is it not likely he was thinking here of the regular clergy? His sarcasm shows that he had no love for 'reformed Franciscans, priests, Jesuits, and similar people of the other, new world'. Through them, he took aim at the most intransigent defenders of religious orthodoxy, both Genevan Calvinists and the champions of the Catholic Counter-Reformation after the Council of Trent. Marguerite de Navarre favoured a simpler, purer form of Christianity and despised the Cordeliers. Théophile de Viau was persecuted on the instigation of leading Jesuits. Béroalde de Verville hinted that he was no admirer of the turn towards extreme fanaticism in the two rival strands of the Christian faith. The closing paragraph of his polemical tract, entitled 'Argument', hints at his true thoughts: 'Tell me: are you really up for finding the path to success? Make sure you read this book in the right way. It is constructed exactly like those pictures that change when viewed from a different angle. A little bird told me that there are some uncouth fellows who have said, "They are the knaveries of blasphemers!"'[40] The work's broad philosophy is indeed aligned with the taste of the spiritual libertines for obscenity and bawdiness and particularly their questioning of the religious dogmatism that was gaining ground before their very eyes. The optimistic culture of Erasmus and the first French humanists, believing man to be capable of great things, was no match for the rising tide of intolerance and pious humanism, which inclined to tragic pessimism. Yet it did not give way completely. Théophile de Viau's works were published in eighty-eight editions over the course of the seventeenth century, five times more than those of Malherbe. *Le Moyen de parvenir* was printed in several clandestine editions over the same period, and more frequently from the eighteenth on, with the author's name on editions after 1757. Some fifty editions have been printed to date.

Odorous wind

An astonishing epistolary dialogue on defecation gives the reader the feeling that the two correspondents may have read *Le Moyen de parvenir*. The pair were ladies of the highest social rank. The correspondence was begun by the Sun King's sister-in-law, Elizabeth Charlotte, Princess of the Palatinate. On 9 October 1694 she wrote to her aunt, Sophia, Electress of Hanover, who replied on the last day of the same month.[41] Elizabeth Charlotte, clearly in a foul mood, complained about having to relieve herself outside in full view on a visit to Fontainebleau. She was out of favour at that point, as the king had not forgiven her for vigorously opposing the marriage of her son, the future regent, to a bride she considered beneath him. Louis XIV was giving her the cold shoulder and she was unhappy about it. Knowing that her correspondence would be read by others, she took the opportunity to slip in disparaging remarks against her enemy, Madame de Maintenon, calling her 'slipslop' and 'the stupid old woman'. The following outpouring of faecal matter, as it were, could well be a way of getting her own back. The words are nonetheless extremely coarse.

> It is very vexing that my pleasures should be upset by turds; I wish that whoever was the first to invent shitting had only been able to shit, he and all his race, when hit with a stick. Zounds, how is it that we cannot live without shitting? Be at table with the finest company in the world, you still must go and shit. Be with a pretty girl, a woman you like; should the urge to shit take you, you must shit or die. Ah! Cursed shitting, I know no fouler thing than shitting. Seeing a fine person, sweet and clean, pass by, you cry, Ah, how fine it would be if only they did not shit! I can forgive it in porters, soldiers, guards, sedan carriers, and others of that calibre. But emperors shit, empresses shit, the pope shits, cardinals shit, princes shit, archbishops and bishops shit, generals of an order shit, priests and curates shit. Admit, then, that the world is full of foul people, for in the end we shit in the air, we shit on earth, we shit on the sea, the entire universe is full of shitters and the streets of Fontainebleau are full of shit, for they lay turds bigger than you are, madame. If you think to kiss a sweet little mouth with fine white teeth, you are kissing a shit-mill; all the daintiest foods, biscuits, pâtés, pies, partridges, hams, pheasants, all just turned into shit when chewed.

The concluding phrase echoes Béroalde's 'teeth making shit'. The princess subtly slipped the knife in, deliberately failing to include kings and queens in her list (the physiological reason for this remains unspoken). Her aunt doubtless scented danger, as the letter-writer's brother-in-law, the most powerful sovereign on earth at that point, had something of a reputation for being pitiless. Knowing that he would have full access to her response via the spies who kept a close eye on court correspondence, she launched into a vibrant paean of praise probably intended to charm him by making him laugh:

> It is a fine, shit argument you make on the subject of shitting, and it indeed seems that you hardly know pleasure, since you know nothing of the pleasure of shitting; that is the greatest of your misfortunes.

One must never have shat in one's life to not feel the pleasure there is in shitting, for it can be said that of all the necessities nature has subjected us to, that of shitting is the most agreeable. One finds few people who shit who do not think their turds smell good; most diseases come to us only for want of shitting, and doctors only cure us by dint of making us shit, and he who shits best, is cured fastest. One might even say that we only shit to eat, and if meat makes shit, it is true to say that shit makes meat, since the finest-tasting swine are those that eat the most shit. [. . .] The most beautiful women are those that shit the best; those that do not shit become withered and thin, and therefore ugly. The finest complexions are only maintained by frequent enemas that encourage shitting; it is thus to shit that we owe beauty; doctors write no more scholarly dissertations than on the shit of patients; have they not brought from the Indies an infinity of drugs whose sole purpose is to produce shit? Shit is used in the most exquisite pomades and powders. Without the shit of martens, civets, and other animals, would we not be deprived of the strongest and best scents? [. . .] Agree, then, that shitting is the most beautiful, useful, and pleasant thing in the world.

The electress concludes by mentioning the bad mood that drove her niece, despite her freedom, to 'shit anywhere when the mood takes you'. It was a very clever way to put down an unruly child who risked upsetting her master even more. In so doing, she revealed a number of practices of the day that are now forgotten. First and foremost is the lack of repression, even in the highest social ranks, since she claims that everyone likes the smell of their own turds. Then there is the use of excrement and urine in many remedies recommended by the medical profession[42] and the importance of scents harvested from animal sex glands.

The Princess Palatine cannot be seen as an exception or a badly educated German boor. She also describes the immodest games played at court, including a farting contest between herself, her husband and their son, the future regent. In 1710, she wrote that the king was careful not to fart, but that the dauphin and his wife would do so. The civilizing process clashed with long-established traditions in France.[43] *La Farce nouvelle et joyeuse du pet* [*The new, joyous farce of the fart*] was already bringing in the crowds in the late medieval period. The year 1540 saw the publication in Paris of *Le Plaisant devis du pet* [*A pleasant dialogue on farting*], and as has been seen, Eustorg de Beaulieu wrote a blazon on the topic three years later. Erasmus's advice to young people, available in French translation in 1544, was not to squeeze their buttocks to hold in a fart to be polite, because it would expose them to illness. It was better to leave in order to let the fart out somewhere discreet, or if that was not an option, to cover the sound with a cough. A century later, the abbot Charles Cotin wrote a series of riddles on the subject:

By me one of the sexes [female] is touched
By a very unfortunate influence
And one blushes at my birth
As one would blush for a sin.

Assailed by a vigorous wave of moral censure, publicly breaking wind came to be considered uncouth, but the practice soon gained ground again, not only at the very top of the social scale, at the court of Louis XIV, but also in Enlightenment medical treatises. In 1754, a certain Doctor Combalusier devoted a lengthy study to the pneumopathology of flatulent diseases. The topic still invited jokes, of course. Breaking the glass ceiling that reserved the topic for men, Marie-Antoinette Fagnan took advantage of mid-century Anglomania in France to publish her *Histoire et aventures de milord Pet* [*History and adventures of Milord Fart*] in 1755. 'I offer here the life of a famous hero, who has filled the entire earth with the sound of his name', she begins. 'Milord Fart was born in Pants, a town in the Netherlands, between the embrace of two twin sisters, his cousins, the Buttocks. His mother Big-Belly did not bear him long.' The abbot Antoine Sabatier de Castres likewise brought a dash of Rabelaisian verve to his *Les deux pets* [*Two farts*] in 1766. The author of risqué tales unscrupulously borrowed the evocative substance of his narrative from Canon Béroalde, whose work he must have read. He updates the style and puts the work into verse, adding details for a refined contemporary readership. However, he insisted on the pestilential air 'that issues warmly from the dirty region', laden with atoms of faecal matter, and the colicky humidity that brings manly vigour low. Less elegantly than his model, he concludes that 'The arsehole / Of an Italian woman / Could only be a sewer.' The scornfully misogynistic, anti-Italian conclusion indicates that bad smells had also become a matter of xenophobia.[44]

All human societies have developed scatological rites.[45] In *Ancien Régime* Europe, these were common, and had a direct link to our sense of smell. The French often made scatological jokes. Pierre-Thomas Hurtault, a headmaster whose first-name initials in French coincidentally spell out the verb 'to fart' (P. T. is pronounced the same as *péter*), taught his contemporaries *L'Art de péter* [*The art of farting*]. The work, initially published anonymously in 1751 with an eloquent engraving, was reprinted in 1775 under his name with an explicit subtitle: *Essai théori-physique et méthodique, à l'usage des personnes constipées, des personnages graves et austères, et de tous ceux qui sont esclaves du préjugé* [*A theoretical-physical and methodical essay for the use of constipated persons, serious and austere persons, and all those who are slaves to prejudice*].[46] It is easy to agree with the author's opinion: 'The sole principle of the indecency attached to farts is the mood and caprice of men.' It is equally easy to follow his advice, using 'coughs and little ruses with chairs, sneezing, or shuffling one's feet, not to be recognized as a farter'. He then sorts farts into categories: provincial, 'less falsified than those of Paris, where all is refined', household, virgin, fencing master, young lady's 'with a little taste of *off you go again*', married women, bourgeois women, country women, shepherdesses scented with wild thyme or marjoram, old women, bakers, clay potters, tailors, tasting of plums, geographers, cuckolds, soft and sudden. His post teaching at the Military School may explain the long-attested tradition of army humour based on flatulence. In the early twentieth century, Joseph Pujol, better known as *le Pétomane*, was able to play *Au clair de la lune* on a well-placed small flute and blow out the stage lights from a distance. He triumphed at the Moulin Rouge and across France with his Théâtre Pompadour, which the Marquise of the same name would doubtless not have approved of. He even attracted famous audience members including the Prince of Wales and Sigmund Freud, who was very curious to understand why the public was so amused by such uninhibited anality.

Ingenious inventors even studied the problem, if the story of a 1785 discovery by a 'famous mechanic', M. de Venclos (whose name sounds suspiciously like the French for 'closed wind'), was not just a joke.[47] He supposedly came up with the idea of a mute for those subject to flatulence. It produced 'rather than a gloomy, disagreeable sound, the very pretty tune of a bird-organ. The music can be matched with the various states of the individual, serious, tender or light, depending on their nature.' There was no word about what happened to the smell, though the noxious vapours of excrement were the main concern of hygienists in the reign of Louis XVI. In 1777, the king appointed a commission of chemists to study the effects of mephitism, a disease which struck fear into the hearts of night soil men, as has been seen. In the industrial era, the bourgeoisie energetically repressed flatulence. Mains drainage became obligatory in Paris in 1894, though the Pétomane carried on performing on stage until the First World War. This heralded a new era in which bodily emissions went unspoken, doubtless due to two convergent phenomena. The first was the slow but steady uptake of mains drainage, which made the urban population increasingly ill-at-ease with residual smells of faeces or unpleasant body odours. The second was moral in nature, driven by powerful cultural forces: the increasingly wide perception that cleanliness was an absolute necessity. Being dirty and smelling unpleasant became synonymous with social inferiority, even marginality. This was the start of a golden age for psychoanalysis, as repression related to the anus and urinary tract was now widespread in the higher echelons of society, bringing in legions of patients who were suffering as a result of the difficult journey to rid themselves of bodily smells.

The pendulum has recently begun to swing back the other way. The taboos surrounding sexuality, bodily functions and smells began to break down gradually in the 1970s. Publishers nowadays no longer censor rude words by printing just the first letter followed by an ellipsis, as the famous bibliophile Jacob did in his 1861 edition of Béroalde de Verville's *Moyen de parvenir*. Veiling Béroalde with countless layers of modesty was a gigantic undertaking. Following the example of the French comedian Jean-Marie Bigard, known for his crude jokes, comics no longer shy away from scatology to make their audiences or TV viewers laugh. In turn, science reassures us about the universality and harmlessness of flatulence. Professor Marc-André Bigard (no relation to the comedian), a gastroenterologist at Nancy university hospital, writes that 'people who never break wind do not exist, they have simply learned to hold it in enough to fart only when they defecate'. In fact, sulphur compounds are solely responsible for the unpleasant odours that assail our nostrils, as 99 per cent of fart molecules have no smell at all.[48] And breathe!

4

Scent of a woman

Why do women appreciate perfumes much more than men seem to? A poetic response might be that it is because they are more delicate, more sensitive, more ethereal. However, the main causes in European civilization are cultural and social. For the past two or three millennia, women have been accused of smelling worse than men. While the charge is now less common than it once was and it is now seen as a terrible sexist insult, it remains an insidious – some might say subliminal – presence.

Chapter 3 demonstrated the absence of anal repression in both men and women in the sixteenth century. In early childhood, learning shame and fear of something that was potentially bad or dangerous was not based on this mechanism. Rather, it was based largely on fear of the female body, seeking to limit male temptation as much as possible and specially to urge young women into modest behaviour by warning them of the terrible power of their sexuality. Not only did they learn to contain their sensuality, described as insatiable by all the male authorities of the time, but they were also taught that they were the source of a universal danger. The source for this belief lay in Antiquity. In the first century AD, Pliny the Elder described women as the horsewomen of the Apocalypse, sowing destruction every month:

> But nothing could easily be found that is more remarkable than the monthly flux of women. Contact with it turns new wine sour, crops touched by it become barren, grafts die, seeds in gardens are dried up, the fruit of trees falls off, the bright surface of mirrors in which it is

merely reflected is dimmed, the edge of steel and the gleam of ivory are dulled, hives of bees die, even bronze and iron are at once seized by rust, and a horrible smell fills the air; to taste it drives dogs mad and infects their bites with an incurable poison.[1]

Women had a disturbing aura that was unpleasant-smelling by nature and terrifying during menstruation. This belief clearly promoted male control over females, reducing the latter's role to pleasuring their masters and producing children since Greek Antiquity. Their smell was ambivalent in a way that male scent was not: it was powerfully attractive to men, but violently repellent if the woman was menstruating, ill or simply old. The female scent was an extraordinary blend of the smells of courtship and death, in a single being. The 1924 work *Thalassa* by Sándor Ferenczi, a psychoanalyst and disciple of Freud, claimed that men copulate with women because female genitalia smell of herring brine, harking back to the primeval ocean to which man seeks to return.[2] The pseudo-scientific formulation is a simple echo of the enduring negative association in the Western imagination between vaginal odour and fish. French has retained traces of this association in the slang terms *morue* (cod) for a prostitute and *maquereau* (mackerel) for a pimp.

The sixteenth and seventeenth centuries saw a considerable rise in this phenomenon. The medical profession decreed that women smelled vastly worse than men, though men still desired them. Fear of menstruation increased. Old women, though they no longer had periods, were paradoxically accused of giving off a dreadful fetid stench like the Devil's, which explains why collective anxieties clustered around the figure of the witch, doomed to be burned at the stake. Coquettes who masked their own disgusting body odour with perfumes were condemned by churchmen who criticized them for going against the natural order to tempt men astray. The swiftly spreading olfactory taboo meant women were demonized much more than previously. Convinced of their own inferiority and ashamed of their own nature, women experienced one of the most anti-feminist periods in European history.

Demonizing the smell of women

The Zeeland-born physician Levinus Lemnius (1505–68) published a Latin work in 1559 that was widely read across Europe and translated into several languages. It claimed, 'Since women abound with excrement, and emit ill smells because of their periods, they make all things worse and spoil their natural forces and innate qualities.' Like Pliny the Elder, Lemnius believed that contact with menstrual blood destroyed flowers and fruit, tarnished ivory, dulled iron blades and gave dogs rabies. Following Heinrich Cornelius Agrippa, he added further harmful effects to the list: menstrual blood blackened warm linen, induced spontaneous abortions in mares, turned female donkeys barren, and made conception generally impossible. The ashes of sheets stained with menstrual blood stripped the colour from purple dye and flowers. He went even further, claiming the same effects were caused simply by female bodily odours. Building on the theory of humours from Antiquity, he wrote that this was because females were cold and moist, while 'so pleasant and sweet a smell issues from male bodies, and such excellent vapours, because of their natural heat'. In the proximity of such nauseating beings, he added, nutmeg became dry, rotten and blackish; coral became 'pale and wan', but became redder when carried by a man.[3]

Lemnius's understanding of nature led him to make a clear distinction between the two halves of humanity. His view must be taken very seriously, given the considerable international success of his work, which reflected views commonly held by the medical profession at the time. He attributes a deep-seated sense of shame to women, for instance, because drowned female corpses float belly down, whereas men float belly up. This is a religious and moral understanding of gender difference, establishing an implicit comparison between maleness, warmth, light and God on the one hand, and femaleness, coldness and moistness on the other: women were naturally attracted downwards, where contemporary beliefs located their subterranean Hell. Antiquity's theory of humours was given a Christian gloss marking the original dichotomy between men and women and the latter's particular relationship with evil.

The idea is explicitly taken up elsewhere in Lemnius's work. Adulterers, he writes, 'can never keep their jewels beautiful and perfect, as they turn cloudy and dark by the foul vapours they contract from those who wear them [. . .] For they draw venomous qualities from corrupt bodies that exhale such virulent vapours, and infect them, just as menstruating women will foul a clean mirror.' Men's natural pleasant smell is perverted by sins of the flesh into a pestilential odour that will cloud gemstones. This promotes an underlying theory of contagion, from harmful physical contact to poisoning the air by the simple act of breathing. The adulteress's sinful body contaminates that of her lover, making him exhale venom that pollutes the purest of things. For scholars and Renaissance poets alike, the physical microcosm was tied to the entirety of divine creation by invisible threads. The nature of womanhood went from merely troubling to outright dangerous when she was menstruating, which is why sex was absolutely out of the question at that time of the month.[4]

Infection, corrupted air and a pestilential stench, all associated with the medical doctrine of contagion, were also attributes of the Devil, as chapter 5 will show. Lemnius writes that filth and corruption breed rats, dormice, eels, lampreys, snails, slugs and earthworms, while snails, bumblebees and wasps are born from cow pats, and flies spontaneously generate. A century later, the German Jesuit Athanasius Kircher (1602–80) still claimed to be capable of producing snakes and frogs by spontaneous generation. Such creatures born of putrefaction and excrement reinforced the link between Satan and womanhood in contemporary thought. Many such creatures, particularly slugs and snails, were used in women's beauty and health treatments at the time. All were considered to be commonly found in Hell and were included in depictions of witches' Sabbaths by artists daring enough to choose the subject.

Lemnius's theories found fertile ground in cultivated circles in the latter half of the sixteenth century, when the optimistic humanism of Erasmus and Rabelais was gradually giving way to a more pious version. The new humanism, disseminated by Jesuit schools among others, was rooted in a tragic understanding of man the sinner, crushed by a vengeful God. This engendered mistrust in the pagan texts of Antiquity, which were carefully expurgated for young readers. In this context, views of the two sexes became radicalized against the backdrop of the eternal Christian struggle between the forces of Good and Evil. Men joined the heavenly army, while women yielded to Satan's lure if not kept wholly under the male authority of a father, husband or brother. A male guardian was considered necessary for female salvation.[5] In the absence of such a guardian, women would unavoidably fall into Satan's clutches. This was a very convenient way of justifying the growing control over women's lives. The medical profession provided scholarly explanations for their 'natural' inferiority, desired by God, in terms that would be understood by their contemporaries, cunningly confining them within a fear of their own bodies, seen as sources of universal danger. Many writers passed on the same diagnosis.

One such was the mysterious Seigneur de Cholières, whose tales are suffused with humanist and medical references and moral reflections drawn from ecclesiastical sources. His 1585 *Matinées* [*Mornings*] make abundant reference to women in tones that are far more critical and moralizing than those of other male writers of his day. He may have been hiding his true identity: the book has been tentatively attributed to a former Protestant, Jean Dagoneau, who died as prior of Abbeville in 1623. His writings include reflections on the traps of Satan, the flesh and the world. The content of the 1585 publication would seem to confirm he was indeed the author. To live a long life, he advises, avoid sex. Women are very harmful to health because 'the flame of their inferno' dries out their unfortunate lovers. In language worthy of a preacher, he refers to their 'gulfs and quagmires of immodesty' and reminds his readers that men are 'the leaders of women'. Castigating a man who has been 'transformed into a billy goat' by his wife, he uses an image of the Devil: the horned, vile-smelling, lubricious goat is an embodiment of Satan at a witches' Sabbath. A chapter on the 'conjugal truce' contains a charge against menstruation, described as a 'red, phlegmy pitch'. Pliny the Elder's diatribe on periods is quoted at length: 'it infects the very air', Cholières writes, adding vital advice on steering clear of 'this poisonous blood' by abstaining from sex for eight days a month, or ninety-six days a year. This opinion would have been shared by a strict confessor. On top of that, coitus was to be avoided for two years if the woman was breastfeeding, as it caused 'the menstrual flowers to blossom anew' and their odour was harmful for the infant: 'Poor man, you would spoil the milk!'[6] He points out that the prohibition is stipulated in canon law but omits to add that the church also advises lengthy periods of marital abstinence in Lent and Advent. In 1587, his work *Après Disnées* [*After Dinners*] expands on his anti-feminist discourse, attributing the female tendency to chatter to the moistness of their brains: 'In the end, chatter is of great use to them, purging the brain and evacuating the bad humours that could at length, if held in, cause them ill.'[7] Women who kept their thoughts to themselves therefore doubtless had the Devil in their heads!

The taboo on sex during menstruation seemed to be on the rise, though it is doubtful how widely it was followed in practice. The medical profession used fear to try and impose the prohibition. In 1585, Jean Liébault wrote that several of his colleagues feared children conceived from sex during the period of abstinence would be born with leprosy, while he himself held they would be monsters.[8] The foul smell of women became a common observation among doctors, who suggested numerous remedies. The royal doctor Jean de Renou, who died in around 1620, offered perfumed mixtures for incense burners, 'for health or for decorum'. He provided an easy recipe for ladies of quality when they fell ill, to be used particularly on the first day of taking medicine. The powder was based on 'orange and lemon peel, cloves, cinnamon, musk and other similar ingredients macerated in rose water, then said incense burner [is placed] on the flame so that the stench of their arse may be dissipated by the fine scent of such perfume'. He also recommended medicines adapted to the part of the body requiring treatment: 'pessaries for the nature [vagina] of women in the form of Priapus, or a suppository for the arsehole in the form of a cylinder'.[9] Loys Guyon, who died in 1617, suggested two ways of overcoming fetid female smells: 'stinking herbs' such as notchweed and rue held the womb in place and stopped it wandering round the body, as Rabelais had claimed. Alternatively, soft scents and perfumes could be used, with a dab of spike lavender or sweet almond oil mixed with a few grains of civet or musk on a midwife's finger to be placed as far up the vagina as possible.[10]

When ladies did not smell of roses

The unpleasant smell of women haunted the collective cultural imagination in the sixteenth and seventeenth centuries. Artists seeking to depict the sense of smell frequently alluded to it. An anonymous print entitled 'The pleasures of life', dating from the seventeenth century judging by the garments, depicts the sense of smell as a young woman of quality sitting at a table, holding a rose in her left hand. Under her left sleeve is nestled a tiny lapdog of the sort women of fashion carried in their muffs. It alludes unambiguously to the fetid smell of a woman's armpits.[11] Man's best friend, known for an unparalleled sense of smell, is commonly associated with women in depictions of the sense of smell (see figures 5 and 12 below). Cesare Ripa's famous *Iconologia*, published in Rome in 1593, read across Europe and translated into French in 1643, offered artists the model of a woman standing holding flowers and a bottle of perfume, with a dog by her side. It clearly inspired an etching by Abraham Bosse in around 1638, though he also added a pipe for the woman to hold (figure 11). From the late sixteenth century on, other artists chose to depict amorous couples with the woman smelling a rose or holding one out for the man to sniff, with a dog's nose in her lap, which holds a basket of flowers (figures 7 and 10).[12] The poetic appearance hides the true meaning: nothing smells worse than female genitalia, as Jean de Renou claimed. The Dutch engraver Crispin van de Passe (c.1564–1637) produced a cruel work on the same theme (figure 6). A fashionable young lady wearing a lace collar holds a flower in her left hand, with a lapdog in her arms. To her right is a man of quality with a ruff round his neck, giving her a sardonic sidelong glance and ostentatiously holding his nose.[13] The new way of depicting the sense of smell through couples drew attention to its erotic dimension while warning the audience, and men in particular, against the fleshly delights of creatures as sinful as they were smelly.

On a visit to France, the highly refined young Italian priest Sebastiano Locatelli wrote of an experience in Saulieu, Burgundy, on 14 May, 1665:

> We went to see the young women of marriageable age dance, as was the custom on feast days. They were dancing the first dance enlivened by the sound of an enormous fife, but the bagpipes under their arms sounded far better! [. . .] This entertaining spectacle was more pleasurable from afar than from close up, as an extraordinary stench spoiled the festivities. [. . .] Filipponi, a cheerful man, started a dance in which people kissed from time to time; as we changed partners with every turn, he kissed all the women before the end. But the pleasure was, I assure you, well recompensed by disgust, as you needed a strong stomach to come close to some of the women.[14]

It is interesting that he mentioned the smell of the women but not that of the men. He also claimed his fellow traveller shared the same sensations. While he himself fully grasped the importance of steering well clear of the devilish temptresses, his fellow traveller was by no means as reticent: rather, he enjoyed their personal scent, breathing it in deeply as he kissed them all. Some light is shed on the scene by the worldly priest's opinion of women, presented elsewhere in the same account: 'Man loses his mind for a visible beauty that passes in a flash, leaving nothing but stench and filth, and once it has gone, nothing but pain and repentance at having loved.' His aversion is the result of strict olfactory training to associate any female bodily odour with danger rather than the powerful erotic invitation it had once been – and that Filipponi still craved.

At arm's length

The demonization of bodily functions developed considerably in the sixteenth and seventeenth centuries. The civilizing process turned the nether parts into bodily hells and excretion into a sign of animality that must be hidden for modesty's sake. The aim of the twofold rejection was to transform the subject's self-perception: increasingly alerted by terrifying warnings of Satan's omnipresence and threat to the everlasting soul, the subject was urged to repress his bestial side and harness his sensuality to soothe his fears. The treatises on civility that were being published in ever greater numbers provided tricks and techniques for reassuring individuals traumatized by increasing moral demands. They promoted a sense of disgust at the human body by recommending certain objects and materials be kept at a distance using tools and gloves. They advised against physical contact such as touching guests at table when serving them, and recommended keeping away from neighbours and not handling food with bare hands. One of the best-known of such works, Antoine de Courtin's 1671 *Nouveau traité de la civilité qui se pratique en France parmi les honnêtes gens* [*New treatise of the civility practised in France by decent people*], forbade impure contact such as putting elbows on the table, picking up greasy food, drinking from the bowl like animals, blowing on food covered in ash, nose-blowing, scratching, burping, and spitting in public. Displays of temper and bad smells had no place in company. It was impolite to pull faces, roll the tongue, chew the lips, straighten moustaches, pluck hairs, blink, rub the hands together gleefully, crack fingers, shrug, burst out laughing, or talk at close quarters, 'spitting in people's faces and often stinking them out with their breath'.[15] Individual bubbles of private space expanded, preventing any bodily contact, immodest or otherwise. Similarly, speakers were to avoid deliberately contaminating the people they were talking to with their breath.

This final point brings us back to the question of the erotic power of smells. The demonization of the body proved to be much more focused on women than on men. Sebastiano Locatelli's account reveals this polarization. It also suggests that the unpleasant female smell foregrounded by the medical profession and in art did not stop men being susceptible to a woman's scent. Yet modern science has shown that men emit fifty times more substances designed to attract the opposite sex than do women – not as pheromones, whose existence has yet to be proven in humans, but as axillary steroids. Androstenone (related to testosterone), present in male sweat and reminiscent of urine, is the only such steroid that seems to have an effect on women, who can identify it in low doses when ovulating.[16] It should be women who send men the letter often attributed to Henri IV or Napoleon, 'Don't wash, I'm on my way'! The product is now on sale in concentrated form to help attract women, particularly in the United States, where the market seems to be flourishing. Unfortunately, customers have indicated that the effects are inconclusive and disappointing. This belies the commonplace that all men are swine, since androstenone is a powerful erotic signal emitted by male pigs. Maybe it would be better to eat celery, which contains the same substance.

Prior to the recent trend for general deodorization, an initial major olfactory shift took place in the sixteenth and seventeenth centuries, leading to the demonization of scents associated with women, including perfumes and beauty treatments. The prejudice, not rooted in any biological grounds in the modern sense of the term, arose purely as a result of the broadly negative attitudes towards women shared by male, intellectual, medical, religious and political authorities of the times. These multiple pressures gave rise to a fear of the female body that literally terrified men. Cholières summed up their fears, taking up the definition of women by the church father Saint John Chrysostom: 'the nature of evil painted with the colours of good'.[17] Likewise, Jean de Boyssières (1555–c.1584), though he also wrote love poetry, displayed considerable misogyny typical of many of his contemporary writers in a stanza on the humours of women:

> Fury of Hells, inflamed by horrors.
> Angered serpent, venomous grass snake,
> Ugly, foul-smelling toad, stinking grass.
> Infectious privy, pestilential stench.
> Preferred to cold hemlock as poison.
> Sole author of man's perdition.[18]

There could be no clearer demonstration that our sense of smell is entirely shaped by cultural phenomena arising as a result of specific historical processes. In the late Renaissance, men learned to fear smells emanating from women like the Devil himself, to the point of wishing, like Montaigne, that they smelled of nothing at all.[19]

Guilty women

Women could not help but feel guilty, or at least deeply uncomfortable, at belonging to the cursed half of humanity. They were taught to hide their evil bodies and mistrust their erotic urges. Where the commonest female sins of the flesh – fornication (sex outside marriage), procuring and adultery – had once been treated with some leniency by the ecclesiastical courts, they now slowly became punishable acts in France, after the sacred nature of the marriage bonds was confirmed by royal decree in 1557. However, few cases were actually tried, around a dozen a year in the vast area covered by the Paris parliament in the last quarter of the sixteenth century, indicating feeble efforts at repression. The same cannot be said for another infraction criminalized by a further decree the same year: concealing a pregnancy.[20] This referred to failure to declare a child conceived out of wedlock to the authorities. If the child were to die, whether by infanticide, by abortion or even simply by accident, the mother risked the death penalty. Between 1575 and 1604, 494 women sentenced to death by lower courts for concealing a pregnancy made their final appeal to the Paris parliament. In 299 cases, or 60 per cent, the death sentence was upheld and the women executed, usually by hanging. These women accounted for over two thirds of all women put to death for all crimes. Over the course of the same period, only 40 of the 234 women appealing convictions for witchcraft, or 17 per cent, were eventually burned at the stake. The deeply sexist legislation, which was applied from 1557 on, principally affected vulnerable young women, particularly servants impregnated by their masters, and widows. The aim was to prevent not only abortion and infanticide, but all sexual activity outside the sacraments of marriage. The hundreds of terrible cases of public punishment indicate that the authorities were determined to come down hard on women who transgressed, adding terror to the fears of unwanted pregnancy at a time before effective contraception. Magistrates saw it as the worst crime a woman could commit. To them, and to all their male contemporaries, a woman had to be married to procreate legitimately, as she did not have ownership of her own body. Since women gave life in the name of God, destroying life could only be done in the name of Satan. The terrifying edict remained in place throughout the *Ancien Régime*, though courts began to show more leniency in the eighteenth century.

From Henri II to Louis XIII, the ban on sex outside marriage was a religious, political and legal priority. Spectacular public executions turned some of the accused into examples for the crowd. The spectacle of their punishment and public repentance was intended to teach the onlookers an edifying lesson, thereby reinforcing social norms. On 2 December 1603, Julien and Marguerite de Ravalet de Tourlaville, a brother and sister from a noble Norman family, were beheaded on the Place de Grève in Paris, at the age of twenty-one and seventeen respectively. Marguerite had committed incest with Julien and given birth to a daughter. The case was aggravated by a blow to the sacrament of marriage, as Marguerite was married to an older man. The chronicler Pierre de l'Estoile commented on their end soberly, adding that their father almost succeeded in obtaining a royal pardon by throwing himself at the king's feet, but the queen stepped in because of the horrible nature of their crime. In 1604, a cheaply printed news-sheet pitilessly condemned their evil conduct. In 1613, François de Rosset devoted the best-known of his *Histoires tragiques* [*Tragic stories*] to the pair: 'Our century is the sewer of all the others', though 'God leaves nothing unpunished.' He added drama to their final moments by having Marguerite give a repentant speech: 'Lord, we have sinned [. . .] Forgive our iniquity [. . .] as loving humans in whom vice is fastened from their very mother's womb.' François de Rosset claimed that everyone present, including the executioner, was moved to tears. His version takes considerable liberties with the truth, recorded in the official court report. When the sentence was handed down, Marguerite and Julien both proclaimed their innocence, while Marguerite swore that 'a bad husband was the cause of her misery!' and called for a confessor. Julien stood proud, boldly affirming he had no fear of death. Emissaries sent by their father then exhorted them to bear their punishment 'patiently'. Marguerite begged her parents, other brothers and her sister for forgiveness, and declared that she too had no fear of death, 'if she should go to paradise'. The court clerk and confessor were displeased, as they were set on making the pair confess that they deserved their fate and beg forgiveness of their Creator and of justice. Marguerite and then Julien eventually gave in and said what was expected of them. Marguerite wept bitterly, prayed to God and kissed the ground. On arriving at the scaffold, she turned to Julien and said, 'Take courage, my brother! Be consoled in God! We have truly deserved death!' She was beheaded first. Then Julien refused the blindfold and wordlessly underwent the same fate.[21] Rather than the exemplary act of repentance imagined by François de Rosset, Marguerite merely spoke words of support to her brother, along with an expression of her own sense of responsibility, while he stubbornly remained silent, refusing to admit his guilt. The disparity in their reactions probably lay in a clear difference in how men and women perceived sexuality. Men were not under such intense guilt-inducing pressure as women.

Many intolerant moralists and preachers demanded the harshest punishments for those who failed to follow their own definition of the path of virtue. In 1570, the Franciscan brother Antoine Estienne (*c.*1551–1609), based at the oratory of Notre-Dame de Vincennes, published his *Remonstrance charitable aux dames et damoyselles de France sur leurs ornemens dissolus* [*Charitable remonstrance addressed to the wives and maidens of France touching their dissolute adornments*]. The work enjoyed considerable success, reaching its fourth edition in 1585. The content was rooted in typical clerical misogyny, but unlike similar works, it reached a wide lay audience of those able to read in French – in other words, principally men. Though in principle it spoke to a female readership, the author in fact told men what they should and should not be allowing their wives to do. His argument is mainly based on the fear of death and Satan.

All flesh, he reminds his readers, is but 'foul, stinking dung'. That does not, however, mean women should be allowed to conceal their true nature. Rather, he criticizes them harshly for their 'dissolute adornments', particularly their open collars ironed into flounces with starched round folds like those of neck ruffs, and their black masks: the former showed off the skin, the latter hid sexual turpitude. He spoke out even more vigorously against the fashion for women to wear wigs, claiming it was dirty to adorn one's head with the hair of a corpse that may have suffered from ringworm or even leprosy. Yet he also thought women were shameless if they showed their own hair. They should avoid doing so because they were 'subject to their husbands'. The long-standing taboo on showing women's hair, with all its erotic, visual and olfactory messages, lasted until the twentieth century. As we have seen, the Pléiade poets wrote that their beloveds played on their charms by scenting their hair with enticing perfumes. Brother Estienne railed against women who used perfumes in their arsenal of seduction. He particularly disapproved of musk and pomanders, while coquettes who used makeup he scorned on the grounds that 'paint marks out the adulterous woman'.[22]

The elegant woman's mirrors, perfumes and makeup gave Satan a gateway into a body focused on fleshly desires, as all women's bodies naturally were (figure 8). Similarly, too much perfume opened the gates to Hell. The Franciscan Philippe Bosquier published a verse tragedy in Mons (then in the Spanish Netherlands) in 1598, subtitled *Petit Razoir des ornemens mondains* [*A small razor for worldly adornment*], in which a terrible God and vengeful Christ angrily denounced the sins of misbelievers. 'I have plague, hunger, war in my hands / I can still cast them on humans', Christ exclaims. He particularly disapproves of the morals of women who wear makeup, gowns and perfume in the latest fashions to tempt innocent young men into sins of the flesh:

And the better to catch young men in love,
They must plaster themselves in purple and ceruse [white lead],
They must change the naïve colours
That they received from me: they shall have scents,
Their garments doused in musk, they shall have balm,
In their hands will be the sweet-smelling apple [a pomander].
My nostril will not endure these scents,
My eyes are dazzled by all these colours,
I will not endure such vain bawdiness
Which does but stoke the fire of fornication,
Which forces and constrains the blind young lord
To run after them like a young bull.[23]

The reigns of Henri III, Henri IV and Louis XIII witnessed a great wave of diatribes against female immodesty. These were part of a broader attack on the sin of lust, both by Catholics following the Council of Trent in 1563 and by Protestants. The Calvinist theologian Lambert Daneau, who in 1564 penned a book intended to eradicate witchcraft, published his *Traité des danses* [*Treatise on dances*] in 1579, arguing that the practice was invented by the Devil to encourage sins of the flesh.[24] Philip II quickly made dancing punishable by fines in the Catholic Spanish Netherlands as a result. Success was by no means guaranteed in either case, of course. Yet this does point to a moral will to keep the two sexes apart physically during practices that generated sweat and desire. The medical profession followed religious censors, heightening fears of the risk of excessive sexual intercourse to men's health, as their natural heat was said to be sapped by the insatiable sexual appetite of women. In 1568, Ambroise Paré advised steering clear of sex altogether to avoid contagion, as 'Lady Venus is the real plague'[25] who diminishes men's strength. One murderer was even readily granted a pardon on claiming that the wounded man died not of the wounds inflicted on him but of exhaustion, having been foolish enough to give his sensuality free rein. The doctor Loys Guyon's *Diverses leçons* [*Diverse lessons*] of 1604 spoke out against lustful practices: 'For what dirty ends are scents used today', he laments. Not only

> do people perfume their clothes and hair, but many also their virile member, and the vulva before coitus, to enjoy greater voluptuousness. Others wear scented rosaries, not for use in their prayers, but solely for glory and to attract people to love each other voluptuously, and to seem more agreeable. But in church, and on the altar consecrated to God, they will be perfumed but with a little incense costing just two or three *sols*.[26]

He adds that he does not reject perfumes completely, as they can be useful in certain remedies, but advises his readers to use them sparingly.

Jean Polman, canon of Cambrai, published *Le Chancre, ou couvre-sein féminin* [*The canker, or female breast-cover*] in 1635. He saw 'the odious chest' as 'the maw of Hell', Satan's pillow, imagining the Devil frolicking 'on those ivory mounts'. The latter half of the work claims, 'Nature teaches that girls and women should be veiled' – a tradition no longer widely followed in Catholicism.[27] That same year, the Parisian priest Pierre Juvernay published a *Discours particulier contre la vanité des femmes de ce temps* [*Particular discourse against the vanity of women in these times*], which also condemned women who exposed their breasts in the streets, churches and elsewhere. It was a venial sin to uncover the breasts slightly, but mortal if they were mostly bare or if anyone passing by should happen to commit a mortal sin as a result of seeing them, he argued.[28] Nudity had formerly had a positive connotation for neo-Platonists such as the artist Sandro Botticelli, who considered that a beautiful body must house a beautiful soul: it now underwent a profound shift, becoming immodest and sinfully alluring in the case of women. Spanish fashion, which spread throughout Europe in the closing decades of the sixteenth century, sought to avoid triggering lustful thoughts by covering every square inch of skin, with gloves for the hands, high collars and ruffs for the neck, hats and coifs for the head, and thick layers of face powder for men and women alike. Moralists raged against such makeup, however, as a seductive trap worn by women of quality seeking to appear more beautiful, as Juvernay commented. For the perfect pale complexion, they applied a thick layer of ceruse, or white lead, to their faces, then added a touch of vermilion to the cheekbones. Some wore eye-catching beauty spots made of taffeta or black velvet that stood out against the artificially pale skin. Pierre Juvernay saw these as devilish tricks that put the elite women who wore them in a state of mortal sin, promising them they would pay for their sins at the Last Judgement. The church continued to express its disapproval of such practices throughout the seventeenth century. As late as 1682, Claude Fleury, later confessor to Louis XIV, was still writing against the dissolute morals of immodest women. Women who sought to beautify themselves, wore desirable gowns, vain adornments or perfume, or walked with a shocking gait were, he argued, bad Christians.[29]

The brilliant jurist Odet de Turnèbe (1552–81), a man of wit who frequented literary salons including that of the renowned literary mother and daughter Madeleine and Catherine des Roches, wrote a comedy entitled *Les Contents* [*The happy men*] in around 1580. The characters discuss female artifice in very realistic terms: 'A woman who uses paint is anathema to me even if she's as beautiful as Helen. I wouldn't kiss her for anything; ceruse is pure ratsbane, I tell you.' A female character goes even further, arguing that 'It's not surprising that these faces all blanched and vermilioned, with a crust of paint thicker than Venetian masks, have lost their credit amongst intelligent people.' The man then lists the unpleasant-sounding ingredients of such compositions:

> Do you think that young men court ladies to acquaint themselves with the taste of arsenic or any of the other ingredients, such as powdered

talc, Venetian ceruse, Spanish rouge, egg white, vermilion, varnish, pignons, quick silver, urine, wine, lily water, ear wax, alum, borax, oriental cosmetics, wild henna, bugloss root and other such drugs with which they plaster and daub their faces to the peril of their health? Before they've reached thirty-five they're as wrinkled as old sheeps' hide, or as old ungreased boots. They've made their teeth fall out and their breath as smelly as a stink worm's hole. I tell you, when I just think about such vileness I can barely hold my gorge.

The heroine is a cultivated, musical young woman, whose own beauty 'is not the kind which you put away in boxes and take out the next morning. She's true to nature',[30] with no need for artifice.

The concept of foul-tasting and foul-smelling substances is tied in with the unnatural artifices used by unscrupulous women to tempt men. But women could not win: the medical profession was also expounding at the same time on the natural stench of women, even when not menstruating. Many women doubtless saw this contradiction as grounds for transgressing moral prohibitions: paints, pomades, hair powder and heady perfumes derived from animal products remained popular until the reign of Louis XIV, as will be shown in chapter 6. Doctors even kindly recommended remedies against unpleasant female odours. In 1637 Jean de Renou sang the merits of two scented powders, 'Cyprus powder' and 'violet powder', the latter actually made from Florentine iris.

There is a custom of enclosing all these powders in little taffeta or satin bags, which stinking women wear between their two breasts to cover and correct their imperfection, and not only them, but also several effeminate young lords at court. But truth be told, using such powders should only be allowed for those who need them to recover their health.[31]

Actual reactions to the erotic power of bodily odours are hard to trace. They cannot have wholly conformed to the descriptions by doctors, churchmen and men of letters, who are the main sources on the topic, as their writings are laden with moralist messages that on occasion distort the phenomena completely. Jean Liébault, for instance, wrote in 1582, 'Sweat with a pleasant smell reveals an excellent temperature of the humours [. . .]. Thus those who are full of bad humours, such as lepers and lascivious people, exude sweat that smells like a billy goat.'[32] In other words, the foul smell arises either from an imbalance in the humours stemming from disease, or from excessive lewdness. Such ideas, originating in the medical writings of Antiquity, are presented as observations but have no real basis. They define a pleasantly fragranced model of masculinity, like

Alexander the Great, referred to in the text. Women are conspicuous by their absence, since they were believed to smell naturally bad. Yet Liébault gives numerous remedies for curing putrid stenches coming from the mouth, feet, womb and so on.

A breath of eroticism

A glance back at the authors discussed previously offers a way to balance this vision with an attitude that is somewhat more attentive to the body's own demands. Women of quality were far less prudish and circumspect and far more lascivious in Brantôme's *Vie des dames galantes* [*Lives of gallant ladies*], published long after his death in 1614.[33] He argued that 'perfumes are a great incitement to love'. The proliferation of works hostile to this point of view in fact proved that far from being in decline, perfume was still widely used. What would one such moralist have said to the grieving widow who cut off the parts 'that she had once so loved, and embalmed them, aromatized and scented them with perfumed and odoriferous musky powders, and then set them in a silver gilt box' to keep them safe? Brantôme admitted he had no idea if the story was true, but the king enjoyed it and shared it with several members of his inner circle. His own version of the adventures of Venus, cheating on Vulcan with Mars, may have reached the ears of Henri IV and later Napoleon. The goddess did not choose the charming young man with the curly hair, but the lover back from the battlefield, stinking with sweat and black with dust, who slept with her while still all bloody from the fight, 'without cleaning or scenting himself in any way'. The erotic thrill felt by women – not men – at their lover's sweat is in fact a better match for the role of androstenone, according to modern science. Brantôme returned to the same subject later, arguing that handsome, delicate men were less liable to sate excessive, unbridled female lust 'than an ugly man smelling like a stinking, dirty, lascivious billy goat'.

A scandalous criminal trial in 1611 saw Louis Gaufridy, priest at the church of Les Accoules in Marseilles, sentenced to be burned at the stake for witchcraft. His confession was published and distributed in Aix-en-Provence in a cheap news-sheet.[34] Such sources were sold in the street, reaching a wide audience, as sensational news stories were passed on by word of mouth beyond the reading public. The *Mercure français* reprinted the story almost verbatim that same year, giving it considerable publicity both in Paris and across France. The short text describes the priest signing a pact with Lucifer to 'take his enjoyment of some girls'. The document is probably not a faithful record of the priest's thoughts. Rather, it is rooted in demonology, the science of the Devil, developed by Catholic theologians to identify and root out humans guilty of complicity with Satan. Gaufridy's lustful turpitude is framed in deeply negative terms as a mortal sin of the flesh. A handful of erotic expressions translate magical beliefs shared by scholars and common folk alike. The Tempter is accused of teaching his disciple the secrets of irresistible charm, explaining 'By the virtue of my breath I would inflame all the girls and women I wished to love me, if my breath merely reached their nostrils.' Gaufridy was rumoured to have breathed on a thousand women with exquisite delight, including Madeleine de la Palud, the daughter of a Marseilles nobleman. The more he breathed on her, the more deeply in love she fell, craving his body. He also confessed to taking part in a Sabbath where the Devil turned Catholic rites on their head, at which he breathed on girls to have his wicked way with them. The text concludes with his execution, witnessed by a three-thousand-strong crowd, according to the narrator.

The priest-sorcerer's erotic breath translates his bodily odour's power of attraction for women. The news-sheet, a propaganda tool for a religion that placed stricter demands on urban populations, turned an old, magical belief in male breath into a devilish trap: breath exhaled via the nose – then held to be an erogenous zone – was held to be a way to charm and seduce women. Male breath also had sweeping curative powers. To this day, in rural areas, some men are still said to have the gift and are able to cure health problems like sprains by blowing on them.

The gutter press

News-sheets, generally consisting of text alongside an engraving, were the ancestors of today's true-crime magazines. The news-sheets' heyday was the age of the witch hunt, from 1580 to 1640. They were a means of disseminating church thinking, wrapped up in the curiosities of daily urban life. The Parisian chronicler Pierre de l'Estoile was a keen collector. They were read avidly by people who passed their content on to others, particularly when watching an execution, filling in the back story. They shaped public opinion by popularizing scholarly texts by preachers, demonologists and authors of tragic literature, another flourishing genre at the time, as will be seen below. One of the key themes of such news-sheets was the fear of women and their all-engulfing sexuality. The anonymous writers cleverly applied the church's traditional anti-feminism in a familiar, accessible style. The sin of vanity was framed in episodes from real life in which female coquetry was harshly punished. Several variants on the same narrative, in 1582, 1604 and 1616, recounted the misadventures of a wealthy, coquettish young woman who hankers after a superb band or magnificent collar. Not finding any to her taste, she loses her temper, blasphemes, and promises to give herself to the Devil if he finds her what she wants. A suitor, or even the Devil himself, comes along, places the desired accoutrement round her neck, and strangles her. The 1616 version takes place in Antwerp, identifies the arrogant, impatient woman as the Comtesse de Hornoc, and adds that the Devil then vanished with a loud fart. The family hid the cause of her death, but at the funeral, the coffin was too heavy to be carried. When it was opened, a black cat jumped out.[35]

One 1613 news-sheet deliberately set out to cause horror in readers. The scene took place in Paris on 1 January 1613. A young nobleman returned home at around four in the afternoon after a dinner in fine company. Outside his house, he met a well-dressed young woman adorned with pearls and jewels. He engaged her in gallant conversation and invited her in to wait for the rain to stop. She agreed, saying she had sent for her carriage. Yet, like sister Anne, she saw nothing coming. The young man then invited her to stay for the night. He came to see if everything was to her liking, then, growing bold, touched her breast. She offered no resistance, so he stole a few kisses, 'which lit the fire in his soul, whose flame consumes our spirits and whose smoke darkens the eyes of our understanding'. He eventually managed to coax her into bed. The next morning, feeling a nameless sense of dread, he went back to check on her. She was cold as ice, without a pulse, and not breathing. He called in the judicial officers and doctors, who all agreed 'that it was the body of a woman who had been hanged some time ago, and a devil had taken over her body to trick the poor nobleman'. Immediately, 'a large cloud of dark smoke rose from the bed, lasting about as long as the Lord's Prayer, offending their senses with an extreme stink'. When the cloud thinned, all that was left in the bed was a 'rotting carcase'. The text insists that it is a true and faithful account, and concludes with the moral of the story: men blinded by their passions run the same risk. God has given them this example to bring them back onto the straight and narrow, as salvation is only open to those who rid themselves 'of all such dirty and dishonest pleasures'.[36]

A literary stink

The fear of divine punishment was also behind the vogue for 'tragic histories'. The new genre, which emerged alongside news-sheets, remained fashionable in the upper echelons of society until around 1630. François de Rosset's *Histoires tragiques de nostre temps* [*Tragic histories of our times*] was highly popular from 1613 on and was translated into several languages. It contains the tale of Louis Gaufridy, clearly borrowed from the news-sheet about his execution and the account in the *Mercure français*, two years earlier. François de Rosset doubtless also had in mind the story of the nobleman seduced by a devil in the corpse of a young woman when he recounted the tale of a demon in the guise of a young woman who approached the Chevalier du Guet's lieutenant in Lyon, their carnal encounter, and the sad end that followed.[37] He added a further touch of spice by having his ill-fated hero share the beauty's favours with his two companions. He then has her reveal her true identity to the men once they have sated their lust, gathering up her skirts to show them 'the most horrible, ugliest, stinking, and rotten carcase in the world'. The men are struck dumb and fall into a dead faint, then die one after the other in short order. The moral of the story is that 'fornication begets adultery; adultery, incest; incest, the sin against nature [sodomy]; and after, God allows men to couple with the Devil'. This sliding scale of sins of the flesh was applied by courts at the time, as such practices were now criminalized and more harshly punished than previously. The last three – incest, sodomy, and witches copulating with demons at their Sabbaths – were punished by the cruellest of deaths: burning at the stake. Jean-Pierre Camus, bishop of Belley, a friend of Saint Francis de Sales, produced hundreds of bloodthirsty, fire-and-brimstone tragic histories from 1628 on, with the legions of Hell sweeping across the earth. His books proved enormously popular with an educated, worldly readership, but eventually fell out of fashion in the 1630s. As in news-sheets and François de Rosset's works, anything originating in the underworld smelled vile. This was borne out by a short piece published in 1630, *Le Puant concubinaire* [*The stinking common-law husband*]. A headmaster, as learned as he was dissolute, a drinker and a gambler, debauched countless women. He eventually took a young beauty as his common-law wife for seven or eight years. He stubbornly refused to be separated from her on his deathbed and died without absolution, 'on the lost woman's breast'. Within the hour, his corpse had turned so rotten and putrid the house was uninhabitable. He was buried six feet deep in the local church, but the stench was so foul that he had to be moved into the graveyard. The stench was such that no one dared enter the burial ground, so the corpse was finally thrown in the river, polluting it so badly that large numbers of rotting fish were cast up. Men of intemperate habits beware, Bishop Camus concludes, damnation is at the journey's end![38]

Satan stank atrociously, as did all those who gave themselves to him, unlike the best Christians, who retained the sweet odour of sanctity even after death. In the sixteenth and seventeenth centuries, faith could be identified by its pleasant scent, while misbelievers sullied their surroundings both physically and morally. The sense of smell increasingly transmitted a message that very clearly differentiated between good and evil. The greatest taboo focused on women, whose insatiable sexual appetite, now closely linked with death, was evoked in terms of satanic putrefaction. This was by no means a recent theme, of course, but it took on a terrifying new dimension as all the authorities were now in agreement. The sense of smell was carefully trained to turn any particularly repugnant odour into an alert signal, warning of eternal peril. The stench of Satan was associated with the plague and the unbridled lubricity of foul-smelling billy goats, as will be seen in chapter 5 on the plague. Unpleasant smells emanating from women were less easy to separate from their power of attraction, despite a constant flow of propaganda designed to keep close rein on their sinful flesh and the desires it triggered in men. The same cultural matrix turned post-menopausal women into witches chained to the Devil, whose deadly breath was akin to that of the Fates or Furies of Antiquity.

Death and the old woman

Renaissance poets inherited a deeply contemptuous image of elderly women from classical Antiquity, particularly the works of Horace, Ovid, Apuleius and Martial. Clément Marot drew on this tradition in his counter-blazon on breasts, as seen in chapter 3. A great wave of writing against elderly women swept the literary stage until the mid-seventeenth century. The age of tragedy and the Baroque considerably worsened the unpleasant features attributed to them as authors vied to outdo each other in unflattering descriptions, drawing on definitions by demonologists of the new crime of witchcraft, which saw many women burned at the stake from 1580 to the end of Louis XIII's reign.

Compared to the furious imprecations against matronly women that were common at the time, comments by Brantôme and the

medical profession seem almost mild in comparison. Brantôme wrote
of having heard tell of 'a very great lady, very great indeed, one of
whose ladies said one day her breath stank worse than a bronze
piss-pot; those were the words she used to me; one of her most
intimate friends, who came very close to her, confirmed it to me
too; it is true that she was rather on the elderly side'.[39] Might this
have been his friend Marguerite de Valois, better known as *la Reine
Margot*? Along the same lines, doctors recommended a whole host of
remedies to mask fetid bodily odours, as has been shown, including
scented pouches to be worn between the breasts.

This makes the widespread, virulent anathema against elderly
women all the more striking.[40] It went far beyond the medieval tradition of the grotesque portrait, as found in the writings of François
Villon, for instance. Significantly, the theme was also popular from
the first quarter of the sixteenth century on among artists working
in the Rhine region, where the Reformation was taking hold. The
greatest artists, including Albrecht Dürer, depicted naked witches.
Hans Baldung Grien even made the subject his speciality from 1510
on, while seizing the opportunity to show off the charms of beautiful
young women in a manner approved by society. One of his drawings,
dating from around 1514, shows two young women in erotic poses
flanking a vigorous-looking old woman with sagging breasts, whose
decrepitude is only clear from her face. An engraving by Niklaus
Manuel Deutsch (d. 1530) is much more worrying. The old woman
is dishevelled – proof of her low morals – and she bears the outward
signs of old age, yet she shows herself off in a provocative full-frontal
pose, grinning lewdly at the viewer. Her shrivelled dugs and hairy
pubis are a morbidly erotic invitation with demonic overtones.[41]
Writers likewise accused post-menopausal women of still being
madly in love with love itself. Erasmus's *In Praise of Folly* (1511)
describes them in tones of ironic scorn: 'Better sport still is to see
those decrepit old women that old age seems long since to have cut
off from the number of the living, those strolling corpses, those stinking carcasses which everywhere exhale a sepulchral odour, and yet
who cry at every moment, nothing is sweeter than life.' Even Pierre de
Ronsard, the most charming poet of the French Renaissance, studied
in every French classroom, wrote of a witch named Catin [whore]
in *Les Folastries* [*Frolics*], while the equally charming Joachim du
Bellay penned the 1549 *Antérotique de la vieille et de la jeune amie*
[*Anti-erotic of the old woman and her young friend*]: 'O old, vile
woman / Old woman, dishonour of this world'. Similar disgust was
expressed by other writers including Agrippa d'Aubigné, Mathurin
Régnier, Charles-Timoléon de Beauxoncles, sieur de Sigogne, and

Marc-Antoine Girard, sieur de Saint-Amant. Spain gave France the character of the procuress, witch and Devil's accomplice Celestina in Fernando de Rojas's tragicomedy of the same name, translated into French in 1527, inspiring Clément Marot and many others.

Such women were held in contempt for their advanced age, unpleasant smell and closeness to death. They could only be servants of Satan, wrote du Bellay and Ronsard, who penned an ode *Contre Denise* [*Against Denise*] in 1550, describing his subject as a witch: 'At the sigh of your breath alone', he wrote, dogs barked in terror, rivers flowed backwards, and wolves following Denise's trail howled. The witch Catin is shown 'By her two conduits blowing / Downwards her stinking breath', before wallowing in graveyard corpses. Joachim du Bellay wrote of his own horror of old women in 1558:

> Old woman older than the world,
> Older yet than squalid filth,
> Older yet than pale fever,
> And deader yet than death itself,

adding that their gaze and breath are enough to douse any 'loving flame'.

While poets were more indulgent when it came to young women, who represented the scent and savour of life, old women could expect no pity from men, or perhaps even from God, since their smell evoked death. An ode written by Agrippa d'Aubigné at the age of twenty in 1572 offers a striking tableau of the two contrasting ages of womanhood.[42] It compares the beloved, his Venus, to her duenna, the Gorgon watching over her. By day, the 'old serpent' with the pestilential breath guards the door of his beloved like Cerberus. At night it is even worse, as the two women sleep naked in the same bed. The poet compares the two bodies feature by feature: the young woman has all the qualities dear to the poets of the Pléiade, while the older woman is described with Baroque violence. The beloved smells delightful, having scented her hair with Cyprus powder and ambergris. The old woman stinks and her ringworm-infested scalp is crawling with bugs and lice.

> An odour funnels out of
> Her pale, rotten face
> Withered by a thousand cankers.
> And the rheum from her eyes.
> And the gutter of her snotty nose.

The young woman's neat, sighing breast could hardly be more different from the older woman's desiccated dugs that resemble a flaccid, empty bagpipe. The nymph's thigh contrasts with the old woman's wrinkly arse, which releases 'Like great smoke / A thousand poisoned flies'. The insects, believed to be generated by putrefaction, were an attribute of Satan and Hell. The beloved's 'little rosebud' has a terrifying antithesis in the deformed red genitals of the older woman, who may be suffering from a prolapsed uterus: judges in trials for witchcraft studied such cases up close in their painstaking search for Satan's mark. Did they feel the same disgust as the young poet?

> Yes indeed, their beards entwined,
> And a thousand patched skins
> And I know not what colour
> Of an old turkey cock in heat,
> A gash like an old slipper,
> Hanging entrails, a spleen
> And two cabbage leaves
> Sullying her knees.

The conclusion is pitiless: 'Thus despicable fate / Combines life with death.'

Later, in the early seventeenth century, descriptions of elderly women's genitals as dirty, dripping, smelly, bearers of disease and death became a commonplace in satirical poetry full of obscene imagery. In many cases, the poems had a sadistic dimension as the authors dreamed up hideous forms of torture for the old women that seemingly obsessed them. Sigogne (1560–1611) took perverse pleasure in the long-drawn-out punishment inflicted on 'the repugnant Perrette':

> We must, like for sorcerers, shave her hair
> Then on market day tie her on the wheel
> Break her with a bar, and when broken, hang her
> Then cut down the rope and throw it in the fire.

It sends a shiver down the spine to realize that the subject of the poem was in fact Mademoiselle du Tillet, a famous marriage broker at the court of Henri IV. Some of our modern-day politicians could take lessons in insults from the poet, who furiously plants his claws in the withered flesh of the old women of his day:

> Colourless carrion, cadaver from the tomb [. . .]
> Dug-up carcase, attacked by a crow,
> Similar to visions that come to us in a dream:
> You are some old body rotting away in snow,
> Or a sorcerer's body hanging from a gibbet,
> Dressed by a demon to terrify men!

Numerous other authors delighted in reviling the physical decline in women as they age, without fearing criticism in return, as male ageing was viewed much more leniently. The poem *Contre une vieille* [*Against an old woman*], published clandestinely in *Le Parnasse satyrique* in Paris in 1622, speaks out against their repulsive sexuality:

> When the old woman gets fucked,
> She runs with sweat all over,
> She burps, farts, and blows her nose.[43]

A number of plays feature older women in a physical relationship with the Devil. One such is Sigogne's *Satyre contre une dame sorcière qui frayait avec le Diable* [*Satire against a witch who associated with the Devil*], published in 1618, in which bad smells are a constant leitmotif. The elderly woman stinks worse than rotting carrion. She exclaims,

> Death and I are one and the same
> We differ on but one point
> For I am pale and she is wan
> But I smell, and she does not.

The author then addresses the reader directly:

> But what was unbearable,
> And what reeked so badly to me,
> Was that the woman and the Devil
> Both stank.

> She farts and passes wind for pleasure;
> He smelled of old cheese;
> And the Devil and the She-Devil
> Vied to out-stink each other.

Demonic pleasure

While these poems were burlesques, not taken entirely seriously by their authors, they did nonetheless express a violent misogynistic fantasy rooted in the image of the witch developed by demonologists. At their instigation, thousands of women accused of being Satan's accomplices, mainly from rural areas and 'decrepit old women', were burned at the stake across Europe. The women's trials opened with their body hair being shaved so that the judges could search them for Satan's mark. The executioner or a doctor would prick such marks with a long needle: if they did not hurt or bleed, the conclusion was that this was a mark left by the Tempter on his new prey. There is no way of knowing what the judges thought of studying the drooping naked flesh of older women, or of their body odour, as no accounts survive. Legal documents do, however, describe sex acts with devils at the Sabbath, as specialist manuals encouraged judges to probe for detailed confessions on this point. The surviving confessions, all along the same lines, are terrifying: demonologists expected to hear accounts of extreme pain, as the Devil's penis was said to be icy cold and covered in spikes. This has on occasion been interpreted as a prohibition on the female orgasm. This is no doubt anachronistic, as medical theory at the time held that the female orgasm was vital in producing fine children, especially boys. The Spanish theologian Francisco Suarez (1548–1617) shared the same opinion at the height of the witch hunt. Many witches did, however, stand accused of enjoying sex for its own sake, since their advanced age meant they could no longer bear children. Rather, Western society in the period of tragedy and the Baroque was giving voice to a fundamental prohibition that involved not pleasure per se, but procreation: sexual activity was to take place only within the marriage bond with a view to conceiving children. Old women therefore no longer really had the right to it. The macabre imagery woven around such old women, closing in on them like a net, made them the Devil's accomplices if they dared express their own sexual needs or desires.

The period from 1550 to 1650 saw the rise of new norms of behaviour. The dominant idea that emerged, taking over from more optimistic views of existence, was man's infinite guilt and God's severity. This gave rise to a fundamental conflict between the hope of salvation and the fear of damnation. Satan was now constantly on the prowl, with the permission of the Creator, who used him to turn sinners into better Christians. The Devil patiently dogged his victims' footsteps, as François de Rosset and Jean-Pierre Camus explained. The most dramatic change affected women. The misogyny of the medieval church was as nothing compared to the wave of hatred against women that swept across civil society in the age of tragedy. Women became legal minors, whatever their age, and lost all independence, at least in theory. Women were considered weak, their humours foul-smelling, their menstrual cycles harmful, while their sexuality sapped male vitality, in what was one of the worst periods in history for the gender. It was generally held that they could not achieve salvation on their own and required constant surveillance by a male authority to avoid doing the Devil's bidding. Marriage was thus an absolute necessity, both to force them to save their souls against their will and to constrain their all-consuming sexual appetite.

Demonizing women was clearly a way to legitimize the male dominion that weighed ever more heavily on women. Only the idolized young women of poets' dreams temporarily escaped the belittling vision of womanhood, because they symbolized life, and because they might be sweet-talked into bed. Marriage was a prison for wives, whose duty was to remain modest and faithful and give their husbands fine children, while carrying the burden of the household like a snail. Then came the descent into Hell. With encroaching age came disaster. Women smelled bad in their early years, though poets affected to believe the opposite; they were nauseating and dangerous when menstruating, and came closer to putrefaction the older they became. Tragic and Baroque culture assimilated older women with death. This sheds light on why witch hunts were pursued with such vigour across Europe, as Satan's decrepit servants were held to be as putrid as the Devil himself. In the final analysis, it simply comes down to men's boundless terror at seeing women of a certain age, often with a new-found degree of independence, trying to wrest back power by pledging allegiance to the Prince of Darkness.

Things only began to change slowly from the mid-seventeenth century on, when the archetype of the old woman became somewhat less evil, and legal proceedings against the so-called devilish sect also lost ground. In 1653, Molière's *L'Étourdi* [*The blunderer*] features a more reassuring image of two matronly women fighting, though one does call the other a witch.[44] The classical age took less interest in the dreadful, devilish smells that earlier generations had learned to fear like the plague.

5

The Devil's breath

Europe saw a sharp increase in cases of the plague in the sixteenth and seventeenth centuries. Many parts of France saw terrible outbreaks of the disease from 1580 to 1650. Doctors and surgeons gave the terrified population a stereotypical explanation: epidemics were caused by the wrath of God, seeking cruel vengeance on sinners. The remedies and steps they advised to avoid contagion focused on the terrible danger of 'venomous vapours' infecting the air. The medical profession saw a direct link between such vapours, caused by the dreadful stench of putrefaction and deadly smells wafting through the air, and the stink of the Devil tightening his grip on the world. It was commonly understood that Satan was literally in charge of carrying out God's dirty work. The stench of the Devil's breath killed people with the full agreement of the Creator. This belief – a way of explaining the inexplicable in religious and moral terms – found its way into the medical profession's armoury of preventions and cures.

Comparing these therapeutic practices with the olfactory rites intended to protect the health of countless societies worldwide, past and present, reveals a number of similarities. Sweet-smelling fumigations, keenly recommended in the Renaissance, echoed the practice in Homeric Greece of burning cedar branches to keep the gods on side. In the sixteenth century, pleasant-scented smoke still created a connection between men and God to defeat the evil deeds of demons believed to live underground. Other rites were designed to keep demonic threats and bad Christians at bay, requiring special impenetrable garments to be worn head to foot and doused in perfume. The protective outfits worn by plague doctors were merely a specialist variant of such garb. Fundamentally, recurring outbreaks of plague were seen as a demonstration of the existence of Hell on earth. Poor mortals all too often caught the stench of Satan in their nostrils. For them, perfumes were first and foremost preventatives, though the most sought after – musk, civet and ambergris – came from animal secretions, from sex glands in the first two cases. As contemporary thought held that like had the power to destroy like, the Black Death could be fought with smells even more foul than those it generated. Of course, all these recipes and protections were hopelessly ineffective, given that the real cause of the scourge remained a mystery: *Yersinia pestis*, the plague bacteria spread by rat fleas. Yet such remedies shed light on an astonishing olfactory realm full of the beliefs, fears and emotions of a world now lost.

Venomous vapours

The second-century doctor Galen believed that the plague resulted from an imbalance in the primary qualities of air, heralded by a powerful smell of putrefaction. The theory was still widely held in the Renaissance, adapted to the Christian context: it was believed that the fetid stench did not descend from Heaven, for everything sent to earth from above is good, but rather rose up from Hell and the underground realm of the dead, who were often buried in very shallow graves. Places and phenomena liable to speed up the process of organic decomposition, such as swamps, cesspools, sulphurous gases from volcanic eruptions, fog and bad storms, were thought to foster the ideal conditions for infection. All were associated with the Devil, as were disgusting, slimy creatures such as toads, and lightning, which left a foul smell in the air. The Devil's agents, witches, were believed to cast curses to bring down drizzle, rain and storms to destroy harvests.

In 1477–8, the famous Florentine humanist Marsilio Ficino wrote the treatise *Consiglio contro la pestilenza*, which referred to 'venomous vapour' rather than simply an imbalance in the qualities of air. The following century saw many more medical works on the plague, whose authors openly attributed the disease to God's wrath against sinners. Ambroise Paré devoted a lengthy chapter to the plague in 1568 before denouncing the 'corruption of air' that he claimed to have observed while fighting an epidemic in Lyon: 'the putrefaction of the plague is considerably different from any other kind of putrefaction, as it has a hidden, nameless malignancy which cannot be explained'.[1] In contemporary usage, a reference to malignancy meant the Devil.

A few years earlier, the Parisian doctor Antoine Mizauld had recorded his own experience dealing with an outbreak of plague in the city in 1562.[2] His aim, he wrote, was to provide simple, practical advice, all tested by himself or his friends. The first thing to do is beg God 'to soothe his ire against us, and withdraw his sword of pestilence, with which he justly persecutes us for our demerits'. As the scourge 'participates in the corruption and imperceptible worsening of the air', he advises steering clear of places known to be infected and avoiding bad humours. Readers should purge on medical advice, use prophylactics morning and evening, light sweet-smelling fires, wear perfume and regularly change their undergarments, which should be white. He also advises against going outside after sunset or before sunrise, and it is important to have 'in hand some scents, and some antidote in the mouth'. It was vital not to come into contact with patients or anyone coming straight from a place known to be contaminated. It was advisable to shun housing close to graveyards, dumps, butcheries, flayers' yards, fishmongers, cesspools and other 'stinking, vile' places, and to steer clear of leather workers, curriers, candle makers, pork butchers, darners, furriers, old clothes dealers, second-hand traders, cobblers and 'similar vile, dirty, and base artisans'. It was crucially important to keep bedrooms clean, spreading sweet-smelling grass and flowers over the floor twice a day. Clothing must be kept clean, folded away in a chest with sweet perfumes. Dogs, cats and poultry should not be kept inside and pigs, pigeons, geese and ducks should not be bred nearby. Rotten food and corrupted drink should be avoided. Dung heaps should not be allowed anywhere near people, nor should stagnant water and faecal matter. 'Making urine in the street where excrement is' was even less to be tolerated. Housing must be well aired but the windows should be kept closed if the wind was blowing from the south or west, and no one should go out at all in fog or rain or if the wind was blowing from the south. To avoid losing heart, one should steer clear of the sick, the sound of bells ringing for the dead, the infirm and the elderly.

Such instructions reflect a theory of contagion. They may indeed have been useful to some degree, keeping healthy individuals away from sources of contagion, if they were wealthy enough to move away to the countryside for a lengthy stay, like the storytellers in Boccaccio's *Decameron*. Anyone who stayed behind in the infection-ridden towns and cities was hardly protected by guidelines that were essentially inspired by a moral understanding of health. The text presents the fight against the epidemic as a struggle between good and evil. Plague spread wherever stench and putrefaction reigned. Anyone wishing to avoid the disease first had to draw closer to the heavenly realm by wearing white, avoiding the bad humours caused by excessive behaviour, living a life regulated by the sun's warmth, lighting sweet-smelling fires, and wearing protective perfumes and using pleasant smells as prophylactics. Yet none of these precautions stopped the Black Death from killing vast swathes of the population. Doctors and surgeons were nevertheless a source of some hope for people who were wholly unequipped to deal with the scourge when it first broke out in 1348, helping them seek to soothe the wrath of God by means of propitiatory rituals that focused on the misdeeds that brought His avenging sword down on them. The sweet-scented smoke rising from towns and cities and drifting up to Heaven bore with it their hopes for mercy.

Plague-ridden towns

Urban centres were considered far more sinful than the countryside and smelled far worse, as has been shown. They also suffered far worse when plague broke out, as it did repeatedly. The authorities responded with exclusionary measures and quarantines, for instance in Arras, capital of the county of Artois, whose twenty-thousand-strong population was under Spanish rule until France won the county back in 1640. Police decrees offer an insight into the fight against the disease. Anti-plague measures were fairly low key prior to 1580. On 18 April 1438, the threat of an epidemic saw the town's paupers and swine driven outside its walls. On 23 September 1489, as plague tore through nearby towns, precautions were taken against cases identified locally. A straw bale was placed outside every house infected, and patients had to carry a white stick when out and about so people could see them coming. They were banned from crowded parts of town. On 26 August 1490, when plague was again feared, the Arras councillors made the case for closing the public bathhouses, where contamination easily spread. By 27 April 1494, the dreadful disease again had the town in its grip. The 1489 rules were brought back and anyone transporting a plague victim had to wear a yellow strip of cloth the width of a palm on their clothes so that people could avoid them. Schools were closed, dumping rubbish and dirty water in the market and in the streets was banned, slaughtered pigs had to be salted down and other animals were driven out of town. The authorities even put a stop to street-sweeping for fear of worsening the epidemic.

The situation took a new turn in 1576. A surgeon was chosen on 31 August that year as the 'plague bleeder', tasked with drawing blood from sufferers. The procedure's effectiveness was far from proven. The surgeon was paid a hefty bonus, half on starting work, the other half at the end of the epidemic, and received a comfortable tax-free weekly wage. All his meals were provided by the authorities and he received whatever drugs he requested at no cost. Wealthy and 'poor honest folk' alike also paid him for his services. In return, he inspected plague corpses and gave free treatment to the paupers listed on the municipal registers. He was not allowed to refuse patients or charge anyone living in the town or neighbouring faubourgs for treating injuries or other diseases including syphilis, or 'Naples disease', first described in 1498. During the 1576 outbreak, plague doctors were obliged to live in the house provided and were not allowed away for more than two days without permission. It proved an extremely dangerous job, particularly as the outbreak was worsened by the large numbers of country folk seeking refuge in Arras – or at least so claimed the local authorities, who took the disease as a pretext to expel them. Following the surgeon's death or hasty departure, a replacement was appointed on 27 October 1580. When he died on 18 July 1582, a third took over, then a fourth ten days later, with no explanation. Texts dating from 1597 insist that no one other than the 'plague surgeon' was allowed to treat the disease. On 13 September that same year, the situation was so dire that a public procession was held to plead for divine mercy, while plague patients were temporarily banned from the streets; later, they had to carry a white rod measuring five or six feet when venturing outside so they could be seen coming. Beggars arriving from elsewhere were driven out. Second-hand clothes dealers were banned from buying their wares in Amiens, Cambrai and Saint-Omer, where the disease had run rampant the previous year. The same precautions were implemented for every subsequent outbreak of the disease. One of the worst led to a long set of rules and regulations on 23 August 1619, decreeing three weeks of quarantine for anyone coming into contact with patients, ordering the expulsion of non-locals and vagabonds and the burning of rubbish, and stipulating the duties of the medical profession, including alerting the authorities. A further rule was added in 1655 placing a ban on feeding pigs, because they smelled bad.[3]

These rules were closely based on medical advice, which saw the human body as porous and hence liable to be permeated by air corrupted by the plague. Direct contact with sufferers was therefore to be shunned. Ambroise Paré advised his fellow doctors and anyone coming into contact with those infected to avoid 'their breath and the steam of their excrement, both solid, liquid and vaporous'. A safe distance was to be maintained in case of interaction with a patient. In Arras, it was clearly defined in 1597 by the rule stipulating patients must carry a white rod measuring some two metres in length. Elsewhere, plague surgeons and grave diggers were often urged to carry similar rods, creating a safety zone against the deadly contagion that mapped onto the individual bubble around each human. It will be shown later that an individual, invisible 'suit of armour' concocted from various scents kept foul smells out of this personal space. Ambroise Paré suggested that urban authorities should take the same precautions as in Arras, enforcing the cleanliness of homes and streets, cracking down on dung heaps and rubbish, ensuring dead animals and filth were taken far out of town, maintaining clean water supplies, and stopping the sale of food unfit for consumption. Bathhouses were to be closed down because they softened the body and 'opened the pores, and consequently the plague can promptly enter the body and bring on sudden death'. Dogs and cats should be slaughtered to prevent them spreading contagion by eating dead bodies or their excrement. Paré did not, however, think there was much point in forcing patients to stay at home; it was better simply to forbid them from coming into contact with people in good health. No property belonging to plague victims was to be sold, and urban centres spared the outbreak were to keep their gates closed to anyone travelling from centres of contagion. Paré recommends lighting large, sweet-smelling fires to purify the morbid air in houses and outside in built-up areas. He refers in passing to the custom of burning gunpowder at night or dawn: 'The violent sound and odour of smoke corrected and chased away the contagion in the air' during an outbreak of plague in Tournai, he explained.[4]

Many other members of the medical profession made identical points. One such was the Rouen doctor Jean de Lampérière, writing in 1620. He told the same story about Tournai, explaining that 'the air violently propelled by the effort of the powder and its smell of sulphur repelled and corrected the plague-ridden air'. He added that some people even fired harquebus volleys in houses to the same end. His opinions are fundamentally similar to Paré's, except when it came to human excrement. He believed that people should not be allowed 'to discharge their bellies and urine in the streets; which has major consequences, and about which few orders are given; public sites should be made for such discharges, along the river', with each seat walled in. He also wrote in greater detail about the use of fires against plague, advising they should be lit after sundown, using wood that withstood rot, such as juniper, laurel, cypress, fir, ash, walnut, broom, heather or pine. Their power could be increased by adding herbs such as rue, wormwood, southernwood, tansy, rosemary and sage. He also presented a theory of contamination through the eyes: 'Many people have caught the plague simply by looking at infected houses.' He goes on to explain: the eyes are 'the gates to the sun, but the sun of that microcosm which is the heart, to which they convey the good or ill that is sent to them'.[5] In the end, it all comes down to a gigantic cosmic struggle between two opposing principles in which each individual human is both battleground and prize. The manifold precautions needed to avoid falling prey to danger are all a struggle against the self to prevent the sin/plague entering the subject's bodily substance in the first place. Lighting a sweet-smelling fire in the morning or evening was a way of keeping putrefaction at bay and dissipating darkness, choosing life over death. The fragrant smoke rose up to Heaven to soothe God's wrath. On earth, good Christians must shun those already suffering the atrocious punishment of hideous contagion. Fleeing the disease in horror, as Montaigne fled Bordeaux in 1585 despite being the city's mayor, was a perfectly legitimate reaction, as the divine scourge afflicted the worst sinners. In 1646, the Toulouse priest Arnaud Baric drew a parallel between the epidemic and the 'worldly, fleshly, and demonic pride' of women, young or mature, showing off their breasts, shoulders and arms below the elbow, 'against all sorts of Christian modesty, to the ruin of souls'.[6]

Urban centres struck by the plague foreshadowed the Hell that awaited misbelievers. These places' usual stench became unbearable, mephitic, sulphurous and morbid, triggering a connection between their olfactory signal and the most terrifying death. The very words and expressions 'to stink like a corpse', 'miasma', 'rot' and 'putrefaction' all conveyed a message of dreadful danger, particularly as some fetid smells that were usually unremarkable took on a much more menacing aspect during epidemics. One example was the smell of animals that ate human excrement. Recommendations were also made for cats and dogs to be culled, though their skins were customarily used to make perfumed gloves to protect against the plague itself, as chapter 6 will show. Similarly, people were advised to avoid going near pigs, whose filth and stench were used to stigmatize the poor, now considered undesirable. 'For when the plague comes to a region, it starts with poor, dirty people, who live clustered together like pigs in narrow lodgings, scarcely differing in their lives, exercise and conversation from wild beasts', in the words of the Italian doctor and chemist Angélus Sala.[7] Driving out vagabonds, non-locals and country folk who fled to urban centres in the vain hope of finding a safe haven was part of a vast ritual to purify the City of God besieged by demons. Christian noses were entrusted with a delicate mission to guide their owners on the path to salvation.

Perfume as armour

When plague was running rampant, Antoine Mizauld argued that it was vital to purify both healthy and infected air by one of three means, fire, fumigation, or scenting it with water, flowers, grasses and herbs. The first involved setting up a brazier or glowing coals in the centre of the room to burn sweet-smelling substances such as benzoin, cinnamon, cloves, myrrh, nutmeg, lemon peel, angelica root, or a mix known as 'oiselet de Chypre' (Cyprus fledgling) placed in a small, bird-shaped pomander. Fire was not advised in sultry weather, as it risked heating the putrid air even further. In this case, it was better to use cooling fumigations made from plants that were thought to be cold-natured, such as violet, water lily, rose, lemon, orange and incense plant. Using scent meant making a concoction of such plants, sometimes with added rose water and vinegar, to spray over the walls and floor. The poor had to be content with potions made of lettuce, sorrel, plantain, vine leaves and other common plants steeped in water from the local fountain and mixed with vinegar.[8]

Even a century later, advice against the plague was still fundamentally unchanged. In 1668, when the disease broke out in Champagne, Pierre Rainssant, professor of medicine at the university of Rheims, gave exactly the same advice. He recommended airing infected houses, sweeping up every scrap of dirt including spiders, and burning it in the courtyard with the patient's bed linen and everything they had touched. Only gold and silver could be purified by hot water or vinegar, he assured his readers. Ropes should be strung across rooms to hang carpets, wall hangings, clothes and household linen that had escaped contamination. Chests were placed on trestles and left open. Windows were closed and chimneys blocked up. Then a three-finger-thick layer of ash was spread in each room and sprinkled with vinegar to stop the floorboards from catching fire. A circular straw bale of the same size and thickness was put on it. Two dishes of perfume made from sulphur, turpentine resin, saltpetre, antimony, cinnabar, sal ammoniac, orpine, galbanum, euphorbia, asafoetida, benzoin, birthwort, arsenic and storax, all ground to a powder, were thrown onto the straw, which was then piled over the mix and sprinkled with vinegar to slow combustion. A fire was set in the straw on the top floor and then on lower floors and all doors closed. After three days, the house was safe to enter: all doors and windows were thrown open to let the emanations out and pure air in.[9] Such remedies may sometimes have been worse than the disease: houses at the time were often made of wood and other light, combustible materials. At least the author expressed an unshakeable faith in the purifying virtues of fire. Like many doctors, he advised fighting fire with fire: his perfume recipe included a number of toxic ingredients such as euphorbia and birthwort, and others that smelled deeply unpleasant, such as sulphur, resin and asafoetida or Persian ferula, associated with Hell and the Devil in the contemporary imagination. Asafeotida, in German known as *Teufelsdreck* or 'devil's dung', was known for its 'strange stink'.[10]

Odet de Turnèbe's comedy *Les Contents*, written in around 1580, sums up the precautions to be taken before venturing out if an epidemic was raging. The heroine's religiously inclined mother wants to take her to the dawn service at church. The heroine protests: 'Don't you know that people are dying of the plague near the church? The doctor told you never to go out before sunrise.' Her mother replies that devoutly reciting Saint Roch's prayer offers protection against contagion, adding 'Put a bit of angelica in your mouth and a vinegar sponge in your hand.'[11] Angelica root had a musky taste and was thought to be a supreme preventive against the plague,[12] while vinegar was seen as a vital weapon in the armoury against the disease, as will be seen below.

Antoine Mizauld frequently sang the virtues of rue, whose powerfully musky, even fetid smell he considered as offering excellent protection against the dreadful disease. The plant was also held to have magical properties. It kept insects, particularly fleas, at bay, which certainly helped prevent the spread of the plague. Mizauld gave much more advice based on smells and perfumes.[13] Readers keen to avoid contagion should start by taking an antidote of mithridate, made of twenty rue leaves, two walnuts, two figs and a grain of salt, ground and mixed with a small amount of good white wine. Or they could suck on roast meat marinated in white wine that angelica root had stood in overnight. The rest of the liquid was used to wash the face, neck, hands and arteries along the arms. The point was not basic hygiene, but rather to strengthen the parts of the body most exposed to corrupt air.

When out and about, it was advisable to carry a piece of angelica, gentian or some similar plant in the mouth and hold a lemon, lime or orange studded with cinnamon bark or cloves to raise to the nose in case of need. This should be changed at least twice a day. Another solution was to hold a sponge soaked in rue vinegar and wrung out so that only the smell remained. It was crucial to carry a pomander that could be held to the nostrils, and a handkerchief full of laurel leaves left to steep overnight in rose water and cinnamon or rose vinegar. The poor had to be happy with washing their hands and faces in vinegar and a bit of theriac or holding a sprig of rue to sniff regularly: Mizauld comments that this was common practice in Paris in 1562. He advises women not to overdo it, however, as he has seen it give some ruddy complexions or even facial ulcers. He adds that it is useful to soak the sprig in vinegar and add 'things with a finer scent' to make the experience less unpleasant.

Pomanders not only helped against contagion, they were also intended to be a source of pleasure. Mizauld suggested filling them, winter and summer alike, with a mix including roses, violets, water lilies, sandalwood, cinnamon, myrrh, benzoin, ambergris, camphor and musk, ground to a powder and steeped in rose water. The same powder was used to fill perfumed rosaries or small taffeta pouches that were carried around to be sniffed, or worn day and night on the breast in a heart-shaped pouch to strengthen the organ. The powder was also used in candles for home and church use and in scented torches to be carried from room to room, when visiting the sick, or leaving the home at night.

Particular care was to be taken with visible body parts vulnerable to contagion, such as the mouth, nose, eyes and ears, and other areas exposed to the air, such as the face, neck and hands. The hands should be washed frequently with a mix of white or ruby wine, rose water and a touch of camphor. Soaking a piece of angelica root in it and adding a splash of rose vinegar made it more effective. Some rue or angelica placed in the mouth offered further protection. Noses and eyes were protected with a dab of spike lavender oil, which smelled delightful, the author claimed. The more delicately inclined could smear genuine scorpion oil, made in Provence, over the arteries in their arms, their temples, neck, throat, 'orifice of the stomach' (anus) and heart. Mizauld swore it was very effective, convincing doubters that 'one venom or poison often cures and drives out another'. As scorpion oil was hard to come by in Paris, he suggested replacing it with juniper oil, which also smelled marvellous. He gave a scented water recipe using sandalwood, aloe, cinnamon, cloves, rosemary flowers, lavender, angelica root, ambergris, musk and camphor, all ground to a powder and steeped in rose water and white wine. A handkerchief was to be dipped in the liquid morning and evening to wash the arms, temples, neck and throat, while the inside of the nostrils and ears should have it dabbed on with a finger. It could also be rubbed over the heart and orifice of the stomach, 'and even the virile parts and genitals, which have some mysterious occult sympathy with the rest of the body, and great consideration in this disease; which is ill thought of today', he sighed. He had the whole body covered, even the anus, which one might think was relatively little exposed to the evil breath of contagion. As well as the open and porous parts of the body, all the most important parts were protected by a carefully constituted armour of frequently reapplied scents. It is, however, unclear how closely such tips from the medical profession were followed in popular practice. Mizauld also praises a highly effective custom from Auvergne, where the locals drank three fingers of urine with mithridate to keep contagion at bay, or cured their buboes by applying the scalding concoction to them. In 1604, Loys Guyon deplored the harm caused to health by old cheese and shared his disgust at a method used by the coarse peasantry to avoid the epidemic: they ate cheese on an empty stomach! It seems cheese had not yet become a source of national pride for the French, setting them apart from less refined nations.[14] Plague and damnation!

Perfumed rituals

In sixteenth- and seventeenth-century Europe, the terrible smell of plague patients led their carers to put up multiple barriers of scent between them. Though perfumes per se were harshly condemned by numerous moralists who saw them as nothing more than erotic traps worn mainly by women to catch the unwary, they came into general use when epidemics broke out, as they frequently did. Doctors and their patients saw perfumes as the sole weapon in their armoury against the Black Death, all sharing a belief in the disease's demonic origin described by Martin Luther, who wrote that evil spirits 'poisoned the air or otherwise infected the poor people by their breath and injected the mortal poison into their bodies'. Perfumes were used to strengthen and stimulate the individual's own physical and spiritual defences. They were also a source of pleasure: doctors advised adding enjoyable smells to the powerful, even nauseating, bases. Musk, civet and ambergris were everywhere, all commonly thought to be pleasantly scented; the first two were also powerful aphrodisiacs. The wealthy made lavish use of such fragrances, splashing them over everything, even their fashionable little lapdogs. Henry VIII of England and his daughter Elizabeth I preferred a combination of rose and musk. Scent enabled the rich to make overt displays of their wealth by purchasing perfumed leather goods such as gloves, shoes, boots, belts and sword sheaths. Gold- and silversmiths invented scented jewels, bracelets, necklaces, rings and gemstones, which according to one contemporary theory were the result of water condensed by a particular smell.[15]

In the case of the plague, however, perfumes were used to keep people at a distance, not to entice them closer. The Toulouse-born doctor Oger Ferrier clearly demonstrated this in 1548, following mainstream advice by telling people to keep sniffing at a pomander, sprig of herbs or flowers, or a sponge dipped in vinegar and rose water when out walking. He also suggested they should take precautions against other people's breath and the nauseating smell of the streets.[16] All such observations repeatedly, almost obsessively, concur in describing people who had escaped the contagion, forced to venture out in public like terrified shadows, shunning all human contact. Not a square inch of their body, including beards and hair, was left without a protective layer of perfume. As Jean de Lampérière wrote in 1620,

> Before leaving home, rub your temples, inside your nose, your lips, palms, the carpals where your arteries throb, even your heart with good Peru balm, which by its astringency closes the entrance to bad air, by its balsamic virtue resists corruption, and by its spirituous and odorous exhalation, cheers the heart and spirits; when going out, you must place in your mouth a piece of one of the following opiates: two drops of clove essence, or a few grains of ambergris, or angelica extract.[17]

This suggests a purifying, expiatory ritual rooted in perfumes. The sinner surrounded himself with a scented bubble to earn back God's good graces. Forcing himself into isolation even in a crowd kept temptation, and the everyday stench of urban life, at arm's length. The sense of smell was therefore called into considerable play. In this context, it would be hard to make the case that sixteenth- and seventeenth-century Europe saw our sense of smell as largely unimportant. Quite the reverse: it was vital to life, and therefore singularly powerful.

Plague doctors were particularly exposed to contagion and took even greater precautions (figure 13). In 1619, Charles Delorme, in the employ of Louis XIII, came up with an entirely hermetic garment for doctors treating plague patients. The Abbé de Saint-Martin recounted, 'He had himself made a garment of goat leather, which bad air has great difficulty in penetrating: he put garlic and rue in his mouth; he put incense in his nose and ears, covered his eyes with glasses, and in this garb attended patients.' The outfit, completed by a stick to examine the patient from a safe distance, was impressive. No part of the body came into contact with the air. A wide-brimmed hat was worn on the head, along with a mask with a beak some sixteen centimetres in length, with two holes for nostrils. The mask filtered the air through herbs and perfumes placed in the beak. The eyes were safe behind their lenses. The ample coat fell almost to the floor and the doctor also wore short goat-leather boots attached to hide breeches, a hide undershirt tucked into the breeches, and long gloves. The leather armour offered twofold protection against the Black Death. The leather itself was a powerful defence against the Devil's breath because it came from a goat, a demonic symbol par excellence whose vile smell drove out contagion, as seen in chapter 3. The leather would also have been scented with herbs and other aromatic substances, such as thyme, balsam, ambergris, melissa, camphor, cloves, laudanum, myrrh, rose petals and styrax.[18] Jean de Lampérière added some further details to the advice of his colleagues. Once they had perfumed all their clothes, undergarments included, they should also carry a waxed handkerchief to avoid breathing in their patients' exhalations. They should also rub their lips, temples and the inside of their nostrils with a blend of camphor oil, Peru balm and galbanum extract, and put in their mouth a small ball of myrrh kneaded with clove essence and ambergris extract. They should wash their hands and faces with houseleek juice mixed with garlic vinegar or rue. The plague patient's eyes and mouth should be avoided, both face on and from the side. Doctors visiting patients should not wear woollen garments or loose knits that let the air through. It was advisable to change clothes straight after the consultation and have them re-perfumed before donning them again. It was also vital to wear an amalgam of mercury and gold or lead mixed with powdered sapphire and jacinth over the heart.[19]

Rue, vinegar and tobacco

Fighting fire with fire was both a major medical theory and a popular practice in sixteenth- and seventeenth-century Europe. Doctors naturally held 'folk' customs in contempt, due largely to their origins rather than doubts over their effectiveness. One such was the thera-peutic use of foul smells by the rural population, who sniffed rotting cheese, drank their own urine, bred goats to keep their homes safe, and breathed in the air from privies first thing in the morning on an empty stomach. One German doctor was still recommending privy-sniffing as late as 1680. In England, the night soil men described in

Daniel Defoe's 1720 *Journal of the Plague Year* followed medical advice to the letter, working with garlic and rue in their mouths and smoking scented tobacco.[20]

Garlic and rue were considered to smell vile. Jean Liébault wrote in 1582 that garlic gave people bad breath and made their excrement stink.[21] In regions outside Provence and Gascony, using garlic as a preventive against plague often meant overcoming a powerful aversion to its smell, as was the case for Henri IV of France, who made abundant use of it. Rue was also considered to smell fetid and was known to cause abortions if ingested in pregnancy. It was also reputed to be evil: Agrippa d'Aubigné listed it among the ingredients used by witches, alongside mandrake, hemlock and white hellebore.[22] It was associated with Satan and was most often described as a cure or preventive for the Black Death, a reputation it maintained for centuries. In the reign of Louis XIV, the chemist Marie Meurdrac, who wrote a number of accessible recipes, made much use of rue, recommending that readers should take five or six drops of rue essence in a spoonful of eau de vie every morning during epidemics as a precaution. She also advised taking pills made of rue extract, tincture of aloe, Venetian theriac, myrrh, lemon and orange peel, and spirit of vitriol 'to protect against any infected air and corruption'.[23] The concoction known as 'four thieves vinegar', still used in Napoleon's day, likewise contained rue, as will be seen in chapter 7. Unlike garlic, rue has lost its anti-demonic properties in the modern imagination. Maybe it was not spectacular enough to ward off the vampires that haunt our cinema and television screens.

Vinegar was a panacea in pre-revolutionary France. The midwife Louise Bourgeois included it in seventeen different recipes to treat toothache, fever, jaundice and kidney pain, to stop lactation for women who wanted small, pert breasts, and to protect against the plague. She advised carrying a vinegar-soaked sponge in a small openwork ivory box to sniff at in case of danger.[24] Ambroise Paré explained that vinegar was used in this way for its cooling properties, essentially in the summer months, and advised washing the whole body in a boiled solution of vinegar with other scented seeds and roots, theriac and mithridate: 'Vinegar is contrary to venoms, warm and cold alike, and prevents rot, particularly as it is cold and dry, which are two things that are contrary and repugnant to putrefaction; which is shown by experience, for dead bodies, meat, herbs, fruits, and other things, are kept in vinegar without rotting.'[25] As late as 1809, the author of the *Parfumeur impérial* reminded readers of vinegar's considerable prophylactic properties, adding that it had long been used for personal hygiene as a 'preservative against contagion and bad air'.[26]

Tobacco also had a role to play in the fight against the Black Death. This is not particularly surprising, since new consumables were often tested as cures before being taken up more widely: the same was true of alcohol, coffee and chocolate. The English scholar Sir Kenelm Digby (1603–65) provided a recipe for scented tobacco, including oils of nutmeg, lavender, cinnamon, marjoram and clove, ambergris, six grains of musk, nineteen grains of civet and a grain of black Peru balm. The musk and ambergris were ground with half a peeled sweet almond, then mixed with the civet, before the rest of the ingredients were added. He described it as excellent against bad air when rubbed under the nose and on the temples. It softened the taste of tobacco when stored alongside it in a box. The powerful scents of ambergris, musk and civet dominated the recipe while fixing and harmonizing the floral notes. Scented tobacco remained in fashion for many years, particularly when aristocrats began using snuff. This may originally have been to protect against foul smells at court and in town or even as a sweet-smelling nasal barrier against contagion. In 1693, *Le Parfumeur françois* indicated that tobacco was compatible with all scents, the most commonly used being orange, jasmine, rose and tuberose. It came in yellow or red, and was scented with musk, civet and ambergris.[27]

The way people thought about the plague in the sixteenth and seventeenth centuries was heavily influenced by the supernatural. The many preventives recommended by Jean de Renou in 1624 included not only mainstream protections such as angelica, scorpion oil, Rufus's pills, mithridate and theriac, but a number of rather more unorthodox ones such as unicorn horn, mercury, viper flesh, dittany with its purple-black flowers, water germander, green anise, Armenian bole, Maltese earth, mummia (a medicine made from powdered mummies), the mythical bezoar (figure 18) and oil of vitriol.[28]

Pomanders

Pomanders are recorded in use as early as 1348. At first they held nothing but ambergris, which was believed to have warm, dry properties. Further ingredients were later added to protect against plague. It became very fashionable to carry pomanders or wear them at the waist in the sixteenth century. Precious pomanders were made from the finest materials for the social elite.

In 1536, the Holy Roman Emperor Charles V owned a hollow

golden grenadine whose 'stalk' held perfumes. The same year, a large golden apple filled with perfumes, designed to be hung from a woman's waist by a flat chain, was also listed. The French royal court had similar accoutrements: two flat golden apples with a mirror on each side, both holding a small copy of the seven psalms, were recorded in 1529; a long chain scented with large grains of musk, ambergris and civet that wrapped round the waist three times in 1591; a golden ship with a small Moor made of perfume, set with pearls and diamonds, in 1599. In 1561, the castle in Pau owned a spherical pomander containing a globe in a crimson satin pouch. In 1598, the Duke of Savoy owned a round pomander in green enamel, one half depicting a chestnut, the other half the branches of a rose bush. In fact, musk had become so common by 1575 that even men of the cloth and professors doused themselves with it, one account complained. A document dating from 1685 recorded that Italians and Spaniards could not do without their fragrances and their scented gloves and leather, while their churches were also highly perfumed with sweet-smelling pastilles and incense.[29] The same was true of France at that period, as the next chapter will show.

Pomanders were part of the arsenal of talismans used to ward off evil forces. Dutch paintings from the first half of the sixteenth century frequently depict pomanders in the hands of people at prayer, or hanging from a belt or rosary, reflecting the desire to keep demons at bay. Miniatures and paintings show plants playing the same role.[30] Jewellery was cunningly wrought in every imaginable shape, from pears and hearts to crosses, snails and Moor's heads. When Henri IV of France's mistress Gabrielle d'Estrées died in 1599, an inventory of her estate included two perfumed chains, six gold and diamond buttons that also held fragrance, a gold bracelet with several scents, a perfumed pear, and a perfumed hand inlaid with gold.[31] Lists of jewellery belonging to Marie de' Medici, queen of France, in around 1609–10 include 'an enamelled and engraved golden apple with a golden pendant to put perfume in' and 'a Moor's head made of musk and ambergris, set with gold and silver and enriched with ten rubies on the hat or garland and eight emeralds'.[32]

The fashion for pomanders was by no means limited to the aristocracy or the wealthy. It was perfectly possible to make one simply by sticking cloves into an orange or lemon or even a ball of clay with various scents kneaded into it. Many people could afford the cheaper models in base metals. When the Pléiade poet Rémy Belleau died in 1577, his possessions included 'a small flat pomander set with gold wire and a small pearl, estimated at thirty Tours sols'.[33] This was no doubt a mid-range model, elegant but not extravagant. In 1557, a glove merchant who sold his wares from extremely well-placed premises inside the Paris law courts, just next to the main hall, stocked at least sixty-two such pomanders, according to his estate inventory. This listed them alongside other items such as gloves and rosaries, creating some uncertainty over their exact value, as twelve pomanders and three small rosaries were estimated to be worth twelve sous in total. The shop price for customers was doubtless not much more than a sou each. A builder's mate earned six sous a day in Paris in the early 1560s, suggesting that most people in employment could afford a pomander relatively easily, particularly since doctors insisted they were vital to stay in good health.[34]

Pomanders and pouches of scent were a crucial weapon in the fight against the plague. The doctor Loys Guyon, writing in 1615, held that if no precautions were taken, 'the venomous vapour conceived in the air' infected the heart and led to death. He showed contempt for folk beliefs such as taking a dose of garlic and a little wine in the morning before leaving the house, sniffing latrines first thing in the morning, or drinking a child's or one's own urine on an empty stomach. Similarly, he reminded his readers that the Sarmatians (Poles) fought the epidemic by throwing the stinking carcases of dogs, horses, cattle, ewes and wolves into the streets on the grounds that 'the horrible stench drives out the pestilential air'. He argued that the most effective preventive was wearing a pomander round the neck or taffeta pouches full of scent over the heart.[35] Louis XIV's doctor Nicolas de Blégny gave an excellent recipe for pomander perfume to be sniffed regularly, incorporating storax, benzoin, angelica and orris root, aromatic calamus, nutmeg, three types of sandalwood, ambergris, musk and tragacanth mucilage, all mixed to a paste with rose water. The pouches, to be regularly applied over the heart, held orris, yellow nutsedge and angelica root, aromatic calamus, white sandalwood, dried mint, marjoram, oregano, aloe wood, carnation flowers and red roses, ambergris and musk, all ground to a powder. As a preventive or cure, he suggested perfuming sleeping quarters with a mix of coarse salt, angelica root, rue leaves, cloves and camphor steeped in three quarters of a gallon of cold vinegar. This could also be used to wash the nose, hands, temples and so on. He added a 'bezoardic balm' against corrupt air in case of danger, made of distilled oil of rue, lemon and orange peel, lavender, angelica, camphor grains, yellow ambergris oil and nutmeg oil, a dab of which was to be rubbed in the nostrils before venturing out.

Nicolas de Blégny also had several even more astonishing recipes to cure those suffering from the dreadful disease. Take, he wrote, large toads in the hottest July days, hang them upside down by a small fire, then dry them and their vomit in the oven. Grind them to powder to be shaped into small flat medallions. Sprinkle these generously with theriac and apply them over the heart in a pouch. The same result could be obtained by placing large toads in a pot over the fire, dissolving the resulting powder in white wine and drinking the mix in bed in the morning, leading to profuse sweating. A third recipe involved hanging the toads by one leg until dead, salting and charring them and eating the ground remains.[36] Nicolas de Blégny was something of a medical buccaneer with a dazzling career; his ideas here took him onto the dark side, offering a clear invitation to fight evil with evil. Toads were believed to belong to Satan's realm. Women accused of witchcraft were often rumoured to breed toads at home for their own poisons and spells. It sends a shiver down the spine to think that such concoctions, steeped in black magic, were available to the royal court and even the Sun King himself as protection against the Devil's breath. It is more reassuring to imagine that La Fontaine might have turned it into one of his fables: *The Lion, the Doctor and the Toads*.

6

Musky scents

All of Europe was swept up in a wave of olfactory enthusiasm following the Renaissance, and France was no exception. Powerfully heady perfumes dominated society for over two centuries. Musk, ambergris and civet reigned supreme in rich and powerful circles, not only at court, but also in lower social ranks. This led to striking contradictions with the dominant austere moral code of the day, which saw artificial scents as demonic traps leading straight to Hell. Louis XIV perfectly embodied this ambivalent attitude: he loved fragrance as a young man, but then came to loathe it. However, the habit was so well established that his disgust had little impact. Madame de Maintenon still wore jasmine-scented gloves, claiming that the smell came from someone else, if her enemy the Princess Palatine's mocking commentary is to be believed.[1]

The endemic presence of the plague had a profound impact on the culture of scent. It was now not only permissible, but medically vital, to ward off contagion with an impenetrable scent bubble that would withstand the Devil's poisonous breath. As such, society naturally embraced perfumes, following examples from on high: as Simon Barbe wrote in his 1693 *Parfumeur françois*, the Old Testament showed that 'the Lord loved perfumes', while the Sun King often enjoyed watching 'Sir Martial in his cabinet composing the scents he wore about his sacred person'.[2]

A vast market opened up for doctors and manufacturers of aromatic substances. The strict code dictating individual appearance forced everyone to deck themselves out in various scents. Books of beauty secrets were published in large numbers, targeting women who wanted to stay fashionable and prevent or disguise the signs of ageing. Doctors proposed rejuvenating cures whose ingredients have much to say about the terrors of the age and the profoundly magical thinking that extended across social classes. Apothecaries came to play a key social role, as did wealthy manufacturers of perfumed gloves. They masked the process of post-mortem decay by cutting up perfume-soaked animal hides, including dog skins, to protect against accidental physical contact. They provided the rich with compositions that transmitted an erotic message, its animal origin carefully sublimated, while masking unpleasant body odours and protecting the wearer against potential olfactory threats. Scent seems never to have been so important as in these centuries, with their omnipresent stench. This may have been a way to come to terms with the extraordinary fragility of life and terrifyingly ineffective medical practices, as mocked by Molière. Smelling plentifully and powerfully, or ceasing to exist: that was the question.

Fountains of youth

The word 'odeur' (smell) crops up very frequently in the doctor Louis Lémery's 1702 *Traité des aliments* [*Treatise on foodstuffs*].[3] The main adjectives used to describe it outline the semantic field of aromas at the turn of the eighteenth century. They were good, agreeable (lemons, limes, star anise, nutmeg, salad burnet, truffles), marvellous (Barbados orange blossom), exquisite (orange blossom, greengage), powerful and pleasant (mint, thyme, basil, grape), aromatic (aniseed, coffee, fennel, pistachio, parsley, mint, thyme, basil), piquant (female nutmeg), powerful and unpleasant (fermented peas and beans, boiled cauliflower), stinking (urine after eating asparagus) or foul (coriander). Garlic was in a class of its own, as 'its smell drives out snakes'; it was good for treating drunkenness and dirty or befouled water and rotten food at sea. Lémery also uses much of the same vocabulary to describe tastes, though here he theoretically had eight categories to draw on: bitter, acid, acrid, salty, acerbic, austere, sweet and unctuous. He describes the pleasant bitterness of dandelions, the piquant taste of vinegar, and the very unpleasant, foul taste of blackcurrants, while classing onion, shallot and ginger as acrid. Chewing angelica root, the cure-all against the plague, was described in a mid-eighteenth-century addition as giving an aroma and taste of ambergris mixed with musk.

This suggests that a relatively detailed olfactory palette was available. Unfortunately, it was not widely used by authors of medical treatises and beauty secrets or by the apothecaries who stocked the requisite products, alongside many others. Ambroise Paré merely criticized the 'malicious poisoners and perfumers' who misled even experts about toxic substances, masking their bitterness and mixing them with sweeter products to hide their unpleasant smell.[4] No further details are given of the smell of the ten or so poisons then familiar – arsenic, sublimate, litharge, realgar, quicklime, orpiment (yellow arsenic), hellebore, hemlock, and snake and toad venom. Some of these were, however, used in beauty treatments. Virgin's milk, used to whiten the skin, contained litharge, which was very harsh on the skin and deeply toxic.[5]

Louis XIV's reign was a golden age for beauty treatments, largely targeting well-born ladies terrified of seeing their bloom fade while they were still young and losing their charm in a society that placed great emphasis on physical appearance. An analysis of four such works published from 1669 to 1698 reveals that the main focus was on women's faces: 58 per cent of the 189 recipes listed are for facial treatments. Then came the hair (14 per cent), hands (10 per cent), teeth (6 per cent), breasts (3 per cent) and lips (2 per cent).[6] The richest of the compilations, by the royal doctor Nicolas de Blégny, devoted fifty-two of its 108 recipes to the face, eighteen to the hair, fourteen to the hands, six to the teeth and six to the breasts.

As early as 1615, Loys Guyon described the ideal complexion, 'which lends the person more grace than any other beauty one may have'. He added,

> The complexion's perfect beauty depends principally on three points: its bright colour, which must be white and vermilion, like the colour of a crimson rose. Secondly, its even expanse, lively and polished in all parts. Thirdly, the purity, cleanliness, delicacy, and transparency of the skin. The complexion that does not have at least a touch of these perfections of beauty is neither good nor fine.

Again according to Guyon, the three worst blemishes were a 'defective colour', or suntan; asperities, fissures, wrinkles, pustules, spots, warts (hairy or otherwise), and smallpox scars; and thick, dirty skin, particularly if it was oily, sweaty or infected.[7]

Guyon could not have known that his definition of the perfect womanly complexion mirrored that used by modern biologists to explain how we choose our partners. The male gaze is subconsciously drawn to female physiognomies whose perfection reflects the owner's healthy immune system. A flawed complexion automatically sends a negative signal, implying the risk of reproductive failure. It is likely that women also focus on the same messages, possibly along with an assessment of the potential mate's physical prowess. But it is above all men who stare at women, carefully studying their faces to avoid being hoodwinked by tricks used to hide physical flaws and advancing age.

Fashion was a cruel business. It did not allow women to grow old. Its archetype was the dazzlingly beautiful young maiden sung by the Pléiade poets. Over the age of thirty, or even twenty in the most competitive arenas such as the royal court, their only hope lay in artifice. This helps explain the dreadful hatred of elderly women in the social imagination of the age, symbolized by the image of the witch to be burned at the stake. Roses smell the sweetest when they have just bloomed. The rest of a woman's life was to be spent trying to hold back time, risking her health in the process as the recipes she desperately put her faith in hastened her decline, made her smell worse and literally poisoned her. However, women had little choice but to turn to the charlatans who claimed to hold the secret of eternal youth. The never-ending quest for eternal youth was not limited to California in the last third of the twentieth century. It was all over sixteenth- and seventeenth-century Europe, the difference being that at that point the phenomenon was not focused on the body. This was not merely because convention, underpinned by the admonitions of strict moralists, banned disrobing in public: anyone caught swimming nude in rivers began to be prosecuted under Louis XIV. It was principally because simply surviving meant keeping a distance from others and shunning skin-to-skin contact (outside of sexual encounters), as defence mechanisms against epidemics. The principal focus was on the face, with the hands in second place. Strangely, the part of the body most associated with individual identity was transformed in the upper echelons of society into a regularly repainted theatrical mask. The fight against encroaching old age produced powdered and daubed ghosts who all resembled each other, adorned with signs of youth whose illusion only worked from a distance, like Francisco de Goya's *Old Women* (1808–12, Musée des Beaux-Arts, Lille).

Female beauty is as plain as the nose on your face. The ideal woman should have dazzlingly white, lustrous skin, not excessively wan but not tanned, with a touch of vermilion, and perfectly smooth – the essence of youth. Pierre Erresalde provided a number of simple skincare treatments, including a 'fine water to make the face appear twenty or twenty-five years of age'. Coquettes could not afford to appear any older. They had to stop time when their attractiveness was at its peak. The 'fine water' consisted of calves' feet, river water, white breadcrumbs, fresh butter and egg whites. The same result could be obtained with Erresalde's other recipes, made from distilled white lilies, white melon water, or asses' milk mixed with eggshell. Medical theory at this time worked largely by analogy with magic. The whiteness of the ingredients was believed to be magically transferred to the skin. Faces could be frozen in permanent adolescence by using fresh foodstuffs with strong germinative power, such as eggs. Not all skin treatments were so mild, however. Facial blemishes, covering every imaginable imperfection, were treated with silver sublimate, white lead and vitriol, while litharge was regularly recommended as a skin whitener. Never was the expression 'beauty is pain' truer. The pressure of social expectations forced women to wear such makeup, particularly at court: 'if she is not powdered she has no grace', particularly when 'wrinkles begin to enmesh her body', as one satirical poet wrote in 1624.[8]

Paul Scarron's 1650 comedy *L'Héritier ridicule* [*The ridiculous heir*] offers a pitiless description of the treatments inflicted on women desperate to sup from the fountain of youth:

> You think to mock such young ladies
> As myself; some are as lovely
> As those ladies of quality in whom often, it is said,
> White, pearls, eggshells, pork fat and sheep's feet,
> Balm, virgin's milk and a hundred thousand other drugs
> Make hairless heads as bald as white cherries
> Mirrors of love, their false lures
> Displaying beauties they do not possess.
> They can be called plush fabric faces.
> A third of their selves is beneath their toilette;
> Another in their high-soled shoes, the worst is in bed;
> Goods from others alone adorn them,
> What they can take from their own domain
> Is flabby flesh, sour armpits and bad breath.
> And as for their fine hair so splendid to see,
> Its roots took hold in another soil.
> It is in most cases a transplanted plant
> Applied with care to toothless heads.[9]

Reality was often even more hair-raising than fiction, as indicated by the advice dispensed by the Sun King's spirited medical adviser, Nicolas de Blégny.[10] His concoctions may not have tasted great, and their smell must have brought a touch of country atmosphere to court. He made abundant use of animal and human excrement in sixteen pages of remedies, and of urine in a further twenty-seven recipes. Dog balm, used for wounds, ulcers, toothache and colic, was made from well-fed dogs killed with a hammer blow to the head then boiled up with mallow, nettles, elder, white wine and five or six pounds of earthworms. Like was believed to cure like, which may explain the curious way the dogs were slaughtered: anyone rubbing the unpleasant-sounding concoction on their temples was supposed to be instantly cured of toothache. Getting rid of warts was easier: it just needed fuller's earth soaked in dog urine. Dog excrement, ground and soaked in vinegar and plantain water, was, in Blégny's expert opinion, an excellent remedy for diarrhoea when applied as a hot, if rather smelly, poultice. Nosebleeds needed a liquid blend of donkey droppings that were ground and mixed with plantain syrup, certainly intended to attenuate the taste and smell. Fresh pig's droppings could also be dried on a fire-shovel, ground, heated and inhaled. Might today's drug addicts think of this as a dirty line to sniff? Gallstones were broken down with borax in eau de vie, with the scale from an earthen pot that once held stagnant urine, all dissolved in wine. The mixture, administered to patients for fourteen or fifteen days, was said to be dramatically effective – at making alcoholics give up their favourite tipple, perhaps? Dropsy of the belly, when the lower abdomen was swollen with flatulence, was cured by placing the subject in a dry steam room and sprinkling the heated stones with the urine of a healthy individual. The patient – who must indeed have been patient – was advised to breathe in the steam to sweat, 'continuing the perfume as long as he can bear it'. 'Stench' might have been a more fitting term.

It is interesting to think that the king, who hired the imaginative doctor in 1682, might have tried out some of his bold ideas. Cruel whispers might suggest he did, as Blégny was arrested for embezzlement in 1693 and died in disgrace long after. Whatever the truth of the matter, his arsenal of treatments cured Louis XIV's bromidrosis, inherited from his grandfather Henri IV, who was told by Madame de Verneuil one day, 'You stink like carrion.' The Sun King's first doctor, Guy-Crescent Fagon, claimed his feet stank.[11] Nicolas de Blégny recommended washing them frequently in warm water containing dissolved alum. Against smelly armpits, he recommended a poultice of artichoke root cooked in wine or thistle root paste, powdered mint, and a liniment of myrrh leaves and liquid alum. The treatments in his treatise alternate between ordinary-sounding concoctions made from plants, and magical flights of fancy that leave the reader scratching his head. For instance, painful tooth cavities can be treated by plugging the hole with partridge brains. If you cannot get hold of a partridge, or if inserting the brains proves tricky, you can simply take a dead man's tooth and repeatedly touch the painful tooth with it until it crumbles.

The treatise also contains dozens of beauty treatments along the same more or less smelly lines. They were certainly widely used, given the author's prominent social position before his fall from grace. He recommended many 'weak meat broths to feed and conserve a delicate complexion'. One such recipe involved white vinegar, borax, mastic, aloe, egg whites and eggshells plus ox bile distilled in a bain-marie, making the skin dewy and lustrous. 'Water of talc' was made from snails farmed in a pot with salt and vinegar. The snails were fed a spoonful of talc a day for three months, then crushed and distilled. To 'improve the water's unpleasant smell', sugar and a small pouch of musk and ambergris were added. Another way of obtaining a smooth, white complexion was to prepare two gutted pigeons stripped of their feathers, turpentine, fresh eggs and limes in an alembic with a dab of musk on the lip to make the smell bearable. Perfumed fancy handkerchiefs, or *mouchoirs de Vénus*, were used by the most elegant women: they were scented with charred chalk soaked in spirits of wine or a mix of alum and white lead, then dried. Other recipes included cosmetic oils made from pearls dissolved in vinegar or pork fat. One recommends pork lard melted in new white wine as 'whitening the face marvellously'.

Then come the 'whites and magisteries', such as a 'white of pearls, admirable for the complexion', made of powdered pearls and white or pale coral dissolved with ground bismuth in aqua fortis. The resulting powder was washed until the smell of aqua fortis had gone, then mixed with pomades or floral waters made from water lilies, lilies and so on. The sovereign remedy for blemishes and tans, which were considered terribly common, was 'cosmetic ox bile', blended with alum and powdered sandiver, left out in the sun for fifteen days in May. It was then mixed with powdered porcelain dissolved in spirit of vinegar, borax, frog sperm (no clue was given as to how to obtain it . . .), camphor, sublimate and sugar candy, and left in the sun for ten to twelve days again. The result was applied to the face when venturing outside, and not washed off until the evening. Blemishes were also improved thanks to a water obtained by distilling half a dozen whelps with their entrails removed and veal's blood, or a thick paste of pigeon droppings, flax seed and barley flour, ground and soaked in strong vinegar. To bring colour to the complexion, nothing beat red sandalwood boiled in distilled vinegar with a touch of alum. Brazil wood, alum, vinegar and lemons were also used to make a carmine base for the complexion.

Nothing was too good to help women meet social expectations, though ruining their health. Blégny's treatise includes recipes for hair removal, putting on weight, beautiful nails and perfect breasts, dyeing hair, eyebrows and beards blond, black, silver or red, and tooth-whitening powders made from coral, stag antler, pumice stone and cuttlefish bone. It also lists several dozen pastes used to remove grease from the hands and soften their skin, and waters to whiten them. He adds five recommendations for making perfumed gloves with orange, rose and jasmine flower water. The bald and sparse of hair are also catered for, though again the recipes are somewhat off-putting. Simply burn bees in a pan, mix the ashes with flax seed, and pour the mix into a concoction of lizards drowned in oil, boiled and left out in the sun for twenty days. The mix was applied as needed to the head for fast-growing, luxuriant locks. A variant used snails, small flies, wasps, bees, slugs and burned salt, left in the cellar in a pot pierced with small holes for harvesting the resulting 'unctuous liquid' to be massaged into bald patches. No need for lengthy head-scratching to uncover the covert meaning behind these recipes. They involve a dash of black magic, as the animals in question, including lizards, were thought to come into being through spontaneous generation, hence to belong to the demonic kingdom. The Devil was not merely in the detail, he got right into people's hair – particularly as the liquid may have been unctuous but probably smelled downright hellish.

The promises of beauty and health held out by such recipes were, of course, empty. Their authors sold the illusion of eternal youth and charm to women who had little choice but to believe them or succumb to the blackest despair. Yet the 'miraculous' fountains of youth they claimed to tap into by creating the impression they held the key to ineffable mysteries were sometimes truly vile-smelling. Excepting the numerous recipes based solely on plants and flowers, the potions they recommended must have stunk horribly. The places where such so-called cure-alls were made, such as apothecaries and indeed the homes and palaces of countless customers, must have smelled equally nauseating. Though powerful scents were used to mask the stench, it still broke through and in fact was worse in rich homes than in poor ones, where following the latest fashions was an unaffordable dream. Worse, women's lives were ruled from late adolescence on by the terror of physical decline. The more women fought to maintain a semblance of eternal youth, adorned with the sweet perfume so beloved of poets, the more their health suffered from the toxic products they rubbed into their faces, scalps, hands and sometimes under their clothes. In fact, they were simply adding more bad smells to those arising from disease and the ageing process. As a captive customer base for doctors who were often little better than Molière's satirical character Diafoirus, they docilely used recipes that were often inspired by a deeply pessimistic Christian vision of the body. The ideal of a lustrous, smooth, white face with a touch of vermilion was at heart merely a religious fantasy defining the supposedly chaste young girl promised the blessings of a fruitful marriage, to the advantage of men.

It was all downhill from there, the rest of a woman's life being considered a vale of tears marked by inexorable decline, suffering and death. At best, doctors could hide the ravages of time. Their theories made considerable use of magical analogies, sometimes influenced by demonry in the case of secret recipes containing excrement, disgusting animals and poisons. Just as they used individual scent bubbles to fight the plague, they used scent shields to place the visible parts of women's bodies off bounds. Curiously, the aromatic armour they concocted for society beauties smelled simultaneously revolting, due to its animal and mineral ingredients, and pleasant, due to the heady perfumes added to the mixture. Anyone going near a woman after such a treatment might be put in mind of death rather than love. The musky base notes amplified and transmitted the unpleasant smells not only of the makeup itself, but also of old age and ill health. Only from a distance could the visual illusion be maintained, as no one would fall for it from close up. It may have been the case that the strategic use of physical appearance had a powerful social meaning, principally dividing women's lives into two highly unequal parts: a fleeting moment of youthful promise followed by interminable years of regret at what they had lost, or never had.

Such practices indicate society's utter rejection of older women. The coquettes at the French court had to put on the appearance of something they were not. The illusion was easier to pull off with their hair than their complexions, which is why moralists thundered against using dead people's hair and Scarron mocked those who wore wigs on their toothless heads. Yet hair pieces were highly fashionable, not just for women. Women's natural hair was seen as a visual and olfactory lure, reeling in men by focusing attention away from their somewhat unappealing faces. In around 1630, the fashion for women was to wear their hair in three parts, with a top chignon called a culbute, from the verb meaning 'to tumble', a fringe or *garcette* worn at first short, then later curled, sometimes with a centre parting, and two tufts of curled hair over the ears (figures 9 and 11). Feathers, ribbon bows and gemstones were pinned into the chignon to draw appreciative male gazes, and the hair itself was scented with orris powder, maréchale powder, Cyprus powder and violet musk to arouse desire. The charming young adolescent girls beloved of the Pléiade poets were much admired for their (sometimes artificial) blonde locks and the delightful clouds of scent from their hair. The same customs persisted in the reign of Louis XIV. Luxury became even more enticing as women shimmering with pearls, diamonds and jewels perfumed themselves with exotic animal scents intended to stir infinite desire despite the heavy layers of face powder.[12] Their dazzling jewels were matched only by their delightful fragrance. The sheer size of the gowns they wore at court, and the rules of politeness that dictated more personal space than previously, meant it was hard to get a close-up smell of the marvellously colourful dolls who wore scented pouches and products to hide their fetid armpits.

As early as 1572, the poet Marie de Romieu discussed the harm caused by some beauty secrets in an imaginary dialogue between a mother and her daughter, freely inspired by an Italian work:

'So you find it ill-advised to use red sublimate and Spanish white and all those sorts of powders I have sometimes heard tell of?' asked the daughter.

'I pray you, my daughter, avoid them like the plague, for if once you become accustomed to them, you will be staggered to find yourself old and all wrinkled at the age of thirty, and the least service you receive by them will be constantly foul breath, and your teeth (which are the principal ornaments of beauty) will soon become black, corrupt and rotten, they will be painful and you will be forced to have them taken out one after the other, and when you have lost those on the side, your cheeks will become sunken, and when you lose your front teeth you will look as though you are constantly pursing your lips at something and unwillingly keep your mouth closed, and only dare laugh with your hand in front of it. And such drugs also often cause your sight to be lost or weakened and the whole body's health is worsened.'[13]

While the medical profession was clearly aware of the deleterious effects of such slow-acting poisons, generations of women still used such harmful beauty treatments in their quest for eternal youth. They then needed even more help from intoxicating perfumes to hide the physical decline forced on them by cultural pressure.

Ambergris, musk and civet

The first perfumery manual in French was published in 1693 by Simon Barbe. His preface to the reader claims that his modest aim was to help bathhouse owners and wig-makers in towns without a specialist perfumer. The profession's star products were ambergris, musk and civet. These were foreign imports, like many of the other ingredients already mentioned, such as Arabian benzoin and storax and Peru balm, sold by spice merchants. Their key significance to the perfume trade gave rise to extraordinary legends, proving their immense symbolic power to society at the time. Barbe wrongly describes ambergris as a sort of sea foam and states that musk comes from hunting an exotic animal, pricking it all over to make blood blisters and then drying the blood in the sun. Civet, he claims, comes from a weasel-like creature placed in a cage surrounded by braziers. The perfume was allegedly obtained by scraping sweat from its armpits and thighs with an ivory knife, and started out white before turning golden yellow when its fragrance was fully ripe. He added that none of the three products was edible or suitable to be applied to the skin other than in tiny quantities mixed with other ingredients. However, all were necessary additions to scented waters and sweet essences to perfume hides and gloves. He carefully avoided giving any beauty tips because 'all powders spoil the face', as had already been repeatedly noted.[14]

Perfume specialists now define three successive notes in a scent. The fleeting top notes form the first impression. Then come the floral or fruity heart notes. Finally, the base notes can be less intense than the top and heart notes but are much longer lasting, with the potential to create powerful olfactory memories. These draw on essences from trees such as myrrh and sandalwood and natural or synthetic animal products. Among today's best-loved perfumes, Chanel No. 5 is dominated by jasmine and rose heart notes, while the highly sensual Shalimar is, its manufacturer claims, rich in balmy base notes and tonka bean. All sixteenth- and seventeenth-century perfumes were saturated with animal base notes made from glandular secretions (contrary to Simon Barbe's claims) that carried the other scents. It is hard to imagine a more direct appeal to the flesh than these historical perfumes. The doctor Jean Liébault even recommended those hoping to conceive boys to make love on a bed 'well perfumed with musk, civet, oiselet de Chypre and other fine scents' in a well-lit bedroom decorated with pleasant masculine paintings.[15]

Only an exceptional 'nose' could now get anywhere close to recreating such heady fragrances, let alone produce a real copy. Would such an experiment prove the medical theory advanced by Loys Guyon early in the seventeenth century that the 'warm vapours' of musk and civet enter the brain and cure headaches?[16] It is interesting to wonder whether today's synthetic perfumes, including several dozen types of musk, have as many virtues. Ambergris came from an oily fluid protecting sperm whales' stomachs. Castoreum came from the abdominal sacs of Canadian and Russian beavers: curiously it

Figure 1. Isaac von Ostade, *Village fair, with a church* (detail), 1643. Royal Collection Trust / © Her Majesty Queen Elizabeth II, 2019.

Figure 2. (overleaf) Isaac van Ostade, *Village fair, with a church*, 1643. Royal Collection Trust / © Her Majesty Queen Elizabeth II, 2019. The animality of country life is evoked by the character defecating in the lower right-hand corner (see figure 1). Dogs were reputed to enjoy eating human excrement, and one is watching him with interest (see pp. 41–2).

Figure 3. (previous page) Isaac van Ostade, *Peasants outside a farmhouse butchering pork*, 1641. Private collection, USA. © The Norton Simon Foundation. The moral message is identical, as pigs also fed on faeces, here from the character shown squatting in the lower left-hand corner. This detail was prudishly censored at one point but was revealed by a recent restoration.

Figure 4. Pieter Bruegel the elder (*c*.1525–69), *Haberdasher despoiled by monkeys*, 1562. Source: Wikicommons. This is an illustration of the idea, widely shared by Renaissance artists and doctors, that human excrement smelled worse than that of animals (see p. 36).

BRVEGHEL INVE

Cork. ixcu 1562

ACER · ODORATO · SEQVITVR · CANIS · OMNIA · NASO

Figure 5. *The five senses and for the first, smell.* Collection of figures from the Jean Mès Bible (1590–1), folio 9. Engraving by Adriaen Collaert (*c.*1560–1618), after Maarten De Vos (1532–1603). Bibliothèque nationale de France.

Figure 6. An engraving by the Dutch artist Crispin van De Passe (*c.*1564–1637). Source: Wikicommons. A fashionable young woman holds a flower in her left hand and a small dog is on her lap, nestled in the crook of her arm. To her right, a young man of quality is giving her a sardonic, sidelong look while ostentatiously holding his nose: nothing smells worse than women (see p. 69).

Quamvis floriferus sit gratus naribus hortus,
Sæpe tamen dulci fel sub odore latet.

Figure 7. Engraving by Jan Pieterszoon Saenredam (1565–1607) after Hendrik Goltzius (1558–1617), *Odoratus*, 1595. Source: Wikicommons. The dog's snout is level with the woman's lap, signifying her unpleasant natural smell, which the large basket of flowers is failing to mask. There are numerous variations on the same theme, for instance figure 10.

Figure 8. (overleaf) *Allegory of the senses*, attributed to Angelo Caroselli (1585–1652), oil on canvas. Private collection. Photo © Christie's Images / Bridgeman Images. The perfume vial is traditionally an attribute of Mary Magdalene, the patron saint of Paris's perfumers and glovers (see p. 120), who also represented sinful womanhood, doused in scent and admiring her reflection in a mirror.

Jayme l'oillet sur toute chose
Pour Luy Je quitte & lis & Rose
Leur odeur ne me peut toucher.

ODORATUS.
L'ODORAT.
der Geruch.

Auant que d'estre separee
De ceste fleur tant desiree
Je me veux laisser deschirer.

Figure 9 (top). *The sense of smell* (1625–7). Bibliothèque nationale de France.

Quand au matin l'Aurore a
Tout ce que le printemps est
L'odorat est charme par les do
Que Zephyre conçoit de l'ess

Figure 10 (facing page, bottom). *The sense of smell. A cherub presents a woman with a rose* (*c*.1662–3). Engraving by Jeremiah Falck (1609/10–77). Bibliothèque nationale de France.

Figure 11 (below). *The sense of smell.* Bibliothèque nationale de France. Reversed anonymous copy of a famous engraving by Abraham Bosse (1602/4–76), dating from *c*.1638. The woman's pipe tobacco is scented with musk, civet or ambergris (see p. 69).

L'ODORAT. 3
Toutes choses sont en leur seve
Tandis que les Gemeaux constans,
Viennent renouueler la terre
De l'Hyuer auec le Printemps.

A ce mois l'odorante Flore
Se plaist à humecter des pleurs,
Qu'icy bas l'amoureuse Aurore
Répend sur l'essence des fleurs.

MARS. 3.
A ce mois le Dieu de la Thrace
Met en campagne ses Guerriers;
Et Diane mene a la chasse
Ses chiens courans et ses limiers.

le Blond excud auec Priuilege du Roy.

Figure 12. *Months of the year: The sense of smell. March.* Engraving by Jeremiah Falck (1609/10–77). Printed by Le Blond (1640–1). Bibliothèque nationale de France. The woman's scent is not simply floral. She is also wearing several powerful animal scents and is inviting carnal sin by showing off her breasts. A stinking billy goat in the top right-hand corner indicates that the Devil lays his traps in the springtime.

Figure 13. *Plague doctor's outfit, Rome.* Copperplate engraving by Paul Furst, 1656. Source: Science History Images / Alamy Stock Photo. The outfit worn by plague doctors, entirely impenetrable and doused in prophylactic scents, was a professional variation on the invisible 'armour' of scent worn by rich and poor alike to keep the Devil's poisonous breath at a distance.

Figure 14. *The sense of smell* (1700). Paris: chez J. Mariette, rue Saint-Jacques, aux Colonnes d'Hercule. Bibliothèque nationale de France.

Figure 15. *The sense of smell* (*c*.1695–6). A woman reclines on a divan, sniffing a flower. Engraving by Robert Bonnart (1652–1733). Bibliothèque nationale de France.

Figure 16. Giuseppe Maria Crespi, known as lo Spagnolo (1665–1747), *Girl with a rose and a cat* (*c.*1700–10), oil on canvas. Pinacoteca nazionale di Bologna, Emilia-Romagna, Italy, Mondadori Portfolio / Electa / Cesare Somaini / Bridgeman Images. The late seventeenth century seems to have witnessed a silent revolution in the use of perfumes. Musk, civet and ambergris began to lose ground. The sense of smell, embodied here by a woman, more sensitive to smells than men according to contemporary science, was increasingly defined by floral essences (see chapter 7). The failure to include a dog (see also figures 14 and 15) implies the rejection of both animal-based scents and a negative view of women as naturally foul-smelling. Women were now seen in more positive terms as charming creatures, though love still came with thorns and claws (see p. 151).

Figure 17. Holder containing a set of four perfume bottles and a funnel, late seventeenth century (ivory, gold, diamond and silk, 7.5 × 6.4 × 4.1 cm). Photo KMH – Museumsverband. The floral revolution in eighteenth-century perfumery led to the production of precious bottles to hold them to avoid inconveniencing those who disliked such scents (see p. 151).

Figure 18. Oriental bezoar mounted on a base shaped like an oak tree with a boar, *c.*1700 (gold and shell, 17.8 cm). Photo KMH – Museumsverband. Bezoars were found in the stomachs of exotic ruminants. They were very rare, precious and expensive, as doctors believed they protected against the plague (see p. 104).

Figure 19. Élisabeth-Louise Vigée-Le Brun (1755–1842), *Portrait of Marie-Antoinette in a white muslin gown*, oil on canvas, 1783. Darmstadt, Schlossmuseum. Photo akg-images. A woman's beauty mainly lay in her face, which was given careful treatments, rubbed with pomade and dabbed with vermilion. Then came the only other parts of the body left bare, the neck, arms and forearms, all whitened with the same treatments and perfumed with the floral and fruity fragrances fashionable in the eighteenth century. At court and elsewhere, all well-born women followed the same ideal of beauty, coming to resemble eternally youthful, pink-cheeked porcelain dolls. The artist has made the queen's hands very expressive while masking any signs of ageing that might detract from the painting (see p. 152).

Figure 20. Élisabeth-Louise Vigée-Le Brun (1755–1842), *Marie-Antoinette and her children*, oil on canvas, 1787. Château de Versailles. Photo Bridgeman Images. Court life required a fine white complexion with pink cheeks, even for infants. Tanning was considered vulgar and rustic. Credit: Château de Versailles, France / Bridgeman Images.

Figure 21. Élisabeth-Louise Vigée-Le Brun (1755–1842), *Portrait of Charles-Alexandre de Calonne*, oil on canvas, 1784. Royal Collection Trust / © Her Majesty Queen Elizabeth II, 2019 / Bridgeman Images. Men also wore powder, as shown by this magnificent portrait of the powerful controller of finances at the peak of his career. His splendid wig, elegantly powdered grey, has left marks on his shoulders. Is this a sly dig by the artist suggesting that the man in control of France's finances was using cheap, low-grade starch, which perfumers complained had little staying power (see p. 148)?

Figure 22. Jean-Baptiste-Pierre Le Brun (1748–1813), *Self-Portrait*, oil on canvas, 1795. Photo Peter Horree / Alamy Stock Photo. Élisabeth-Louise Vigée-Le Brun's ex-husband paints himself as a man of importance: he had recently been appointed an expert curator at the Musée du Louvre. The French Revolution did not put wigs completely out of fashion (see p. 154), though for the triumphant bourgeoisie of the nineteenth century, they came to symbolize an age they held in contempt.

Habit de Parfumeur

Figure 23. Anonymous, *The garb of a perfumer*, *c.*1700. Paris, Musée Carnavalet. © RMN-Grand Palais / Agence Bulloz. The original engraving was printed in around 1695 in a collection of 'grotesque garb' (Paris, Nicolas de Larmessin). It was reversed and coloured shortly after. It shows the social significance of Paris's perfumers and glove-makers and features many of the products they sold (see p. 120).

was never used by French perfumers in the sixteenth and seventeenth centuries, though beaver-fur hats were fashionable. Civet is a honey-like secretion extracted from the anal glands of the Ethiopian wild cats that gave the product its name. Musk is a red jelly harvested from the glands of the Asian musk deer. Rutting males produce some thirty grams in an abdominal pouch: in the past, the animal had to be killed to obtain the musk, which is still worth a fortune to this day. Women can apparently detect this musk in tiny quantities, since it is chemically similar to testosterone and steroids. Like ambergris, castoreum and civet, it is reputed to trigger a sexual response in humans. Countless users past would agree. When first extracted, civet had a decidedly faecal note and needed ingenious treatment to become a heady, aphrodisiac fragrance.[17] Little known in modern France, it survives in the two adjoined red cones used as the familiar sign for a tobacconist and sometimes in the shop's name, in twofold reference to the days when it was used as a scent for tobacco. Simon Barbe recommended using just a touch of civet as it was easy to overdo it. These days we might see this as one of the dangers of untrammelled sensuality, as the erotic base notes of musky aromas heighten the pleasurable memories associated with smoking.

Perfumery was not an independent trade in the sixteenth and seventeenth centuries. The need for professional perfumers had become clear as early as the Crusades, when master glovers in Paris had been given more or less explicit permission to use and sell scent.[18] Their statutes were renewed in 1582, but they faced stiff competition from haberdashers, who also dealt in perfumes and were lobbying for the sole privilege of the title 'master perfumer'. A 1594 decree disappointed them on this score but did grant them the right to 'perfume, wash, and embellish their merchandise'. Twenty years later, in January 1614, a royal decree allowed 'master glovers' to call themselves 'perfumers' but banned them from selling anything they had not manufactured themselves. The plague and the passion for fragrances were major factors in putting perfumery on a solid footing as an independent profession. It had its own stars, such as René Le Florentin, who also dabbled in poisons, who came to France in 1533 with Catherine de' Medici, and Martial, the king's brother's *valet de chambre* and perfumer, consulted by Louis XIV in his youth. Marie de' Medici had her own Italian perfumer, Annibal Basgapé, recorded in 1632. Such prestigious positions were often handed down from father to son. In 1686, Pierre Le Lièvre was perfumer to the royal wardrobe; in 1740, Claude Le Lièvre inherited the title of the king's apothecary and distiller, which he passed down in turn to Élie-Louis Le Lièvre on 1 February 1750.[19]

The statutes of 18 March 1656 took the perfume and scented glove trade up the social scale, authorizing those working in it to handle all leathers and fabrics. They were allowed to take on an apprentice for four years and had then to employ him as a journeyman for a further three years to let him produce his own masterpiece, if he were not a master's son. The entrance exam consisted of producing five pairs of gloves, one fingerless, all perfumed, dyed and finished to professional standard. The first pair with five fingers had to be made of otter hide or some other similar animal, padded and lined with fur. A pair of falconry gloves made from a single piece of dog-skin or similar and a pair of low-cut lined gloves made from a single hide were also required, together with short-fingered kid gloves for a woman and low-cut sheepskin gloves for a man. Widows who had not remarried were allowed to keep their late husband's trade, but not to produce their own goods. Master craftsmen were authorized to sell ambergris, musk, civet and other 'strong smells and scents' alongside washed, perfumed or whitened hides. The profession's religious fraternity was in Saint Anne's Chapel at the Church of the Innocents in Paris. Saint Mary Magdalene (figure 8) and Saint Nicolas were the trade's two patron saints. Perfumery took up a lot of space, requiring a shop, storage space, and laboratory with room for cauldrons, coils, presses, mortars, kilns and boilers. As will be seen below, some master craftsmen specialized in gloves or even a particular type of animal hide. The Paris trade was clustered in various neighbourhoods, around Saint-Germain l'Auxerrois, Saint-Eustache, the tour Saint-Jacques, the pont au Change bridge, the Palais on l'Île de la Cité, and Saint-Sulpice.

An anonymous engraving now in the Musée Carnavalet in Paris gives a precise, if rather imaginative, idea of how a fashionable perfumer might have dressed in the late seventeenth century, his outfit a metaphor for his art.[20] The male perfumer wears an incense burner on his head, wafting clouds of scent. His wig is clearly perfumed, while his white complexion, particularly clear on the coloured etching, indicates that men of quality also wore face powder and scorned suntans as vulgar. His shoulders are adorned with perfumed fans. Every part of his outfit is certainly scented. Not a square inch of skin can be seen other than his face, which is coated in heavy makeup: his perfumed garb forms an impenetrable defence against the plague. It is easier to tell from the coloured etching than the engraving that he is wearing perfumed, skin-coloured gloves to protect his hands. Such gloves were part of the perfumers' and glovers' guild coat of arms, with the motto 'From azure to an argent glove'; a variant coat of arms had an incense burner and the motto

'From argent to three gules gloves, to an azure chief with an antique gold incense burner'. The perfumer is shown holding small round Boulogne soaps in one hand and fine Spanish skins in the other. On his chest is a small portable display unit with four shelves, containing, from top to bottom, various vials of essence, pomades from Rome and Florence, soaps from Naples, scented waters, eau de millefleurs (made, as has been seen, from cow pats and a touch of musk), orange flower water, and Queen of Hungary's water. From his coat tails dangle more products for sale, including long gloves, tobacco, cedar, Maltese earth, pastilles to sweeten the breath and for incense burners, Spanish wax and Spanish red, rouge *en tasse* (i.e. made in small porcelain cups), myrtle water (still used today against wrinkles), Cyprus powder containing benzoin and musk, angel water made from benzoin, rose, ambergris and musk, jasmine powder, and Cordova water, similar to angel water with added rose water. Simon Barbe tells us that angel water and Cordova water, perhaps with a splash of ambergris essence, were excellent for hands and handkerchiefs. The model's elegant shoes were also certainly doused with protective scent. However, they would have been made or sold not by perfumers but by cobblers: many other perfumed leather goods such as doublets, pouches, purses, hunting bags, bags, linings for justaucorps and gowns, belts and saddles were supplied by leather curriers and specialist craftsmen. Simon Barbe also advises perfuming wigs in their boxes and two days' worth of clothes by putting them in small chests filled with pleasant fragrances.[21] The habit of constantly wearing scented pouches shaped like the organ in need of protection has already been seen. Simon Barbe's preference was for violet powder. Even when no contagion threatened, homes were perfumed with pastilles of fragrances placed in incense burners on tripods (figure 15) or hanging from the ceiling, oiselets de Chypre for burning, powders hidden in decorative bird ornaments, strewn on the floor, and scented fountains. Hands were sometimes washed in rose water poured from special ewers, though perhaps less often than in the sixteenth century. Diners could keep unpleasant smells at a distance by taking shelter in their own personal space, scattering scented water from a small ring or sprinkler.[22]

The perfumed glove trade

At this point in history, water was feared as a threat to good health, leading to the closure, for example, of bathhouses that were also accused of harbouring venereal disease. Hygiene was not a relevant concept at this time.[23] The population should be imagined as filthy, crawling with vermin and scabies-ridden. The disease was as common as it was hard to treat in an age when soap and washing were infrequent health treatments. Most scholars and doctors considered dirt, particularly on the heads of newborn babies, to be a form of protection. Standing close to other people might have been a superhuman feat of endurance, worse than a crowded underground train in rush hour, if people did not douse themselves and their possessions in fragrance. Just as frequent changes of white shirts were a necessity, refreshing the perfume bubble was vital, and that meant a trip to the perfumer for a pair of scented gloves. What people found hardest to bear was probably not the terrible stench that reigned in urban areas, but the smell of other people – particularly as, as has been seen, even the worst smells lose their power after some fifteen minutes as long as they remain static. People also generally grew accustomed to the more or less ripe odour of their immediate family or people alongside them in workshops. The same could not be said for the thousands of fetid waves of scent trailing in the wake of people walking the streets, strolling round the palace and grounds at Versailles and bustling public squares and inns. As one smell faded, another arose in its place as new people constantly passed by. Fortunately, purveyors of perfumed gloves held the antidotes needed to soothe noses constantly assailed by foul smells. Their scented gloves, developed as a protection against the plague, became even more important in daily life, making the air breathable once more.

Apothecaries sold the ingredients needed to make fragrances. Estate inventories show that some even rivalled professional perfumers for the extent of their stocks. In 1514, the Paris spice merchant and apothecary Jehan Eschars stocked roses, white and black hellebore, thyme, cardamom, lapis lazuli, emeralds (used in beauty treatments), sweet almonds, various unnamed drugs and unguents, distilled waters, and moulds used to make scented communion wafers. In 1522, his colleague Robert Calier sold everything a perfumer might need, including verdigris, incense, litharge, coral, storax, asafoetida, sulphur and musk. He also stocked a variety of distilled waters.[24]

Jean Binet, who died in 1557, was a very prosperous glove merchant on the Île de la Cité in the heart of Paris, with two shops offering a wide range of products. As well as pomanders, as previously discussed, he sold small rosaries, sachets of scented powder estimated at a sou for four, sachets of violet powder, musk and civet. His main trade, however, was in gloves, with something for everyone: his extensive stock included gloves in calfskin, goatskin and calfskin, curried kidskin, white calfskin, sheepskin, buck and goatskin, dog-skin, lined dog-skin, Venice style, Vendôme style padded with silk, women's short-fingered gloves, and fingerless gloves. Some were luxurious indeed, embroidered with gold and silk, worth a livre a pair, or a third dearer yet if embroidered with fine gold or gilded copper. Calfskin gloves embroidered with gold and silk were described as 'washed with scent', while those in goat and calfskin were 'perfumed'. Binet rented a house nearby on rue de la Vieille-Pelleterie that he also used as a workshop and storage space. It was perfect for his trade and for the numerous dyers who worked in the little street on the left bank of the Seine, between the Pont Notre-Dame and the Pont au Change, as it gave them direct access to the river through a water gate, like those in Venice. The house held a stock of finely worked falconry gloves, long kid and sheepskin gloves, fencing gloves (sold at around three sous a pair), Millau-style gloves, two luxurious pairs of velvet and satin wrist cuffs at five livres each, a large quantity of benzoin, and nine bottles of rose water and melissa water,[25] estimated at an impressive sixteen livres. These, along with musk and civet stored in a box, were undoubtedly used to perfume his hides, which he stocked in abundance, with over 2,000 white calf hides. Nearly half of these were stored in a 'small' attic alongside many other types of hide, such as white goatskin, white curried kidskin, kid, chamois, Morocco, sheep, dog (thirty-four skins, with hair). An unknown quantity of cat and hare fur was certainly intended for glove linings. The notary and his assistants produced a highly professional inventory, recording no disgust at the doubtless appalling smell of the treasures heaped up in this Aladdin's cave when they visited it on one late April day. Nor did they pass comment on the discovery of sixty-five dozen calves' heads – 780 in total. Were these waiting to be sold to butchers? A century later, calves' head soup featured in recipe books. The heads were estimated to be rather low in value, just eight livres, alongside several other small goods and nine large pairs of scissors, vital for the leather trade.[26]

The estate inventory of one less well-off colleague was not quite so lavish. When Guillaume Degrain died in 1549, he left twenty-six dog-skins 'left as they are', estimated at one sou in total, while eighteen cat-skins were worth four sous. He sprinkled his skins with rose water and 'mollyet' water, estimated at four and three sous a pint respectively.[27] There is little more of interest in such documents until the reign of Louis XIII. In 1613, the perfume merchant Dominique Prévost, who married in 1566 and set up business in 1582 in the rue des Deux-Portes in the Paris parish of Saint-Germain, also sold perfumed gloves, estimated at four sous a pair, though he was not officially a master glover. He also owned weapons, swords, daggers and a halberd, which suggest his neighbourhood may have been rather unsafe. The inventory estimated a chain of perfumes with two strands at ten sous, a chain of musk and olive wood at twenty sous, a three-stranded chain of benzoin at forty, and perfumed rosaries at fifteen sous the dozen.[28]

The eroticism of leather

A faster pace of cultural development can be seen from the 1620s–1630s on. Ruled by a warmongering king and with a principal minister, Richelieu, eager to carve up the declining Spanish empire, France became home to one of the most refined courts in Europe. Not only the immediate royal circle, but Paris as a whole, was forging a new national art of polite social behaviour and appearance. The ideal model of behaviour was laid down in Nicolas Faret's *L'Honnête homme, ou l'art de plaire à la Cour* [*The honest man, or the art of pleasing at court*] (1630), reprinted six times by the time Louis XIV came to the throne, and copied by many others. This was a new set of social practices rather than a simple updated version of the supposed virtues of the aristocracy. The new professions who provided the structure for the modern state – jurists and administrators, all supporters of the monarchy – were eager to climb the social ranks, copying the tastes and pomp of the old aristocracy. French style grew in confidence, rejecting the dark fabrics and composed postures of the Spanish court. Unusually, male fashions were even more splendid and eye-catching than those for women. The figure of the well-born man tricked out in lace, ribbons, a feather in his hat, pointed goatee, and long sword by his side was to inspire Alexandre Dumas's famous musketeers. There was no need for blue blood or a military career to stride the streets of Paris or preen at well-frequented salons in such new fashions. Boots, long or short, made the man, to the point where satirists poked fun at those who wore them 'at all times, without horses, without mules, and without donkeys'. Boots, worn very loose at the top from 1635 on, were made of leather that was, of course, perfumed. At the end of Louis XIII's reign, elegant men added studied gestures to their repertoire, walking on tiptoe and 'waggling their heads in rhythm and in speech'. Doused in aromatic essences, always ready to greet acquaintances with a deep bow, 'they wear clothes not to cover themselves but to uncover themselves pleasurably', as the poet François Maynard gibed. The streets of Paris were filled with 'powdered, curled, musked Adonises', trailing clouds of scent that announced their glory and left – so they fondly believed – admirers disappointed when they moved on. They wore gloves, naturally, to dazzle women and other onlookers with their charms. Women also cultivated an alluring presence, wearing as much erotic scent as men, if not more. In such elevated social circles, even children were gloved, booted and perfumed.[29]

Stock inventories reflect this orgy of consumption. In 1631, the estate inventory of the late wife of Pierre Francœur, the king's perfumer and *valet de chambre*, certainly left much out. It did, however, list the shop's stock of gloves, some with little taffeta ribbons, others made of scented curried kidskin and sheepskin, and Cyprus powder for dusting on the body. This was a mix of oak moss, jasmine blossom and musk rose, with a powerful, lasting scent. The inventory also lists 'perfumed toilettes', or scented canvas pouches for storing chemises or nightwear.[30]

In July 1636, a major inventory of the estate of Antoine Godard, a perfumer and glove merchant on Rue de la Pelleterie, right by the Seine on Île de la Cité in Paris, at the Sign of Notre Dame, filled almost thirty pages.[31] The detailed list gives a rare glimpse of the richly decorated wares sold by an extremely prosperous master craftsman. One of his rarest possessions was a pair of small silver portraits of Louis XIII and his queen, Anne of Austria. Under their august patronage, customers could purchase frangipani-scented gloves trimmed in yellow and red, gloves made of lambskin, gloves made of curried kidskin and lambskin, double-stitched gloves, frangipani-scented sheepskin gloves, black double-stitched sheepskin gloves, red-trimmed sheepskin gloves, trimmed and washed gloves, broad-trimmed and washed gloves, untrimmed Vendôme-style gloves, white and waxed or white and yellow, double-stitched suede style gloves trimmed with lace, scented with frangipani, and lined with tabis (a sort of moiré silk), gloves made of Flemish lace, large gloves of buckskin and sheepskin lined with ratine (brushed wool or serge) with braiding and fringes, buckskin gloves, large gloves of calfskin and sheepskin padded with panne (silk plush) and embroidered, sheepskin gloves padded with panne in various colours, large buckskin gloves, white or coloured, worth one livre ten sous a pair, dog-skin gloves, small black sheepskin gloves, small coloured buckskin gloves, low-cut buckskin-style sheepskin gloves sewn on the reverse, tight gloves with red fingertips, embroidered with English rabbit fur, sheepskin gloves embroidered with silk on the back of the hand, lined with taffeta and padded with satin, white low-cut chamois gloves, white low-cut buckskin, deerskin or chamois gloves, falconry gloves, low-cut reverse sheepskin gloves, and buckskin gloves decorated with a Jews' harp motif, embroidered with gold and ribbons, 'both white and washed'. Antoine Godard also sold woollen gloves in various colours, very expensive gloves of gold and silver embroidery, for men at six livres a pair, or for women with a removable fold-over mitten or ribbons at seven livres. There were also washed gloves for girls, various types of gloves for children including fingerless ones, and expensive pale gloves from Vendôme, reputed far and wide for its delicate kid-leather gloves.

Gloves were available for all hands, all budgets and all occasions. Scented gloves were the absolute height of high-society fashion in the reign of Louis XIII. Paired with fashionable boots, they drew death's sting in two ways, transforming the hides of countless pitilessly slaughtered animals, including cats and dogs, into armour against the plague and into erotic adornments saturated with powerfully attractive essences stripped from the sex glands of exotic animals. Human noses were accustomed from early childhood to breathing in the scent of death transmuted into olfactory ecstasy. Simon Barbe explains this very straightforwardly in his recipes for treating leather for perfumed fans and gloves.[32] For fans, each fold was scented with floral fragrances, then the finished fan was treated with a civet-heavy composition. For gloves, the hides were first soaked in orange flower water, then cut and dyed, for instance with brown, red and yellow to mimic the colour of frangipani flowers, then left in beds of blossom. Sponges were also used to soak them with a mixture of ambergris, musk, civet and a splash of eau de millefleurs, for which he gave several recipes. They were then dried and shaped, with the exception of dog-skin gloves (or kid gloves made to imitate dog-skin), which were moistened from the inside out, 'which is known as washed'. Frangipani referred to both a reddish colour and a powerful scent close to that of red jasmine. It is hard to tell which of the two meanings, if not both, the 1636 inventory referred to.

The Elizabethan playwright Philip Massinger has one of the characters in his 1623 tragicomedy *The Bondman* say, 'Lady, I would descend to kiss your hand / But that 'tis gloved, and civet makes me sick.'[33] Did English nostrils hold out against the hegemony of animal base notes that was taking over France after conquering Italy and Spain? At the very least, the comment shows that the new social norms of behaviour required men to skim a woman's gloved hand with their lips. That may have been why women's gloves were so often fingerless. Manicured nails and fragrant pomades doubtless kept the bare skin safe from the danger of contagion breaking through the protective armour of scent. Fetishists would have had little opportunity to get their kicks, while women led their swains around by the nose, sheltering behind leather fans that trailed heady clouds of scent.

The fashion lasted in France until at least the mid-seventeenth century, as indicated by the estate inventories of Nicolas Rousselet, a glover and perfumer in the rue Saint-Honoré in 1641, Charles Mersenne, a perfume merchant in the rue du Louvre, the following year, and Pierre Courtan, who ran a shop at the Sign of the Cross of Lorraine in rue Saint-Honoré in 1649.[34] The following only indicates new products listed in their inventories. Rousselet sold many types of gloves, some washed with pumpkin oil, some Vendôme-style the colour of orange blossom, or long gloves with reinforced gussets between each finger, and single-colour perfumed dog-skin gloves for women. He also used orris powder as well as pumpkin oil. Mersenne had a wider range of fragrances on offer, with grey or white Cyprus powder for the body and orris, violet, cedar, Maréchale and musk-infused Cyprus powder also available. He also sold orange flower water and rose water and had 200 pints of benzoin-scented angel water in stock for sprinkling on gloves and clothes. Soaps on sale at one sou each suggest water was used sparingly. His shop also stocked rose wood and cedar wood, dried roses, scented silk toilettes and buttons, and luxurious perfumed embroideries carefully stored alongside animal hides in six chests full of scents, which were estimated at forty-five livres. In 1649, Courtan sold gloves, small soaps and hair powder, whose scent is not detailed. His shop held as well a large number of skins in many colours, often scented, sometimes with jasmine. He also owned moulds to make dangling earrings and rosaries in scented paste.

Nothing new under the Sun King?

The 1640s saw the peak of the erotic combination of perfume and leather as part of the male repertoire of seduction. Charles Sorel wrote an amusing commentary on the fashion in a delightful short piece of 1644, *Les Lois de la galanterie* [*The laws of gallantry*]:[35]

> As for clothing, the great rule to be given is to change it often and to be as fashionable as possible, and by clothing we mean all the main garments and their accoutrements, whatsoever part of the body they serve. Those who stick to a fashion that is no longer current because it seems convenient are to be taken for good Gauls and people of the old court. [. . .] As for the knee-frills worn over them, we approve of their simplicity when they are broad and made of well-starched batiste, though it has been said that they resemble paper lanterns, and a Palace

washerwoman used them as such one evening, putting her candle into one to keep it safe from the wind. To adorn them yet further, we also wish them customarily to have a double or triple row of linen, either batiste or Dutch, and indeed it would be better if there were two or three rows of Genoa stitch to accompany the jabot of the same adornment. You know that as the drawstring and fly are called the *little goose*, the *jabot* is the opening of the shirt over the stomach, which must always be seen with its lace decorations; because only indolent old men wear them buttoned right up. Being also warned that because men no longer wear braided or reticella lace collars, several have added such to their shirts: we forbid them from having recourse to such, which feels too much like meanness, because a true Gallant must not have anything that is not new, beautiful and purpose-made. To get back to boots, they must be long in the foot, though it has been said that one must conform to nature and keep its measurements. It is well known that at the same time as long feet came into use, hats were also worn that were so high and pointy that a coin would have covered the top of them: yet the fashion for those hats suddenly gave way to a flat, round shape, while long-footed boots and shoes stayed, which shows in what esteem they are held. Someone once drove a nail through the tip of another man's boot while he was busy talking, so that he stayed nailed to the floor; but far from making the fashion hateful, on the contrary, if the foot had reached the end of the boot the nail would have pierced it right through, and that is what use it proved to that Galahad. After the boots, if you think of spurs, you will have them in solid silver, and change their style often without complaining about the cost. Those who wear silk stockings will have none but from England, and their garters and shoe bows will be such as are dictated by Fashion, and be warned generally that as soon as some novelty is brought in, there is honour in observing it, such that one appears almost to be the author of it, fearing others might imagine that one is merely a follower. On this subject one must take care to hurry along one's tailors; for some are so slow and fashions last so short a time that they have gone before an outfit is ready. [. . .] Some small things cost little and yet are extremely decorative on a man, showing him to be wholly devoted to Gallantry [. . .], such as for example a fine gold and silver ribbon on one's hat, sometimes interwoven with some fine-coloured silk, and seven or eight fine satin ribbons on one's breeches, in the brightest colours that can be seen: people may say that it is making one's own person into a shop front, and displaying as much haberdashery as if one were selling it; one must still observe what is current, and to show that all these kinds of ribbons contribute greatly to showing off a man's gallantry, they have been called gallants in preference to anything else. Since when, seeing that most ladies, rather than bracelets of pearls, amber and jet, are content to simply tie a plain black ribbon round their wrist, we have found it fitting that young gallants should wear one too, to show off the whiteness of their hands when they remove their gloves. Nor do we disapprove of the intention of those who added a crimson ribbon, joining the two together or wearing them separately, as the two colours suit the whiteness and delicacy of the skin and heighten its radiance. But permission is expressly refused to those of encroaching old age who have black, dry, wrinkly or hairy hands who wish to do the same, particularly as to do so would simply lead to their confusion and mockery. Our fine-complexioned Gallants will still be permitted to wear round, long beauty spots or somewhat large black emplasters on their temple, which is called a sign for toothache; but because it can be hidden by their hair, several have recently begun wearing them on the cheekbone, which we have found a great source of decorum and delight. If critics think to reproach us for imitating women, we will astonish them greatly by responding that we cannot do other than follow the example of those we admire and adore.

A further passage confirms the presence of soaps in the inventories of perfumers in the 1640s. Water and bodily hygiene seemed to be making a timid comeback, nearly a century earlier than generally recognized by historians, who frequently see their use as a result of English customs being taken up in France. In truth, the reappearance of regular washing late in Louis XIII's reign can probably be explained by the social pressure of new standards of attractiveness and fashion.

One can sometimes go to bathhouses to have a clean body, and every day one should take care to wash one's hands with almond cake. One must also have one's face washed almost as often, and one's cheeks shaved, and one's hair washed sometimes, or dry it out with good powders; for if one takes such care having one's clothes cleaned, and even keeping the rooms and furniture clean in a house, there is all the more reason to take care of one's own body. You will have a *valet de chambre* trained in such duties, or you will use a barber who has no other functions, not one of those who bandages wounds and ulcers and who always have a faint smell of pus or unguent.

Sorel is referring here to the establishment of a professional category of barber-wig-makers in 1637, as distinct from barber-surgeons. The new profession had a bright future powdering wigs and looking after men's hair. A barber will 'curl your hair or leave it puffed out', Sorel continues, and care for your beard and moustache to give you 'more grace'. Once the habit had gained ground, it never went away. A royal edict recorded in parliament on 23 March 1673 established no more than 200 combined barbers, wig-makers, bathhouses and steam rooms in Paris and other towns and cities across France. Their premises were indicated by a yellow sign that read 'Bathhouse, steam room, and wig-makers: we care for your facial hair.' They were entitled to sell hair in bulk or retail and to make soaps, pomades, essences, powders and pastes, but were not allowed to carry out surgery.[36] So swiftly did the new hygiene standards take hold that the first edition of the Académie Française's dictionary in 1694 gave one meaning of 'muguet' (lily of the valley) as young men who washed and wore perfume to make themselves attractive to women.

Perfumed glove sellers also carried new stock lines to meet the new demand from customers, who doubtless also included ladies of quality. In 1735, the Paris glove merchant Jean-Baptiste Douaire had vast quantities of starch in stock for wig powder, ninety-eight dozen cakes of soap, fifty pounds of soap by weight, various powders, unidentified except for some Cyprus powder, potpourri (then highly fashionable), powder puffs, almond paste for cleaning the hands, toothpicks, packets of beauty spots for the face, and unscented pomades.[37]

In the latter half of the seventeenth century and the opening decades of the eighteenth, what changed was not so much perfumes per se as the body odour of those who followed fashion. Louis XIV's anti-perfume stance of the mid-1680s may have given the misleading impression of sparking an olfactory revolution, when it was in fact a passing fad given undue importance by the king's hangers-on. Since the only fragrance he could stand was orange flower water, it has sometimes over-hastily been assumed that this proved influential both at court and in the perfume trade.[38] Yet as has been seen, orange flower water was already listed in two inventories of Parisian perfumed glove merchants decades earlier in 1641 and 1642. Before that, it was popular in Italy, and Marie de' Medici and the Marquise de Rambouillet were both known to have loved the fragrance. In the late sixteenth century, thousands of orange trees were planted outside Grasse, then best known for the quality of its animal hides. Aside from the tiny quantities of costly essence made from their blossom, the flowers themselves, too fragile to be transported, were used to make scented gloves much appreciated by Marie de' Medici and Anne of Austria. In around 1650, jasmine joined orange blossom in the Grasse trade, with tuberose coming two decades later, in around 1670. This is when the local perfume industry truly began to develop, with Grasse-based perfumers supplying orange flower, jasmine and tuberose essences and pomades for merchants in Montpellier who traditionally specialized in scented waters. Innovations in fragrance were by no means the sole preserve of the royal court or of the capital. Neroli water and bergamot water (later known as eau de cologne) were invented in around 1680 and 1690 respectively. Neroli is made from Seville orange blossom, with a scent similar to bergamot. It came into fashion thanks to a French princess living in Italy who used it to perfume her gloves and bath water. Bergamot water, a more complex scent, earned a fortune for Giovanni Maria Farina, an Italian perfumer based in Cologne. Bergamot oranges and small Chinese oranges, now known as mandarins, brought new aromas and flavours, with nose and palette working together. Leathers may have become more lightly scented in the latter half of the seventeenth century when orange flower became a popular scent.[39]

The three animal-based scents of ambergris, musk and civet only gradually lost ground. Not until the mid-eighteenth century did they fall out of favour, as the following chapter will show. A crisis, or at least slowdown, in the production of scented gloves may explain why Grasse took a change of direction to focus on the perfume industry. Estate inventories for perfumed glove merchants in Paris become much scarcer and briefer at this point and are thus less useful as a historical source. This may, however, be a misleading impression based on the state of those records that have survived. It is impossible to make any definitive statements on the matter, as further detailed research is required. It is, however, possible to point to considerable continuity in discussions of the subject and in recipes by specialists. In 1637, Jean de Renou (who first published his treatise in Latin in 1609) referred twenty-nine times to ambergris, fourteen times to musk and nine times to civet, often all three together. Rose water crops up forty times, roses themselves nine times and oranges eight times, twice as peel and once as blossom, whose fragrance he praises.[40] The highly successful third edition of Marie Meurdrac's book, published in 1687 (after the first edition in 1666), aimed at a female readership, has five references to ambergris and/or musk, adding civet for the sixth. One of the first references is to improve the smell of a water of talc made of snails crushed with their shells. She also mentions orange flower water three times and orange flower oil a further three. Rose water features thirty-four times, being used in a pomade for the face and hands along with fresh butter, Venice turpentine and lemons, scented with a touch of orange flower water and cloves.[41] Nicolas Lémery's collection, the first version of which was published in 1681, does not point to a sudden shift in practices, except perhaps for civet, used just once, compared to seven for musk and fifteen for ambergris. He refers to rose water eight times, barely more than orange flower water (seven times) and essence (once). The 1686 edition teaches the more impecunious, or less scrupulous, perfumer to make cheap 'Western' musk from small quantities of the original product: in the last three days of the moon, feed the blackest rough-footed pigeons you can find with spike lavender seed and sprinkle them with rose water. Then feed them on beans and pills for fifteen days, slit their neck on the sixteenth and catch the blood in an earthenware dish standing on hot ashes. Skim off the top, then crown each ounce with a drachma (one-eighth of an ounce, or 576 grains) of genuine Oriental musk dissolved in spirits of wine. Add four or five drops of billy goat bile, leave the mixture to steep in good, hot horse manure, and warm it through again.[42] Satanic witchcraft is bubbling just under the recipe's surface, with the colour black, the goat bile and the (hell)fire. Animal perfumes were still a powerful presence in the late seventeenth century, judging by these sources. In 1693, the perfumer Simon Barbe argued that musk, ambergris and civet were enough to perfume gloves, with no need for flowers. He did, however, provide a recipe for ambrette scent, based on civet and orange blossom, and a 'composition from Rome' containing the three animal extracts with orange blossom. A variant blended orange blossom or jasmine essence with essence of ambergris and civet.[43]

Drawing death's sting

In the sixteenth and seventeenth centuries, the extraordinary stench in towns and cities and at court did not weaken people's sense of smell. Quite the opposite; they were perfectly convinced of the need to create impenetrable olfactory barriers against infection and the foul smells that heralded and accompanied plague outbreaks. They paid attention to the messages their noses sent them, alert to imminent danger and fully enjoying the finer fragrances in life. The poet Jean de Bussières made the point forcefully in a curious ode to tulips in 1649:

> Dear friend, I lose myself in joy,
> I can hold back no longer,
> My sense of smell again wishes to unite
> With this dazzling faith:
> It believes that a pleasant scent
> Lends flowers the sweet vigour
> That makes the charm of their life;
> That delighting the eyes is such a small matter,
> If the soul, too, is not delighted
> By a delicious spirit.

But alas! Where are your riches?
Your tulips have no scent;
And all that is fine about them
Lends itself but to vain caresses:
They flatter indeed our gaze,
With their charms that are scattered thin,
Beneath a deceptive appearance,
But the void within their fine bodies,
Having no other consistence,
Means they must pass for dead.[44]

While tulip mania was getting under way in Holland, where the bulbs – a recent discovery for Europeans – were selling for a king's ransom, French culture attached more worth to the scented eroticism of powerful animal smells and secondary floral notes than to such scentless 'princesses'. Heady fragrances were everything! The wealth of riches accumulated by the bourgeoisie by means of trade put the Calvinist United Provinces on the path to deodorization much earlier than France, thanks to the emergence of a society built on trade, in which money had no smell. The dominant elite had little truck with that in the glorious France of the age of conquest led by warmongering kings. They considered powerful perfumes as vital for life, overcoming the terror of death, as de Bussières's ode suggests. Scentlessness was not acceptable, as it undermined the psychological defences built up against the terror of omnipresent putrid smells signalling imminent deadly threats, fought by donning invisible all-over armour and helmets made of perfume. And such danger was omnipresent. Human life was short – life expectancy was on average half that of today. The medical profession was of little help. At best, doctors helped their contemporaries face the fear of death with their countless secret remedies, wholly ineffective from our point of view, yet used with equal parts of piety and hope. Bleeding a plague victim, an old man or a patient on their deathbed only makes sense in an economy of hope underpinned by religion.

The great animal slaughter

But there's more. Sixteenth- and seventeenth-century society exploited animals pitilessly. They were used for everything, like pigs, not a scrap of which went to waste: their bristles became brushes and even their bladders were turned into lanterns and balls for children to play with. There have probably been few periods in history more disastrous for animals. Wild game was hunted with cruel enthusiasm by the king and his nobles. Farm and household animals were used as forced labour before machines came along to replace them.

Animals were needed for travelling, for transporting heavy burdens, for farm labour, and were of course eaten in vast quantities. It is often forgotten that they also provided leather for many uses, including saddle-making and adornments. Their blood, meat, excrement and hides were vital raw materials, used even in many medical potions. Dogs ended up with their skin being worn as gloves by elegant men and women, with cat and rabbit fur making a warm, comfortable lining. The vast slaughter, hinted at by the hundreds of calves' heads found in a master glover's attic in 1557, meant the reek of death constantly hung over towns and cities. Then there was the smell of bodies buried in and around churches, often in shallow graves, before a 1776 decree banished graveyards to outside urban areas. Heady perfumes painfully extracted from the sex glands of exotic creatures were used in extravagant quantities to hide the ever-present stink. Ambergris, musk and civet were commonly believed to offer twofold protection against death, by keeping plague at bay and more concretely by transforming its very nature through scented leather. This led to the emergence of an erotic culture in the upper social strata and those who sought to emulate them. The lamentations of moralists and preachers had little success in reining in the desires expressed in the vigorously fragranced ritual of seduction. Sexual scents borrowed from animals masked the smell of human flesh, mingling with that of the sacrificial victims that were seen as little more than perfumed decoration. Is this really so different from the practices of the many peoples round the world that linguistic decorum now defines as indigenous populations? Feathers, beaver-skin hats and scented gloves and boots were trophies marking out the power and wealth of our European forefathers.

Paradoxically, animals were slaughtered to perpetuate the human race by triggering physical desire. Our noses are indeed linked to our genitals, as della Porta claimed. From the Renaissance to the classical period, noses were trained to spot potential opportunities for physical release by picking up notes of ambergris, musk and civet from the opposite sex. Contrary to treatises on civility that encouraged men of decency to quash their animal instincts, the cultural ritual shaping how men and women became couples discreetly transformed the scent of animal genitalia into not only an essential sales pitch, but also an instrument of male domination. Such heady fragrances masked an individual's own 'natural' scent, which had highly negative connotations in the case of women. Men were held to smell pleasant, according to the medical profession, notwithstanding a total indifference to basic hygiene that was common currency until the age of Louis XIV. The gradual return of baths and washing heralded a far-reaching olfactory revolution that did more for women than it did for men. Its underlying cause may have been a shift in the meaning of death, whose miasmas were driven out to the distant fringes of urban areas where the new hygienist movement relegated graveyards and slaughterhouses. Yet it also reflected a slow change in gender relations, based on a new perception of the body, love and perhaps even other living creatures. The fashion for men's perfumes dominated by ambergris and musk base notes gave way to a new wave of feminine, fruity, floral heart notes. Which, in turn, gave way to the recent diktat of scentlessness.

7

Civilizing floral essences

Can tastes and fragrances shed light on the decline of some European powers and the rise of others in centuries past? It has been claimed that the Spanish empire was undermined in the first half of the seventeenth century when its reputedly invincible military leaders were softened by the new habit of taking chocolate lying down. Meanwhile, tea, drunk quickly standing up in a tea emporium, did much to develop the trading and military capacity of the English.[1] While such hypotheses are somewhat far-fetched, the underlying principle does have something to say about how societies develop or stagnate. France, which accounted for nearly one-fifth of Europe's population, now set the terms of the debate not only politically and linguistically, but also in terms of *art de vivre*, taking up the mantle from Spain. Its hegemony enabled Louis XIV to stand up to a formidable coalition. His successor, Louis XV, inherited the continent's most powerful army, but still found himself hamstrung in the Seven Years War by the young Prussian monarchy's more hardened, aggressive troops. At the same time, the British navy was conquering vast swathes of France's colonial empire, officially ceded to the victors in the Treaty of Paris in 1763.

The decline of the West's leading power is difficult to explain. Between the Sun King's reign and the Revolution, the population increased sharply for the first time in centuries, rising by nearly 50 per cent. Prosperity brought new commodities in abundance. France's maritime trade, essentially built on West Indian slaves and sugar, brought wealth to urban centres along the Atlantic coast, built roads, and led to a more refined lifestyle across the country.

Yet it seems a hidden spring had stretched beyond its capacity. The French now led an enviably comfortable lifestyle, as suggested by the German proverb 'As happy as God in France!' Even the lower social rungs shared in the progress. After the last great outbreak of plague, in Marseilles in 1720, constant fears of the Black Death subsided. Vauban's extensive network of fortresses kept warfare away from the country's vital nerve centres. Famine was on the wane. Medicine was making advances. Tastes and fragrances were improving thanks to France's exceptional culinary culture. Times had moved on from the sexual, animal scent of boots and leathers worn by horsemen riding out to conquer new territories under the two previous kings. Wars were now fought in lace, as exemplified by Fanfan la Tulipe, the fictional hero with his scentless emblem. Living in a land of milk and honey in times of peace, the French army grew soft. Like the king, his cousin the Prince de Conti and the Maréchal de Richelieu, they preferred 'swordplay' in bed with beauties to fighting on the battle-field. The greatest marshals, the Maréchal de Saxe and the Maréchal de Lowendal, renowned for France's last great victories including the Battle of Fontenoy in 1745, were foreign mercenaries; the Prince de Soubise was thrashed by Friedrich II at Rossbach in 1757, and Richelieu preferred to promote his own personal interests rather than those of the monarchy.

Before the French took their revenge on the British in the Anglo-French War of 1783, the smell of defeat often floated over the plethora of marshals and generals, primped with powder, makeup and floral scents. The cantankerous nineteenth-century bourgeoisie, deeply envious of such decadent aristocrats and closely copying their furniture and decor, claimed they were dancing on a volcano. Yet the aristocrats themselves certainly had no idea they were part of a world that was soon to end. Far from it: they saw themselves as the masters of the universe, enjoying all the delights of an idyllic lifestyle shared by aristocratic men and women alike. The art of seduction had become their *raison d'être*. The subtle eroticism of the times required lighter clothes, new textiles such as floral perse, and softer fragrances hinting at pleasures to come. However, the court and Paris still lay in a foul fug, made considerably worse by the city's demographic boom. The situation only truly improved in the late nineteenth century, when mains drainage was built. The sudden diminution in tolerance of bad smells in the mid-eighteenth century can therefore only be marginally attributed to the hygienists and their obsession with eradicating the sources of putrid smells.[2] Relative advances in medicine and chemistry and the end of major plague outbreaks were certainly of greater significance, without wholly explaining the phenomenon. It also drew on the rise of a new, powerfully hedonistic culture in celebration of the body since the reign of Louis XIV. The natural body, praised by philosophers, was washed in baths, subjected to lavish treatments, and scented with exquisite floral and citrus fragrances. Individual protective bubbles of masculine, musky, quasi-military scents, worn to protect against attacks of the plague, fell out of fashion for good. They gave way to the expression of the narcissistic self, centred on a positive view of the body, as religion weakened its grip and Satan was no longer a source of terror. Jean-Jacques Rousseau suggested starting the sentimental education of children in their infancy by taking babies out of the swaddling they wore for years, stewing in their own filth and excrement. Decent, civilized men should not reek of powerfully exotic perfumes; rather, they should have their own light, delicious, attractive individual scent.

The perfume revolution

Attitudes to the body began evolving in the mid-seventeenth century, when soap and water started to make a comeback in terms of bodily hygiene, as has been seen. The movement then began to accelerate, though at a rate as yet unexplored by historians, until it triumphed in the 1750s. This decade by no means saw a new revolution in smells. Rather, it was the culmination of a long, slow, silent process of development. The shift basically lay in rejecting powerful animal fragrances, used to the very tips of the wearer's gloved fingers, sparking a torrid sense of eroticism. In 1693, the perfumer Simon Barbe still gave such scents pride of place in his treatise. This gradually gave way to a sense of disgust at such expensive, exotic substances, often copied by forgers. These products' powerful smell eventually came to be felt as unpleasant. The reasons for the shift are easy to understand, bearing in mind that their notes were more or less similar to human excrement: the Swiss doctor and astrologer Paracelsus, who died in 1541, published a secret recipe for turning excrement into 'civet or Western musk'.[3]

Antoine Hornot published his *Traité des odeurs* [*Treatise on smells*] in 1764, the year Madame de Pompadour died, using the pseudonym M. Dejean. He noted that ambergris and musk were falling out of favour, though they were still at that moment considered the point of origin for perfumes in the trade. Furthermore, he added, 'These smells are still very expensive, though little is consumed.' Quintessence of ambergris was still made, but the name was used for a variety of concoctions made from musk alone, or mixes of musk and ambergris or civet, musk and ambergris. Selling them under the names of those ingredients meant no one would buy them, he explained. Perfumers were keen to cut corners, particularly for ambergris, by far the rarest and most expensive ingredient. Yet they had to reckon with the public's 'aversion' to musk. Dejean also gave a modern recipe for angel water, once held in the highest esteem by his earlier colleagues. 'People of taste and distinction used it for bathing in. According to M. Lémery, it was sprinkled on gloves and clothing, a habit now lost. Scents are now only carried in vials, for fear of bothering those who do not like them.' He added that gloves were the only unscented items now sold by perfumers. To bring a bit of sparkle back to an 'almost forgotten' recipe and its equally unloved cousin Cyprus water, he advised using orris root, storax, rose wood, benzoin flower, white sandalwood and *Calamus aromaticus* (sweet flag). Then, 'to conform to today's tastes, musk must be taken out completely, leaving just a few drops of quintessence of ambergris to showcase the other scents', rose water and orange flower water having been added prior to distillation. Elsewhere, he admits that ambergris 'has been largely forgotten', but is still liked by some. The preference for civet and musk have stopped it from coming back into fashion, though 'a very little ambergris makes mixes come together admirably well'. Civet was still in widespread use 'some forty years ago, but since then this scent has lost all its credit, particularly in France'. Eau de millefleurs, which 'the ancients' made from cow pats, was later made from musk, ambergris and civet. Dejean recommended only using flowers, with sixty drops of quintessence of ambergris for eight pints. He stated that the only floral waters long available to perfumers were made from orange blossom and roses; they were now joined by waters scented with spices, for use in the kitchen, or with thick-rind fruits. Such waters were often used by perfumers in liquid pastes, liqueur manufacturers, and women, who added them to their baths or rubbed a drop or two into their hands.[4]

The revolution of smells was clearly under way. As early as 1764, Dejean was already arguing that the profession had become an art form, frequently describing his colleagues as artists and aiming more basic advice at 'amateurs'. His intellectual curiosity led him to borrow 'old' information from the works of Nicolas Lémery and Nicolas de Blégny, enabling him to define what was new about his own day in comparison with a historical overview harking back to the 1680s. He seems to be a reliable source in pointing out that civet had fallen out of favour since the 1720s, musk was losing ground, and ambergris was to be used sparingly as what would now be called a base note. The major shift therefore involved moving away from animal fragrances and towards floral and fruity scents. Unfortunately, he does not give any further chronological details on the change. The process was certainly complete by the mid-eighteenth century, taking his book as an overview of olfactory fashions of the day. His *Traité raisonné de la distillation* [*Considered treatise on distillation*], which he frequently cross-references, dates from 1753. The shift in tastes from 'excremental' scents to floral perfumes thus took place at least half a century earlier than has been argued.[5]

The turn seems to have been irreversible, judging from *L'Art du parfumeur* [*The perfumer's art*], by Jean-Louis Fargeon, supplier of perfumes to Marie-Antoinette and, later, the imperial court. Musk features nowhere in his recipes, published in 1801. His estate inventory, dating from 1806, likewise reveals his shop had very little musk in stock. He used just a few drops of quintessence of ambergris to make the other scents stand out.[6] His fellow professionals now displayed a significant preference for flowers, spices and thick-rind fruits to create waters with one or several ingredients, spirits, essential oils, beauty waters, waters for washing and quintessences. The latter were available in several categories depending on the number of distillations, from spirit of eau de vie to simple wine, rectified wine and ardent spirits. The last of these were very strong, subtle and inflammable, and could only be made by professionals as they evaporated easily in the hands of a careless distiller.

In 1764, Dejean's ingredients included citron, lemon, lime, Portuguese and bergamot orange, four-fruit recipes, orange flower water and lavender water. The names of his specialities are often misleading, as his angel water, Cyprus water and eau de millefleurs had little in common with the concoctions of the same name from previous centuries. His orange flower water was available in a very delicate scent that cost a small fortune. The tastes of the Age of Enlightenment tended to be for lighter, more delicately erotic scents, like Dejean's sensual water, made from seven pints of unscented cognac, quintessence of citron, neroli, orris, mace and docus (a very rare and expensive seed). The pleasant, soft scent should delight the ladies, he thought. Who would dare claim that love and intoxication do not go hand in hand? He also recommends Adonis water made from flowers, spices and four drops of ambergris, giving an 'admirable whole', a spring bouquet and a delightful *eau mignonne*. One of the most pleasant and popular scents, he wrote, was jasmine, 'the most agreeable of all the flowers', superior to violet. Since it was very difficult to obtain, specialists generally made jasmine-scented hair oil by soaking the flowers in sweet almond, hazelnut or moringa oil and spreading them on canvases that were placed in a large, hermetically sealed box. Another method involved alternating layers of flowers and crushed almonds in a chest. The flowers had to be changed frequently. When the almonds had soaked up enough scent, they were cold-pressed for their oil, which made 'a very delicate, highly scented essence'. Jasmine water was made from the oil mixed with rectified spirit of wine. All such concoctions were as costly as they were delicate, creating a 'perfume so exquisite and so fashionable'. In other words, jasmine was the star fragrance of its day in the fight against putrid miasmas.

The fashion for musk-scented leather goods now being over, gloves lost much of their erotic power, giving way to a gentler, more elegant aesthetic. They were now softened with a paste of refined rye flour, egg yolk, alum and salt. Chamois leather gloves were often given a final extra treatment of several layers of fish oil. Only white gloves were acceptable for public wear. If scented, only a light perfumed oil was used, mainly orange blossom or jasmine. Hands and arms were beautified by sleeping in gloves dipped in a warm mixture of wax, egg yolk and sweet almond oil.

Luxuriating in baths of scent

Dejean devotes around 25 per cent of his treatise to perfumes and nearly 60 per cent to scented products for the face, teeth and hair. The head was beyond question the most significant body part for women, not only as the seat of their beauty in contemporary understanding, but also as the focus for social relations. All their charm lay in their head, amplified by its discreet trails of scent. In the same way as for gloves, these were no longer musk-based.[7] Unlike that of the previous period, clothing was rarely perfumed, though 'perfumed sachets' were still widely used. They were simpler in form, now only square or oval, rather than shaped like the organ they were intended to protect. 'They are filled with potpourri, scented powders, and cotton perfumed with aromatic plants.' Designed to 'cheer the melancholy and strengthen the brain', they were kept about the person or placed in furniture, particularly bedside tables. The powders were made of flowers with added bergamot orange and orange peel or spices, depending on the recipe. Cotton wads were heavily dusted with the powder, with a few drops of ambergris if desired, and placed in a drying oven. In 1693, the perfumer Simon Barbe discussed much stronger assemblages, including Peru balm, civet, ambergris, eau de millefleurs and musk. All his scented sachets included at least one animal scent.[8]

Bathing was important for Dejean, who held that it was vital in maintaining good health. He did, however, describe a range of practices. Some people followed the old-fashioned custom of bathing just once a year, eight or ten days in a row. Others bathed once a week, fortnight or month. Baths could conveniently be taken either at a bathhouse or at home. Three types of bath were on offer, with water up to the neck, sitting in water up to the waist, or up to the calves for a foot bath. Bawdy anecdotes record how the second practice was sometimes a source of embarrassment for male servants who watched ladies of quality relaxing bare-breasted in the bath in front of them, royally ignoring their presence. The master perfumer recommended making up a paste made of sweet almonds, *Enula campana* (elecampane), pine nuts, flax seed, marshmallow root and lily bulbs, to fill one large and two small pouches. The bather sat on the first and rubbed himself or herself down with the other two. Pleasant scents were sometimes added, from orange flower water, thick-rind fruits and spices ('much in use') to storax, benzoin and ambergris for those who liked it, to leave the body white, 'clean and rid of all bad smells'. Dejean devotes six pages to soap recipes liable to lead to rough, even wrinkly skin, being heavy on soda ash, quicklime and olive oil. This had to be softened to make small cakes of soap by the addition of a sweet-smelling paste of orange and lemon peel, orris powder, spirit of wine, a few drops of orange flower, jasmine and clove oil, and two drops of ambergris. Other recipes included white sandalwood, mace, orris and sweet flag, and occasionally benzoin, cloves and nutmeg. Soaps could also be scented with angel water mixed with a tiny dab of ambergris or the essential oils described above. 'Musk-scented soaps' were in fact perfumed with flowers, spices and a few drops of quintessence of ambergris. Soaps made with honey were used to clean, whiten and soften the skin and to heal burns. The author also discusses the rise of a fashion over the previous twenty-five years, since about 1740, of 'toilet vinegars' for the bath and the teeth, claiming that they had come into increasingly widespread use until mid-century and still remained popular. These scented vinegars were made from essential oils from fruits including bergamot orange and citron, and flowers including orange blossom and lavender, as well as thyme, wild thyme and spices. A splash was added to bath water.[9]

Washing was now once more a popular practice among the upper social ranks. The Marquise de Pompadour had an elegant bathroom installed in her new castle in Bellevue, decorated with Boucher's sensual paintings *La toilette de Vénus* [*Venus at her toilette*] and *Vénus consolant l'amour* [*Venus consoling Cupid*]. It had a superbly ornate bidet with a rosewood lid decorated with marquetry flowers and gilded bronze, ormolu decorations and feet, and a tin bowl and douche. It cost her the princely sum of 360 livres in 1751.[10] Bathtubs became a symbol of luxury and sensuality, to the point of becoming a feature of eighteenth-century erotica. In 1746, Claude-Henri Fusée de Voisenon published a bawdy tale entitled *Le Sultan Misapouf et la princesse Grisemine*. His hero, Misapouf, underwent numerous transformations while retaining the power of sight, hearing and thought. While a bathtub, he bore the weight of 'a large, oily, black behind belonging to the fairy'. Freed eight days later, the impish fairy told him, 'You did such good duty as a bathtub, I think you are not angry at everything I showed you in so little time.' The fairy must have been obsessed with cleanliness, or at least sensuality, as she then turned the bonze Cérasin into a 'bidet in Saint-Cloud porcelain', while allowing him the use of his legs. Her sister then jumped astride the bidet and pushed it to a gallop to take her revenge on the poor bonze, giving the reader a delightfully bold mental image.

There are many similar examples. Yet it must be borne in mind that for the majority of those who indulged, the pleasure of bathing (which may also have included self-pleasuring) was its role as a fashionable pastime that prepared the bather to play their role and display their charms on the social stage. Making the body clean, white and pure and scenting it with gentle floral and fruity fragrances was a vital first step in attracting, rather than repelling, the opposite sex, at least in the upper social echelons. Dejean gives perfumes two key purposes, 'Either [. . .] driving out bad smells, or [. . .] reviving people from a faint if rubbed on their temples and nostrils.'[11] This explains why he gives detailed explanations on how to scent the face and hair, which charm the eyes from afar and the nose from up close. The nose is thus the final, pitiless judge of a woman's beauty, triggering – or not – the signal of desire that sparked a couple to form, lastingly or otherwise.

Sensual faces

'It is not enough for perfumers to flatter the sense of smell, they must also preserve the beauty of the skin, particularly on the face, to give it all the glow it should have', Dejean writes at the start of a chapter on virgin's milk. A woman hoping to attract a swain first washed off the dirt in a scented bath. She then set to work on an elaborate ritual to improve the appearance of her face or disguise the ravages of time, depending on her age and the state of her charms, pitilessly scrutinized by men's probing gazes and keen noses. The very name of virgin's milk points at the gargantuan task facing women, who had little choice but to appear young and beautiful. Dejean is familiar with the long-standing recipes, stating that he had taken two from Nicolas Lémery and thirty-four from Nicolas de Blégny. He knows that the concoction was customarily used as a cleanser and beautifier and contained either benzoin, then called storax, or 'vinegar of Saturn' (containing lead), litharge or silver or gold, alum and sulphur. Dejean himself gives eight recipes, some old, others newer, to get rid of spots and red patches and whiten the skin. He believes that they are potentially worth a fortune for perfumers, though they are simple enough for women to make at home.

He then gives thirty-three waters for treating various blemishes, spots and freckles and removing any trace of suntan. They include new ingredients rarely used previously, such as flowers, fruits including strawberries, wild blackberries, and melon, lettuce, cress, chicory, cabbage, fresh eggs and vinegar. One extravagant recipe involved heating a gold coin until it glowed red in the fireplace, then putting it in a quart pot of good wine, five or six times in a row, then adding a touch of lime-scale and using the result as a face wash. Several other recipes echo the widespread use of animal flesh and excrement in the previous two centuries. One recipe called for a freshly killed white hen whose blood was to be rubbed on spots or freckles and left on to dry. This simple method 'really works', claims Dejean, who had not left earlier beauty practices behind completely. Similarly, to avoid a suntan he recommends various recipes using half a dozen whelps mixed with calf's blood, pigeon droppings, a pigeon with its innards stripped out, the 'blood of a male hare' mixed with 'an equal part of urine from the person who is to use it', and ox bile. Despite this, he was a man of the Enlightenment, warning his readers not to use such concoctions without medical advice if suffering from redness, spots or blotchy skin, all of which can be signs of disease. The preparations can, however, be used safely to whiten the complexion or lose a tan, freckles or marks. The safety of such preparations seems highly dubious, given that he recommends using mineral poisons such as litharge.

He gives a further twenty-seven recipes for cosmetic waters to feed the skin, make it soft and dewy, and give the perfect rosy pink complexion. Some he borrowed from Nicolas Lémery, containing white lead, litharge and animal products including pigeons and, in several cases, calves' feet. Others were more modern, with fashionable ingredients such as goat's milk, plants and fruit, including jasmine blossom, melon and lemons.

There are some sixty recipes for facial treatments, indicating they were much in demand among his customers. All women wanted 'fine, white, even skin, a beautiful complexion, a rosy-pink flush, soft skin, with plenty of radiance and even vermilion'. The ideal was pale, lustrous, resplendent elegance, a flawless complexion heightened by a touch of rouge made from cubeb pepper, grains of paradise, cloves and Brazil wood scrapings, all soaked in eau de vie and repeatedly distilled. A 'cosmetic water for a youthful appearance' was made from myrrh, white frankincense, quick sulphur and rose water.[12] Dejean completes his range of facial treatments with a number of easy recipes for tinctures and potions, as well as talcs, oils, pomades for disguising wrinkles, and guides to making *mouchoirs de Vénus*, used dry as and when needed for a fresh, dewy complexion. The market then was as flourishing as it is now.

The abundance of recipes points to one clear obsession: a society woman's beauty was as plain as the nose on her face. But choosing her secret weapons to showcase her beauty was just the first step. She then had to paint her face like a work of art. First, she rubbed it all over with a carefully home-made concoction that meant dabbling in alchemy. She mixed small cakes of white lead into a pomade – Dejean wrote that the finest recipes were made with sheep's feet, snails or May butter – mixed with powdered bismuth white, lead, pearls or calcined Venetian talc, to make the complexion 'fine, radiant and ready for the rouge'. She had to be careful not to produce more than she needed in one go, as any pomade left over lost its radiance overnight. Beauty was hard work!

The last step in Dejean's description was adding rouge, available as loose powder or in pots. The ingredients were the same – Brazil wood, red sandalwood and dyers' bugloss, mixed with gum when sold in pots. Sometimes carmine powder and talc were added to adjust the colour to the customer's requirements. 'These are real recreations for the toilette', Dejean claimed, apparently without irony, though the women who used them may not always have shared his thoughts on the matter. For one thing, it took a degree of dexterity to apply the rouge. A touch was lightly brushed onto the parts in need of colour, then more was delicately added 'to the parts that must be brighter, such that the red appears by degrees, as if natural, and that is the substance of the art'.

The exhausting quest for beauty was not yet over. 'The lips are an ornament for the face: when they are beautiful and vermilion, they are a sign of good health.' Cracked or chapped lips brought the rest of the face down. Pomades were available to care for the lips and make them shine, 'which gives beauty a new lustre'. It was equally important to draw attention to the eyes, the windows to the soul and the emotions, 'the most beautiful, delicate part of the face' and 'an essential part of our selves', Dejean explains. He leaves medical treatments to eye-doctors, offering simply three recipes to strengthen the eyesight while beautifying the eyes with a few drops morning and evening: take distilled snow water and cornflower water, white wine and marshmallow stems, or fennel and euphrasia, still used against eye infections to this day.[13]

Did the Marquise de Pompadour owe her famously sparkling eyes to such tricks? She clearly wore makeup as described above – an absolute necessity for life at the French court until the fall of the *Ancien Régime*. Élisabeth Vigée-Le Brun's portraits of Marie-Antoinette (figure 19) and other high-ranking aristocrats showcase makeup fashions perfectly. The queen and her three children, painted in 1787, all have fine white complexions with rosy pink cheeks (figure 20). Men also wore face powder, using rouge with a lighter touch but sometimes highlighting the shine of their lips.[14] The dominant society and erotic practice was for women to highlight their pale complexion with black taffeta beauty spots of various sizes and shapes – circles, ovals and even crescents. As Dejean wrote, 'Their value lies in the artfulness of their placing.' Beauty spots hid blemishes and sent secret messages of love that were easily decoded by those in the know. The final step of the beauty ritual was looking after the teeth. Dejean lists three kinds of whiteners – waters, powders and 'opiates', referring to tooth powders mixed with various syrups. The latter two stripped teeth of their enamel, an irreversible process that gradually ruined the teeth by removing the best part of the 'mouth's sole ornament'. Tooth powders often contained ground abrasives like coral, alum, pumice stone, marble, cuttlefish bone and stag antler. Dejean argued that tooth waters were better, though some customers complained that they were not effective whiteners. He gave seventeen different recipes, adding that marshmallow was the only root used for the teeth now that ivy root no longer featured in recipes. Powders were sometimes needed to improve looks spoiled by black teeth, but the mix must first be strained through a silk mesh to remove all but the finest particles; the mouth had to be well rinsed before and after. Bad breath could be banished with pastilles made from flowers such as violets, narcissus, jasmine, roses and tuberoses, and other ingredients such as citron, orange blossom, cinnamon and ambergris, and with scented tablets.[15]

Bodily hair care

It was probably social mores that prevented Dejean from alluding to women's intimate care routines and what they did with their pubic and armpit hair. It is likely that women continued to use sachets of scent as they had done in previous centuries to mask unpleasant smells in public. He had much more to say about hair fragrances, which fill almost one-fifth of his book. In the eighteenth century, he wrote, 'almost everyone is content to keep the hair it pleased nature to give them, thanks to powder, which is the general taste and makes the hair uniform in colour'. High-ranking ladies and gentlemen still preferred wigs, which saved them from spending two hours a day at the bathhouse having their hair done, and let them hide a receding hairline. Since beards were out of fashion, only eyebrows and eyelids had to be painted to modify colours generally considered unpleasant, such as fiery red. They were blackened with soot made by burning resin of turpentine, incense and mastic.

Other blends, including one based on gall nuts, were to be used on the hair once a week. Various secret preparations were available to promote hair growth or prevent hair loss. A large number of oils and essences were scented with fruits such as citron, bergamot, orange, lime and lemon, herbs and spices such as cloves, rosemary, thyme and wild thyme, and flowers such as violet, wallflower, jasmine, narcissus, carnation, white musk rose, orange blossom and tuberose. Flower scents were particularly popular. Such products were intended to nourish the hair as well as add fragrance. 'As the head's warmth diffuses the scent', hair products would soon become unbearable if they did not smell pleasant, Dejean argued. The most widely used products in his day, outnumbering oils, were hair pomades made from pork and sheep fat, wax, almond oil, moringa nuts and various essential oils distilled from jasmine, thick-rind fruits and so on. The commonest sort, white pomade, was the base for all the others. Being unscented, it was popular with the few customers who disliked fragrances. The other pomades smelled the same as hair oils. Orange flower was the most highly prized scent, since of all the flower scents it was the one that lasted the best. Narcissus oil was very difficult to make and very costly, but its perfume was 'admirable'. The most exquisite of all scents, Dejean argued, came from Italian rind fruits. Some more whimsical blends were made for particular clients, such as a potpourri unguent perfumed with bergamot. Wigs could be rubbed with sticks of scented pomade. Such concoctions were designed not just to keep the hair in good condition, but also to 'prepare it for the powder' and hold curls. The pork fat in them was sometimes known to turn rancid.[16] In 1693, Simon Barbe recorded the opposite custom, with floral pomades used only for the hair, not the face. He also recorded them as being on the decline, as customers preferred oils, which were more convenient for wigs. Pomades proved necessary to keep women's heads clean, however. 'Only jasmine, orange flower and tuberose pomade can be made and keep well, the other flowers are too weak to give a long-lasting scent', he wrote.[17] Seventy years later, the olfactory palette had considerably expanded and improved.

The scent of powder

The finishing touch to the toilette was powdering the hair or wig. Dejean notes that powder was used in great quantities, suited and perfumed to all tastes. The best hair powder was made from high-quality starch washed with spirit of wine. It was very white, fine and dry and had excellent staying power on the hair, so that the wearer need not fear it dusting his clothes. It came in a variety of light scents, most commonly iris, but also violet (in fact made from Florentine iris root: Dejean states that it was formerly used to perfume clothing), Cyprus powder (the only recipe still using ambergris, musk and civet), maréchal (containing ambergris), carnation, bergamot (a so-called 'superior' mix), imperial (orris, lavender, thyme, bay leaf), 'maritime' (cuttlefish bone, incense, myrrh and sandalwood), the very popular Boulogne (orris, sage, sandalwood) and ambrette (cypress, sandalwood and ambergris). All these powders came in yellow for blond hair, red for light chestnut, and grey, the most widely used, to give hair a silvery sheen. Some, intended for high-born customers, were scented with pure flower extracts of narcissus, jasmine, orange blossom and tuberose or orris 'violet' powder. Other powders were scented with rosemary, lavender, thyme and wild thyme, but these were not popular with customers, unlike orange blossom, which was in high demand, he added, concluding that it was perfectly easy to make one's own blends at home.[18]

Perfumers who also sold scented gloves were granted the right to describe themselves as powder-makers in 1689. Their products catered for a vital social ritual for courtiers and aristocrats that lasted as long as the *Ancien Régime* itself. Visual evidence of the practice can be seen in the magnificent curly wig worn by the controller-general of finances Charles-Alexandre de Calonne in Élisabeth Vigée-Le Brun's *portrait d'apparat* of 1784 (figure 21). Traces of white powder on the shoulders of his sumptuously shimmering black coat show off the artist's virtuoso talent. Or was it a sly touch of impertinence? Vigée-Le Brun disliked hair powder herself and wore it for none of her self-portraits. Was she pointing out one of its downsides? Or perhaps suggesting that the great financier facing up to the disastrous French economy was scrimping on his own personal expenditure and buying cheap hair powder which, as Dejean lamented, had little staying power?

The urban population, rich or otherwise, who wished to follow the diktats on personal appearance often showed off their love of hair powder. The Comte de Vaublanc's memoirs describe the 'new fashions' on a visit to Paris in 1782, wrongly seeing women's use of beauty spots and abundant rouge as a new trend. More interestingly, he recorded that they 'all' carried around a small box of beauty spots, rouge, a brush and a mirror to touch up 'their fine red cheeks wherever they were, at their convenience'. He also drew a quick verbal sketch of their hairstyles: fringes worn crimped, stiff with pomade and powder, standing at a ninety-degree angle to the forehead, a large round powdered bun on both sides of the neck, held in place with brooches, and at the back powdered plaits, loose locks, or a bulky chignon. He also thought that the dominant trend for yellow powder was new, though in fact it was one of the three colours listed by Dejean in 1764. The preference for yellow may have indicated a new-found love of blond hair, enhancing its natural colour. The abominable filth generated by such powders, as noted by the count, hints at low-grade starch and perhaps an increasing uptake of hair powder by less wealthy consumers. Men also wore extravagant powdered hairstyles with evocative names such as *à l'oiseau* (bird style), *au cabriolet* (cabriolet style), *en marrons* (chestnut style) and *à la grecque* (Greek style). The count described the final stage of the toilette: the person put a protective layer on over their clothes and stepped out onto the landing of their apartments to be powdered with a puff held at arm's length by the hairdresser, creating a cloud of dust that was a nuisance for anyone passing by. Wealthy individuals had their own powdering room at home. The hairdresser would puff the powder up towards the ceiling so that it drifted gently down onto the wearer, a style known as *en frimas* (wintry) or *aux oeufs* (with eggs). The hair on the back of the head was still heavily powdered and worn in a black taffeta pouch, though these were gradually growing smaller. The count clearly enjoyed describing the spectacle of wig-makers, heavily dusted with white powder, dashing through the streets clutching a brush and comb to visit their customers.[19]

Unfortunately, the count had nothing to say on the delicate perfumes that must have wafted from such carefully coiffed heads, the crowning achievement of the perfumer's art. It is true that the scent would have worn off for anyone close to the wearer for fifteen minutes, as has been seen. The wide range of scents was also more recognizable for the keen noses of perfumers than for the man in the street. Almost all the scents were soft, sweet, floral or fruity. With the exception of scarce musk-based recipes, still used by a minority, they were all variations on a similar theme. This olfactory revolution was the result of insidious social pressure that side-lined the carnality of animal scents in favour of more discreet plant-based fragrances.

For Dejean, people wore scent for two reasons: 'to satisfy the sensuality of our sense of smell, or of necessity. Sensuality leads us to perfume our apartments and drive out all smells that might be thought unpleasant; we perfume our household linen and even our clothes, not with these strong, violent scents, but with soft fragrances that we can neither distinguish nor define.' Perfumes were used of necessity to drive out bad smells, often caused by contagious diseases. When someone died, 'the dead person's bedchamber must perforce be perfumed', as should hospitals, for the same reason. 'But such violent scents are not part of this book': they fell under the heading of medicine.[20]

There was thus a radical division between exquisite scents used for pleasure and powerful prophylactic smells. This was a new departure compared to the sixteenth and seventeenth centuries, when the two categories had overlapped. The former were now closely associated with life, the latter with death. In 1751, Diderot defined the sense of smell as a driver of sensual pleasure, third behind sight and hearing: 'I consider that of all the senses the eye was the most superficial, the ear the proudest, smell the most voluptuous, taste the profoundest and most philosophical.'[21] Judging from evidence from surviving written sources and works of art, the cultural shift, doubtless sparked in the opening decades of the eighteenth century, had slowly but surely reshaped contemporary olfactory perceptions. In earlier centuries, noses were trained to sniff out the threat of plague so that individuals could protect themselves behind an impermeable scent barrier. Now fragrances were the gateway to life's great pleasures, including the expression of sexuality free from moral and religious trammels. The shift is reflected in contemporary iconography, with new themes making their appearance. The unpleasant natural female smell, traditionally suggested by a dog with its snout in a woman's lap, gave way to a more positive image of womanly charms, for instance in an allegory of smell and taste by the Italian painter Giuseppe Maria

Crespi (1665–1747), in which an attractive woman holds a beautiful pink rose over her left breast, with a cat peacefully nestled in the crook of her left arm (figure 16).[22] Love might come with thorns or claws, but it is as wanton as any alley cat. The role of smell in Enlightenment erotica is worth a full-length study in its own right.

In fact, eighteenth-century eroticism was rather tame. It was generally subtle, with the spectacular exception of the Marquis de Sade, and was governed by social expectations of love that were very different from those of the modern era. Like the fragrances that played a role in developing and sustaining it, it spread slowly, leaving discreet traces in the memory when desire was thwarted by social taboos. Delicate, luxurious items heightened passion, such as bergamot boxes, a Grasse speciality that came into fashion during the *Régence*, made from bergamot orange peel and often decorated with mildly erotic scenes. These were a popular gift between courting couples. Some could afford much costlier gifts such as perfumes in precious holders (figure 17). Some containers made of Chelsea porcelain were made to hold two scents and were decorated with scenes from mythology or Italian *commedia dell'arte*, fables or animals. Now in the international perfume museum in Grasse, Marie-Antoinette's travel kit, made of porcelain, gold, silver, ebony, ivory and leather, was used for her toilette and basic medical care.[23]

It was almost impossible for potential suitors to judge a woman's body, well hidden by clothing. Dejean never mentions care products for any parts of the body below the neck, except the hands. The breasts, stomach, legs, calves, feet, buttocks and genitals did not feature at all. They must clearly have been cared for in some way, however, beyond bathing for health. This was the preserve of the medical profession, who prescribed remedies for strong body odours, and of motherly advice. It must also have fed into the erotic imagination of the times, driven by stolen glimpses of young ladies on swings that sparked heady fantasies. *Le Jeune homme instruit en amour* [*The young man trained in love*], a brief tale published anonymously in 1764, demonstrates that women also sometimes wanted to see the naked truth. The young man was bathing in a river near a château when the cool water sparked his 'flame'. Dressing slowly,

> From the quiet, bucolic place
> He spied at the window
> The countess, who, with her right eye,
> And telescope in hand, was watching him.[24]

The only visible parts of the body – the head, face, hands and sometimes a woman's forearms – were almost never left unadorned in society. Heads were bewigged, powdered and covered in makeup, while hands and arms were coated in pomade. The wafts of scent they generated served to attract the opposite sex while creating a sense of floral, fruity beatitude. Hands were an important weapon in the arsenal of charms. They were often used expressively to catch the eye, as seen in Élisabeth Vigée-Le Brun's portraits, such as that of Marie-Antoinette holding a rose, dating from 1783 (figure 19).[25] Dejean devotes nearly thirty pages to hand care, indicating the vital importance of hands in social rituals of personal appearance: they revealed the signs of ageing hidden by face powder (as today's stars, with their face lifts and Botox, sometimes learn to their chagrin). Hand care was broadly the same as facial beauty treatments. Hands had to be lightened, the ideal colour being a soft rosy pink, and softened with various potions that were often scented. The best powders were made of sweet almond and essences made from flowers (orange blossom, jasmine, tuberose and white rose were commonest) or thick-rind fruits with added neroli. Some recipes rid the skin of blemishes and suntan. Nails had to be perfectly clean, white and with no marks.[26] It is important to bear in mind that the rules of politeness had long required men to show their respect for women with a kiss on the hand. They may no longer have always kissed a woman's glove, as these had lost much of their importance as accessories in the eighteenth century, when the practice spread to the bourgeoisie and wealthy urban milieus. It may have owed its success to being a socially approved, pleasurable form of initial physical and olfactory contact with a woman, particularly if she was beautiful. Hands seemed to have greater erotic powers than before, which may explain why Dejean dwells on them at length in his guide to perfumes. Hands and forearms (when left bare) were scented with floral and fruity fragrances that echoed the sweet perfumes emanating from a beautiful woman's face and hair, as if hinting at future delights. In another reading, they demanded respect for women bravely fighting the signs of ageing.

Only a novel, Patrick Süskind's *Perfume*, could have featured an eighteenth-century Parisian obsessed with the natural smell of young women in the full flower of their youth, murdering them to capture and distil their individual essence.[27] The natural bodily scent of the more coquettish sort of woman was not only buried under her clothes, but also covered by artificial fragrances wafting from her hair, face and hands. In the case of fashionable young women of the Enlightenment, the individual olfactory fingerprint unique to each human, according to modern science, could only be detected from up close as a weak, fleeting head note, attenuated by bathing and discreetly perfumed sachets worn about the body. It was largely dominated by the floral and fruity heart notes worn by the woman, the most popular being orange blossom or thick-rind fruit.

Eighteenth-century society developed a new set of olfactory expectations governing a complex ritual of appearances. Most high-born people shared the same norms of politeness and sociability and felt comfortable with each other because they smelled similar. A minority clung on to the ambergris-based scents of the past or preferred to stand out from the crowd by choosing an unusual scent. Foul smells long stigmatized the lower strata of society. Smell was an instant indicator of an individual's social standing. It also encouraged the development of a new, sensual, hedonist approach to life. The body was no longer seen as a stinking prison for the soul. Destiny was no longer considered a dolorous journey through a vale of tears, with Hell and its stenches at the end of the journey for the sinful majority. Delicate natural perfumes reflecting a new urge to enjoy life carried the day, while new philosophical ideas and a new wave of eroticism triumphed. Women rose to new social prominence such as they had never experienced before. Women in the upper echelons of society now had as much sexual freedom as men of the same class: to give just one example, Madame de Pompadour's sister-in-law, the Marquise de Marigny, openly paraded around with the Cardinal de Rohan, one of her lovers. Far from being the target of violent social disapproval, as in the sixteenth and seventeenth centuries, older women found ways to hide the ageing process with numerous tricks learned from the art of perfumery. Such women were still often the object of mockery for their subterfuges, but it was worlds away from the earlier anti-feminism that rejected women in disgust for their so-called original stink as daughters of Eve, and the hatred of old women accused of witchcraft, said to reek as badly as Satan himself.

The understanding of the end of days had undergone a fundamental shift. Death and Hell were no longer obsessively evoked on a daily basis by layers of leather exuding sexual animal scents or doused in musky perfume. Nature now meant more than the power of a wrathful God. The flowers and fruits that lent their scent to perfumes made nature a rational, amiable, attractive place that created Rousseau's noble savage. This marked the start of a gradual process in the West of marginalizing death by removing it from the public gaze, starting with bodies being buried outside urban centres in the time of Louis XVI and eventually leading to the sight of suffering and death being confined to hospitals. The psychic economy was gradually transformed by a process of modernization that engendered multiple strands of progress. Smell was a key factor in this process. One of the reasons why artificial paradises of floral or fruity scents transformed men and women into walking fragrance diffusers was to fight the rising tide of foul smells, worsened by the dawn of the industrial era.

The emperor's perfumer

André-Michel-Roch Briard was a Parisian perfumer with a shop on rue Antoine, on the corner of what is now the rue Vieille-du-Temple. It was not well stocked when his estate was evaluated for auction on 14 February 1800.[28] The notary's record is brief, doubtless because he saw little point in going into detail for such a modest business. He did, however, note the presence of over 7,000 kilos of two grades of 'Paris starch suitable for making powders', 46.5 litres of orange blossom (estimated at 86 francs and 40 centimes), 4.3 kilos of bergamot orange, 1.1 kilos of lavender, and various scented waters and essences (no further details are given). Briard also had five and a half grains of musk worth 35 francs and 55 centimes and 2.7 kilos of ambrette worth 19 francs and 25 centimes. The considerable difference in price explains in part why the second was much more widely used to add a touch of spice to perfumes. His stock also included ivory, tortoise-shell and horn combs, toothpicks, whalebones, swansdown puffs, toothbrushes and beard brushes, powder boxes and soaps. He also had a stock of hides for making and selling gloves in models 'number one and number two', long glossy gloves, glossy kid gloves, chamois leather-style gloves, and glossy white gloves for men. The 7,000 kilos of starch are something of a mystery. Maybe he sold it in bulk? Whatever the truth of it, the abundant stock of the raw material needed to make wig powder indicates that the practice had not died out with the *Ancien Régime*, though wigs themselves were no longer much in demand. The fashion had taken some time to die out: in 1795, the art dealer Jean-Baptiste-Pierre Le Brun, ex-husband of the famous portraitist Élisabeth Vigée-Le Brun, who was then in exile, painted his self-portrait (figure 22). He depicted himself as a person of note in the new post-revolutionary regime: at the time, he was doggedly requesting the ministry for a position at the Louvre, newly open to the public. He is very well dressed, with a fine wig elegantly powdered grey, and a large black hat.[29] It seems that by 1800, starch was being used to powder natural hair rather than wigs. Was this a way of standing out from the British, then at war with France, and their new tax on hair powder, introduced in 1795 to finance the campaign? During the First Empire, the fashion for women to change hairstyles several times a day meant wigs came back into fashion to a certain extent.

C. F. Bertrand's 1809 work *Le Parfumeur impérial* sheds considerable light on changes in the social role of perfumes, nearly half a century after Dejean's treatise. The author remains something of a mystery: he never refers to Dejean but draws extensively on his work, borrowing its basic structure. Baths – generally scented with lavender, rose or sweet-smelling herbs – are relegated to the closing pages of the book, for example. It frequently attests to the survival of long-standing practices such as toilet vinegars, described as 'preservatives against contagion and bad air'. He lists the ingredients of the best-known recipe, four thieves vinegar, used as a prophylactic since the outbreak of plague in Marseilles in 1720. It contained cloves, garlic, gentian, rue, angelica, juniper berries, wormwood, rosemary, lavender, sage, mint, onion and asafoetida.[30] Like Dejean, he devoted many pages to facial treatments. His pomades were floral-scented, with new fragrances including lilac, mock orange, lily of the valley and mignonette. His recipe for eau de millefleurs no longer contained any cow pat. Another recipe containing ambergris and musk had fallen out of fashion in the 1760s, but he brought it back and updated it with vanilla. A venerable old recipe using snails had been wildly popular with the customers of the famous Jean-François Houbigant, who died two years before Bertrand's guide came out. Like Houbigant, Bertrand described the recipe as one of the 'first rank' of secrets for beautiful skin, and gave what he claimed was the original list of ingredients: sheep's fat, rose water, lily bulbs, marshmallow root, lemon, sugar, benzoin, storax, borax, and two dozen snails with their intestines stripped out.[31] There is nothing particularly original in his skin-lightening pomades, virgin's milk or powders for sachets of scent. He does, however, state that oils were now more popular. These were made with numerous spices, cassia, heliotrope and, in several cases, ambergris and musk. As oils were costly, customers were often palmed off with cheaper imitations.

Starch hair powder, used for more than a century by the highest ranks in society, had 'so many advantages for the cleanliness and elegance of the toilette, that it was in common use and the fashion has spread across much of Europe to the present day', Bertrand writes. There is a note of embarrassment in his discussion of the symbol of pre-revolutionary times. He gives no guidance on how it should be used, but does cleverly give it a modern gloss by explaining that improvements to the starch manufacturing process mean it no longer needs rinsing with eau de vie or spirit of wine. It can now be made at home with the raw materials and a grinder, so that anyone can make their own hair powder as well as an expert. He describes powders scented with flowers, vanilla, heliotrope, 'maréchal' (ambergris and musk), 'musk' (containing ambergris), and an 'imperial' mix of orris, vanilla, ambergris and musk. Others colour the hair grey, blond, red or pink. The latter two shades were a new touch of whimsy unknown in pre-revolutionary France. The complexion was still ideally fresh, clear, lustrous, untanned and free from blemishes. Rouge was still added after white powder. It was made of carmine or saffron and came in darker shades for the theatre and in brighter ones for everyday wear. Nor were there notable changes in care for the teeth, the main remedy being coral powder. Bad breath was banished with catechu drops or gum mixed with rose water or orange flower water, or parsley for garlic breath. Unpleasant household smells were masked by long-standing methods such as burning pastilles on burners, or liquids that might contain catechu or ambergris that evaporated when heated. Potpourri, which had enjoyed a resurgence in popularity in the eighteenth century, was taken up by the new social elites.[32]

Bertrand mentions ambergris and musk relatively frequently, confirming they had come back into fashion to a certain extent after a period in the wilderness during the Enlightenment. Gloves, which perfumers neglected to manufacture, he lamented, were again worn scented with floral essences, with ambergris and musk for a 'stronger and more agreeable' fragrance. He clearly had a fondness for animal scents, though he did warn readers to use no more than a touch of civet, or else the concoction would smell terrible.[33] His contemporaries seemed once again to have a fondness for the powerful, slightly excremental scent of such substances. Might this be the result of the rise of the military in Napoleonic France? The resurgence of such base notes, so popular under the warmongering kings of the sixteenth and seventeenth centuries, may point to the return of triumphant virility as a social virtue in reaction to the sweetly flowery, fruity indolence of the decades prior to the Revolution. The question remains as to whether the trend remained popular or tailed off once again.

Bertrand described himself as a distiller: 'Stills with coils are now used to perfect the operation so that there is no need for rectification.' This produced simple waters, spirits or extracts of flowers and spices, including quintessence of ambergris, essence of musk and civet, and scented waters made from the extracts. These included eau de cologne: Bertrand boasted his recipe was the finest, incorporating essences of bergamot, citron, lemon, lavender, Portugal (orange peel), thyme, neroli, rosemary, all dissolved and blended with melissa water (also known as carmelite water), and sometimes orange flower water for further refinement. To attain perfection, the mixture was then rectified by distillation to make it finer and whiter. This was, however, a lengthy step, often left out.[34]

For a better understanding of the place of such perfumes in society, Bertrand's book can usefully be compared with the estate inventory of one of Paris's leading perfumers, Jean-François Houbigant, who died in 1807.[35] He was born in Paris in 1752 to parents employed in service. He trained with a master perfumer and set up in business in 1775 in the fashionable rue du Faubourg-Saint-Honoré, at the Sign of the Flower Basket. He supplied perfumes to the court and leading aristocratic and bourgeois families. His son Armand-Gustave was said to have created a new scent for the Empress Josephine in 1807, when he was just seventeen. The business expanded rapidly in the late nineteenth century by using organic chemistry to develop new specialities. The brand exists to this day.

The inventory of the shop and its mezzanine store-room at 19, rue du Faubourg-Saint-Honoré, corroborates Bertrand's *Parfumeur impérial*. The shop itself stocked slightly over 164 litres of double lavender water with ambergris or bergamot, valued at 3 francs a pint (493 centilitres), half as much ordinary lavender, vinegar, various unspecified scented waters and toilet waters, pomades, garters, bracelets, combs, tongue-scrapers, toothpicks, toothbrushes, beard brushes and hairbrushes. A powder-mill worth 48 francs indicates that Houbigant probably ground his own powders. He also had dozens of powder puffs for sale; André-Michel-Roch Briard's estate inventory had listed swansdown puffs seven years previously. This seems to suggest that elegant women were now readily powdering their noses at home or while out and about. Were they trying to patch up their traditional face powder or replacing it with a less restrictive alternative? The pink powder featured in Bertrand's 1809 guide would make sense in either case.

The mezzanine store-room, lit by a window giving on to the street, held dozens of kilos of scented white and coloured powder, Cyprus powder, porcelain pots full of rouge, Peru balm, virgin's milk, pomades, some sold as sticks, herbs, coral, red vinegar, chignon and eyebrow combs, fans, pins and large quantities of soap. The main treasures, however, were scented waters and essences. The shop stocked several scented waters for the hair and others for the beard, now back in fashion. The scent is listed in some cases. Tuberose was the main fragrance for powders, with over 100 kilos, followed by orange blossom, jasmine and orris. Over 83 litres of water were perfumed with rose, orange flower and melissa, all valued at 2 francs a pint. Eau de cologne must have been much in demand, with

164 boxes, at 3 francs 50 centimes each, in stock. The most costly essences were made of bergamot, wallflower, lavender, neroli and rose. The rose essence must have been very special, as it was given the highest estimate by the notary's valuers, at 50 francs an ounce (30 grams and 59 centigrams), far more than the value of 9 francs an ounce for neroli essence, which in turn was twice as valuable as lavender essence. The last must have been a good seller, as the storeroom had 13 kilos on its shelves. Vanilla essence was also popular, with 10 kilos in stock, and cheaper than lavender at 16 francs a livre, the same as ambergris and musk, with 4 kilos in stock. Essences of thyme, wild thyme, rosemary and myrrh were four times less dear again. The inventory also lists 1 kilo of essence of lemon zest. The relatively large quantities of animal scents confirm Bertrand's more theoretical writings, particularly as the shop also had 61 grams of untreated ambergris valued at 80 francs, or nearly 40 francs an ounce.

A quick glance at the lengthy stock inventory from another perfumer indicates that the olfactory revolution sparked in the eighteenth century lasted well into the Napoleonic era. Jean-Baptiste-Alexandre Briard's shop on the rue de la Grande-Truanderie in Paris was mainly a bulk supplier for other perfumers. The highly detailed estate inventory from 1810, which would richly reward further scholarly exploration, reflects the major trends shaping a rapidly modernizing profession.[36] The inventory lists large quantities of various grades of starch, including some of very high quality: powder was still in fashion. Briard produced his own powder with special mills, including one used to grind almonds. He stocked soap, especially from Naples, sponges, lots of toilet vinegar in square bottles, and waters for similar purposes that harked back to old customs, though the packaging was updated. He provided containers suited to his customers' needs, such as small coral pots for pomades and square Morocco leather holders with room for six pots, whose use is unspecified. Might these have been used by women on their travels to keep looking fresh and lovely? Flowers were the main scents, particularly orange blossom, lavender and branching iris, alongside fine neroli, bergamot, marjoram, thyme, wild thyme and vanilla. He also sold floral waters scented with rose, orange blossom, bergamot and vanilla, and oils, including sweet and dry almond oil, orange flower oil and 'vanilla number 109'. The inventory also listed a wide range of eaux de cologne, the finest bottles being numbered ten, twelve, fifteen and eighteen, with no explanation. The establishment of such categories, also applied to other products in stock, points to the increasing professional specialization of perfumery. Representatives of the profession, who guided notaries conducting evaluations of this sort, used their own trade jargon to refer to major differences in quality, while three years earlier, when Houbigant's estate was inventoried, the only clue to differences in the grade of precious essences was the estimated value.

In 1810, Briard owned a small quantity of musk, valued at 10 francs – too small an amount to make the case for the renewed popularity of excremental scents of animal origin indicated by Bertrand's book and the 1800 and 1807 inventories of the two other perfumers. It may, however, have been the case that such rare, costly ingredients, liable to be replaced by cheaper substitutes, were only sold via a highly specialized trade network rather than by bulk suppliers. For instance, civet could be purchased in Holland, where the exotic animals were bred, according to *Le Parfumeur impérial*.[37]

In the final analysis, a degree of uncertainty is perhaps not a bad thing, arousing our curiosity as to exactly when the powerful base notes rediscovered in the triumphant age of Napoleon fell out of fashion, or at least lost ground. The sources suggest it was a relatively minor, if captivating, trend. Further research is needed to shed light on the scope and chronology of this resistance to the eighteenth-century floral and fruity revolution that still largely cast its shadow over the opening years of the nineteenth century. The Age of Enlightenment, whose rampant inequality was scorned symbolically in the distaste for wigs, paradoxically survived in Napoleonic France by delighting the noses of the new elite with the sweet perfumes of happiness and progress – two fruitful ideas invented by Enlightenment philosophers.

Conclusion

Smells still have immense social value. The binary code governing them, triggering a cerebral signal of imminent threat or a positive feeling of safety or even pleasure, can readily be applied to the major concerns of human communities. Our flexible, adaptable sense of smell alerts us to danger, helping us steer clear of toxins, and to potential sexual encounters, vital for the survival of the species. All human cultures, past and present, have learned to manipulate our sense of smell by associating one end of the scent spectrum with extreme disgust, and the other end with the utmost sense of well-being. How an individual perceives a given scent is not innate. A brief neuronal flash triggers an initial warning of potential danger, before the sense of smell kicks in, defines the scent as good or bad and memorizes it. Learning the difference is a lengthy process. In today's society, children enjoy the smell of their own excrement until the age of four or five, or even as late as eight in some cases, despite efforts to teach them the contrary. However, today's norms are by no means universal. It has been shown that Renaissance France lived in a foul-smelling fug, without showing the least disgust at human excrement or urine. The literature and poetry of the day saw them as Rabelaisian 'joyous matter' fit to entertain the highest ranks of society. The medical profession made much use of them in remedies and beauty treatments for women. Anal repression had yet to be invented. Far from being seen as nauseating, such smells led people to enjoy excremental scents of animal origin.

In the sixteenth and seventeenth centuries, learning about smells had powerful moral overtones.[1] Western Europe went through a period of great intolerance, particularly from 1560 to 1648, when pitiless, fanatical world views clashed in bloody wars of religion, and developed a binary vision of a world divided into good and evil. The Catholic Counter-Reformation planted the image of a wrathful God punishing unrepentant sinners, and that of an omnipresent Satan, allowed by the Creator to tempt men as a way of urging them into the effort needed for salvation. Their sense of smell came into play to underline the two opposing paths that lay open to Christians. On the one hand, pleasant smells were among the heavenly delights heralding God's presence on earth, like the 'odour of sanctity' arising from the earthly remains of saints. On the other hand, foul smells were strongly associated with the putrid odour of the Devil, who ruled over the mephitic vapours of Hell that awaited doomed souls. Bad smells still triggered reactions of terror, even when they were wholly natural, since medical theory blamed repeated outbreaks of plague on airborne contagion via corrupt smells. A metaphor for Satan's omnipresence on earth, the explanation led doctors with precious few weapons in their arsenal to recommend fighting disease with even worse smells, fighting fire with fire. Saturating homes with powerfully repellent smells, bringing live billy goats indoors, and sniffing latrines before setting foot outside were all recommended as protections against ill health. Women, traditionally suspected since the fall of Eve of consorting with the Prince of Darkness, were living in one of the most misogynistic periods in history. While the poets of the Pléiade sang the charms of beautiful young women, hoping for something in return, the women found themselves increasingly under the thumb of men, who justified their dominance by the threat women posed to the male sex and indeed to the rest of God's creation. Women were cold and damp, according to the theory of humours, and as such smelled infinitely worse than men, who doctors claimed were warm and dry. The menstrual cycle was deleterious, sowing death and destruction. Women were no less suspect after the menopause: older women were the targets of extraordinary spite in the literature of the day. They stood accused of spreading pestilential stench, sparking great fear in men. Was the unpleasant smell of old age a reminder that all men are mortal and that terrible torments awaited them in Hell? The theological doctrine of demonology that led to witch hunts in many European countries distilled men's fears into the single myth of the elderly woman who joined a secret nocturnal sect devoted to the triumph of Satan. Thousands of women were burned at the stake, proving the myth's power despite the far-fetched nature of the accusations. Women were alleged to have flown to the Sabbath where they cooked up revolting messes as putrid as Hell from the remains of unbaptized children, took part in demonic rites, and sowed destruction by casting evil spells on people, livestock and harvests. It is tempting to read the myth as a reinterpretation of the Antique tale of stinking Harpies devouring everything within reach.

Christian thought was dominated by eschatological anguish against a backdrop of social disorder and massacres. It worked its way into everyday life through terrifying sermons by churchmen that were passed on by increasing numbers of lay moralists who studied in radical religious schools. On an individual level, the fear of the end of the world led people to seek protection. Their hope was not only to save their everlasting souls, but also to protect their bodies against the forces of evil, thought to be at their strongest during outbreaks of plague, when Satan's breath was dangerously close. This explains why people sought to protect themselves behind impenetrable barriers. The medical profession believed the body was porous and could contract plague through contact with water. Medical advice was strongly against bathing and washing until at least the mid-seventeenth century. As the main risks to health were airborne, an all-over scent barrier was thought to be a vital form of protection, creating a sort of isolation bubble around the individual. The perfumes, dominated by the heady animal scents of ambergris, musk and civet, were principally used to keep invisible corruption at bay. They were also intended to ward off infection from plague victims, generating an impassable barrier used by those still in good health who were terrified of getting too close to the disease while out and about. After the final major outbreak of plague on French soil in 1720, the practice gradually declined.

Prior to this major shift in behaviour, people living through epidemics acted like individual Cities of God besieged by the legions of Hell. Like babies bundled up tight in their swaddling, adults wallowed in their own fetid sweat. Cleanliness was a rare concern, and almost every square inch of the body was constantly swathed in layers of clothes that were doused in scents as strong as the perfumed gloves people always wore. The need to keep the body completely covered was underpinned by the customary use of powerful fragrances thought to ward off contagion, protecting the ears, nose and mouth. Heads were permanently covered and necks hidden. Ruffs, collars and wigs eventually became commonplace, playing a dual role of decoration and protection for their high-born wearers. The face was the only part of the body that remained visible, and even then attempts were made to hide it when venturing to places known to be infected. The faces of the rich and well-born were protected by layers of white and red powder, while their hair was kept safe by perfumed oils, pomades and essences.

Once the threat of plague had faded, the same panoply of scents was used as a form of social display. The three major animal scents, all very powerful, were obligatory base notes for the cut and thrust of courtship, much appreciated in a society that held military prowess in high esteem. The custom of using such scents to keep plague at bay maintained their erotic reputation, decade after decade, as their widespread use as protection was a strong argument against the constant threats of damnation brandished by moralists against men and women who used perfume as a source of sensual delight. The prohibition on perfume could be got around with just a dash of hypocrisy by claiming a medical exception. Ambergris, musk and civet thus came to play a central role in contemporary culture. They were an omnipresent addition to leather, which was used for a multitude of purposes. Their long-lasting fragrance was also on occasion used to fix and extend floral heart notes, though these had little scope to develop as the majority taste put them firmly in second place. It is true that delicate scents were no match for the powerful individual olfactory fingerprint typical of the day, particularly as women washed no more frequently than men. The resulting smells were certainly far from exquisite, even though women made abundant use of powders worn strategically about their person and scented sachets hidden under their perfumed clothing. Their male companions may have smelled even worse, as there was no comparable cultural pressure on them to mask their natural scent, held by the medical profession to be sweet and pleasant. The truth of the claim may be doubted. The plentiful use of musk-based fragrances cannot have completely hidden the rancid, 'shoulder of mutton' smell of armpits, rotten teeth and bad breath in both men and women. Medical advice simply reflected a sexist prejudice inherited from ancient Greece that claimed that women suffered worse from such afflictions. Yet Henri IV and Louis XIV are known to have had horribly smelly feet, as has been shown. The underlying reason why men were generally oblivious to their own body odours doubtless lies in the different status of the sexes in terms of social attitudes to courtship. Virile men on the hunt for a woman were allowed to reek without attracting too many barbs from the people around them, while the women who were their prey were quickly denigrated and suspected of harbouring disease or being on their period if they smelled bad.

The sense of smell was terribly gendered. Sight let men select a robust-seeming sexual partner from a certain distance, the aim being to sire healthy children, vital for the future of the species. Close

up, the nose took over, particularly in sixteenth- and seventeenth-
century society, when all the women at court and the bourgeoisie all
looked more or less the same. The body was generally hidden, except
for a brief period under Louis XIII when bare breasts were fleetingly
fashionable in elegant society, sparking a flood of indignant protests.
At least young men could indulge in a rare visual treat, while unwit-
tingly furnishing evidence for modern-day biologists interested in
the innate mechanisms governing couple formation. Normally, only
faces and hair were on display, sometimes the forearms and more
rarely the hands, as fashion dictated that gloves should be worn.
There is a ready explanation for why perfumers focused their attention on women's heads: they could earn a fortune selling countless
beauty products. However, the aim was by no means to highlight a
woman's individual beauty, but rather to make her conform to an
archetype. Her face had to be white, lustrous, smooth and flawless,
with well-placed rosy highlights. Tans and wrinkles were beyond
the pale. Her smile revealed impeccable, coral-white teeth. The onus
was on women to look eternally young and fresh. The white makeup
base they used on their faces was often made from dangerous, even
toxic, substances, camouflaging the flaws of the many women who
failed to meet the highest standards of beauty. All these women came
to look the same, like porcelain dolls with rosy cheeks. Their various
face powders were also infused with the same scents, as were their
hair oils, pomades and powders, and the coloured powders used
to highlight the blonde, chestnut or grey of their wigs when these
came into fashion in the seventeenth century. Women's physical
appearance was undergoing a constant process of harmonization.
Keeping face required constant effort and ended up masking individual identities. How could men tell which was their ideal partner
in a bed of identical, gorgeously blooming flowers? One way might
have been to follow the sixteenth-century scholar Giambattista della
Porta's suggestion that the size of a woman's genitals matched her
mouth and lips, while a man's was indicated by the size of his nose.[2]
However, on such a delicate matter, it was best to try and gather
more reliable evidence. Up close, only the sense of smell could help,
detecting unpleasant whiffs under the generously applied powerful
perfumes then in fashion. This gave the potential suitor clues as to
the woman's age and state of health, otherwise hidden beneath the
obligatory mask of makeup. Above all, his nose guided him to differentiate young women, symbolizing life and love, from rank-smelling
older ones, who represented demonic danger and death in the culture
of the day. The sense of smell clearly played a greater role than is the
case today, contrary to widely held opinion.

The eighteenth century witnessed a genuine olfactory revolution. Its roots lay back in the mid-seventeenth century, when baths and body care made a timid comeback. Ambergris, musk and civet also gradually fell out of favour. The attitude of Louis XIV, who loved perfume as a young man but could no longer stand it after the 1680s, except for orange blossom, was probably not the main cause of the change, particularly as his reaction was shaped by fear of sinning and Hell, based on the traditional message of moralists on the dangers of the social uses of fragrance. The reasons underlying the shift are, of course, more complex. Given the difficulty of pinning down the chronology of the change, which requires further research, I have sought to identify key turning points and put forward hypotheses to explain them. The revolution in floral and fruity scents took place earlier than historians have claimed. It seems to have taken hold in the opening decades of the eighteenth century before triumphing in the 1750s, as Dejean's *Traité des odeurs* shows. I read this as a development tying in with broader trends affecting the whole of French society. It shifted from a belligerent culture ruled by warmongering kings, following a moral code laid down by a guilt-inducing religion, to a hegemonic civilization sated with pleasure, admired by all of Europe. While philosophers challenged the church, now considerably weakened, economic progress developed a love of fine cuisine and exotic aromas shipped in from France's colonial empire. The moral code loosened, even in the lower social strata, and eroticism worked its way into people's minds and even their home decor. Pleasure became a driver for change, helping undermine the fanaticism of earlier generations. Plague was no longer a threat; major famines were a thing of the past, and wars were no longer fought along France's borders. The newly peaceful, hedonistic, pleasure-seeking society needed fresh, sweet, soft fragrances to match its progress, drawing on the natural world made so fashionable by Jean-Jacques Rousseau. The court and urban centres, suffering more and more from odour pollution as a result of demographic pressure and the dawn of the industrial era, rejected heady, musky scents in favour of these new perfumes. Advances in medicine, chemistry and perfumery played into this trend until the Revolution. The only thing that remained unchanged was the faces of high-born women, who were still the same white and pink dolls mimicking the appearance of eternal youth, thanks to the tricks of the perfumery trade. Even in Napoleon's day, perfumers kept coming up with new beauty treatments or adapting old ones, such as the snail pomade that made Jean-François Houbigant's name. True, the snails' entrails were removed in the updated version printed in *Le Parfumeur impérial*. . . . The threshold of disgust had indeed shifted. Specialist guides no longer included animal excrement in their ingredients, let alone human waste.

Floral, fruity and spicy fragrances now dominated. The Napoleonic Empire did, however, see a certain resurgence in musky scents, particularly ambergris, limited to a category of customers whose specific characteristics require further research. I have hypothesized that this was perhaps due to the increasing influence of military values in an age when France was conquering much of Europe. Further study is needed here. For the vast majority of Napoleon's contemporaries, however, the world of scents had changed for good, with the exception of women of quality, whose faces were still identically standardized, white and smooth, as had been the case prior to the Revolution. Their bodies, including their powdered hair, were now perfumed with delicate fragrances. The most marked shift was in terms of their individual smell. Subtly scented baths and forms of personal care, including waxing, recorded as early as 1809, destroyed or at least limited fetid body odour.[3] There was therefore no longer any need to mask it with the powerful musky base notes that long wafted from gloves, clothes and sachets of scent. Courtship now took a decisive step away from animal secretions, heightened by persistent body odours, preferring much lighter heart notes that transmitted and enhanced personal scents that were more attractive now that washing had become common practice again. The shift was all the more fundamental for forming a clear break between the sense of smell and the earlier double-edged perception, when fragrances were used medically as repellents against the plague and socially as attractants for the opposite sex. It is hardly surprising that as early as 1751, Denis Diderot counted smell as the most voluptuous of all the senses. The sweetly fragranced bubble that now enclosed men and women of fashion was no longer a protection against deadly disease, but an open invitation to life, love and pleasure.

Though there were further later turns that lay outside the scope of the present work, that message has survived to the present day. Since bourgeois standards of decency required the body to remain clothed, even at the beach, a woman's attractiveness was measured by the beauty of her face and paleness of her complexion, until the twentieth century ushered in further far-reaching social developments. Hair had to be covered until relatively recently, including among the popular classes, due – if one dare say it – to its powerful sex appeal. For centuries, a beautiful woman's scent was the main signal of her charms, while also generating waves of aesthetic pleasure. In the long term, a woman's seductiveness has remained closely associated with the floral or fruity scents that still dominate the market in the early years of the third millennium. Natural products were, however, replaced by synthetic molecules from the late nineteenth century. Perfumes have also become significantly democratized, while fragrances for men have been taken up much more widely, adapted to male or female myths of virility.

Western society is currently by no means as deodorized as has been claimed, with the notable exception of the United States, where a widespread rejection of scents seems to go hand in hand with the Californian cult of the body beautiful, with no need for unsightly body hair or chemical scents to draw admiring gazes. Furthermore, germ phobia and a general avoidance of skin-to-skin contact, even as a merely friendly gesture, gives the sense of sight a crucial role in romantic relationships, particularly as bodies are on open display at beaches and by hotel pool sides – much to the chagrin of men and women who have to go on strict diets in readiness for summer, guilt-tripped by countless media reports on the importance of staying on top physical form to avoid body-shaming. In some cases, particularly on the West Coast, people choose not to wear perfume in public places such as restaurants for fear of inconveniencing other clients: many Americans are sensitive to smells, good or bad. Their ideal is complete scentlessness and hairlessness, particularly on the male torso and even on the head, as reflected by fashionable magazines. Young women remove the body hair from their pubis, armpits, legs and sometimes even chins with permanent laser treatments. The rejection of any hint of man's animal nature doubtless corresponds to a deep-rooted desire to halt the passage of time, as if it were possible to put a stop to the ageing process and death. This fearful attitude, the cultural expression of an individualism that inclines to powerful narcissism, is exploited by countless vastly profitable businesses that market the dream of delaying the onset of bodily decrepitude and preserving youthful attraction. From this point of view, any powerful scent, pleasant or otherwise, triggers a signal of extreme danger, raising the spectre of putrefaction that scentlessness was designed to keep at bay.

Europe today is more hedonistic, less guilt-ridden, and still embraces smells, including strong cheeses in France that other peoples find distinctly unappealing. Systematic deodorization does not appear to be held up as an ideal. Perfumes play a positive role, particularly in rituals of courtship, following short-lived fashions.

It might be thought that there is nothing left to invent perfume-wise in Europe and North America. However, this would be to misjudge the inventiveness of the human mind. I was tempted to conclude with a somewhat ironic word of advice to perfume designers to try playing with musk-based scents, once so popular with all-conquering masculinity, to add a touch of spice to the olfactory monotony of our standardized world and break with the trend to reject our animality, as expressed in North America. But, to my surprise, that is exactly where it was already happening. In 2013, a company based in Toronto, Canada, started working in an unusual niche market that was at complete odds with North American tastes. Zoologist Perfumes has started developing animal scents, hoping that a fraction of the Millennials born after 1980 would appreciate them.[4] The company's early experiments were a flop, as *Beaver*, launched in 2014, was considered too strong by the target market. The formula was modified in 2016, adding fresh notes to make it more attractive, with linden blossom, musk and citrus head notes, castoreum, orris and vanilla heart notes, and musk, ash, cedar and amber base notes. It seems young consumers, regardless of gender, only appreciated the return of such forgotten notes, now entirely synthetic, when combined with the established tradition of floral and fruity scents. The company did, however, expand its range rapidly, suggesting there was indeed a market for its perfumes. In early 2017, its products included *Bat*, *Civet*, *Macaque*, *Panda*, *Rhinoceros*, *Hummingbird* and *Nightingale*.

This has set capitalist noses quivering, and American businesses have now joined the sector. One New York-based company is selling *Ma Bête*, another *Suédois*, with fine leather notes. Then there is the civet of *Cadavres exquis* and the castoreum of *Salome*, both reputed to waken our darkest desires. One journalist has hypothesized that this is a way for Millennials to lay claim to their own animality in a technological, virtual world. She interviewed the head of the boutique perfume workshop that makes *Suédois*, who explained that there is a 'death drive' in such smells, adding that Grasse was not only the centre of the French perfume industry, but also a tannery town, where 'the smell of death and the smell of flowers went hand in hand'.[5]

It seems unlikely that North American customers are fully aware of what is driving their choice of perfume, other than an urge to break with the dominant tradition of scentlessness. In doing so, however, they are reconnecting with a long-overlooked sense, reacting to scent signals that tie sexuality to a degree of bestiality. It may be the case that the powerful wafts of scent they release are automatically encoded in our olfactory memory, like Proust's madeleine, automatically triggering a torridly erotic reaction. At least, that is what the enticing advertisements selling the dream claim. Is it a cause for complaint or rejoicing that, unlike their Canadian rivals, whose references come straight from nature, the American perfumers play with the cliché of French masculinity, redolent with voluptuous odours and driven by amorous urges? *Ma Bête* is directly inspired by Animalis, a base developed in France in the 1920s with genuine extract of civet, castoreum, musk and costus (a plant). Its rather unappealing scent evoked body odour, sweat and stables. It had to be combined with other products to become an irresistible perfume. The same is true of the latest version of *Ma Bête*, which contains floral scents including jasmine, neroli and patchouli. The ensemble is somehow a civilized, subliminal nod to the myth of seduction that did much to further the careers of French actors such as Maurice Chevalier. Its creator described it in interview as 'the tension between Beauty and the Beast' and a reminder 'that we are animals'. Reading between the lines, she sees the women who wear her perfume as embodying Beauty or the victim who falls under its spell, both attracted and repelled by the blend. All that is left for men is to take on the role of the Beast by splashing on the scent and becoming a French Don Juan bristling with pheromones. 'Because you don't wash, I'm on my way!' could be the modern American woman's equivalent to the famous plea attributed to Henri IV and Napoleon: many Americans are firmly of the belief that French men are strangers to deodorant.

It is hard not to be staggered by the extraordinary power of capitalism, which seems to be capable of attributing generous surplus value to this critical, moralist vision by making at least some Millennials susceptible to the eye-watering scent of *Pepé Le Pew*. The popular cartoon skunk, who first appeared in 1945 and won an Oscar in 1949, is a parody of the American view of French masculinity, constantly harassing the beauties he courts in the springtime Paris streets, trying to charm them with his boundless confidence and inimitable accent. Several of his adventures draw on America's olfactory nightmares, for instance when he uses deodorant to beguile his beloved. The creators of musky perfumes will certainly find inspiration in the 1952 episode *Little Beau Pepé*, where he douses himself with eau de cologne: combined with his natural aroma, it literally drives the object of his affections mad with love.

Does this mean that musky fragrances will soon come to dominate once more in a globalized world facing the threat of fragmentation, in which nationalism and populism are reviving the belligerence of the younger generations that have so far kept their heads down and their noses clean? This would require the guarantee of vast profits driving perfume manufacturers to invest heavily in the hope of bringing long-repressed urges back to the surface. That would mean convincing a huge potential customer base of the ability of such products to soothe the angst of civilizations haunted by the fear of decline, the increasingly rapid breakdown of social bonds, and far-reaching changes in romantic relationships. Is the need less pressing in Europe? Only a handful of French perfumes now use Animalis as a base: *Kouros* and *Parfum de Peau*, at their most popular in the 1980s, were joined in 2017 by *Mad Madame*, *Denis Durand Couture* and *Vierges et Toreros*.

The binary olfactory code is one of the simplest of all sensory monitoring systems, yet one of the most fundamental for the human race. Since the dawn of time, it has helped people tell life from death and danger from safety, constantly adapting to social and cultural developments. As long as humans have not morphed into robots, our sense of smell will be a crucial tool in spotting triggers for fear or pleasure and adapting our behaviour to them. To keep moving on the path of life, with its lot of sorrows and joys, we must learn to follow our noses.

Notes

Introduction

1 Norbert Elias, *The Civilizing Process*. Oxford: Blackwell, 1969, 1982 (1st German edn 1939).
2 Translator's note: Jean-Antoine-Nicolas de Caritat, Marquis de Condorcet, *Condorcet: Political Writings*, ed. Steven Lukes and Nadia Urbinati. Cambridge: Cambridge University Press, 2012, p. 147; emphasis added.
3 Robert Muchembled, *L'Invention de l'homme moderne: culture et sensibilités en France du XVe au XVIIIe siècle*. Paris: Hachette, 1994, pp. 55–61; and see below, chapter 3.

Chapter 1 Our unique sense of smell

1 Caroline Bushdid, Marcelo O. Magnasco, Leslie B. Vosshall and Andreas Keller, 'Humans Can Discriminate More Than 1 Trillion Olfactory Stimuli', *Science* 343, 2014, pp. 1370–2.
2 Richard C. Gerkin and Jason B. Castro, 'The Number of Olfactory Stimuli that Humans Can Discriminate is Still Unknown', *eLife*, 7 July 2015, http://dx.doi.org/10.7554/eLife.08127; Markus Meister, 'On the Dimensionality of Odor Space', *eLife*, 7 July 2015, http://dx.doi.org/10.7554/eLife.07865
3 Anne-Sophie Barwich, 'What Is So Special about Smell? Olfaction as a Model System in Neurobiology', *Postgraduate Medical Journal*, November 2015, http://dx.doi.org/10.1136/postgradmedj-2015-133249
4 Lavi Secundo et al., 'Individual Olfactory Perception Reveals Meaningful

Nonolfactory Genetic Information', *Proceedings of the National Academy of Sciences of the United States of America* 112(28), 14 July 2015, pp. 8750–5.

5 This trend can be traced back to Alain Corbin, *Le Miasme et la Jonquille: l'odorat et l'imaginaire social, XVIIe–XIXe siècles.* Paris: Aubier-Montaigne, 1982, published in English translation as *The Foul and the Fragrant: Odor and the French Social Imagination*, tr. Miriam Kochan. Cambridge, MA: Harvard University Press, 1986.

6 Sébastien Doucet, Robert Soussignan, Paul Sagot and Benoist Schaal, 'The Secretion of Areolar (Montgomery's) Glands from Lactating Women Elicits Selective, Unconditional Responses in Neonates', *PLOS One* 23 October 2009, http://dx.doi. org/10.1371/journal.pone.0007579

7 Regulation (EC) No. 1334/2008 of the European Parliament and of the Council of 16 December 2008 on flavourings and certain food ingredients with flavouring properties for use in and on foods.

8 Aurélie Biniek, *Odeurs et parfums aux XVIe et XVIIe siècles.* Master's dissertation, supervisor Robert Muchembled, Université de Paris-Nord, 1998.

9 As reported in *Le Monde*, 17 September 2015.

10 Patrice Tran Ba Huy, 'Odorat et histoire sociale', *Communications et langages* 126 (2000), pp. 84–107. See also Corbin, *Foul and the Fragrant*, and Annick Le Guérer, *Les Pouvoirs de l'odeur*. Paris: François Bourin, 1998.

11 Robert Mandrou, *Introduction à la France moderne: essai de psychologie historique, 1500–1640.* Paris: Albin Michel, 1998 (1st edn 1961), pp. 76, 81.

12 Rachel Herz, *The Scent of Desire: Discovering our Enigmatic Sense of Smell.* New York: William Morrow, 2007, pp. 32–9, 183–6. Italics in the original.

13 Ibid., esp. pp. 53, 84, and Patrick Süskind, *Perfume: The Story of a Murderer*, tr. John E. Woods. New York: Vintage, 1986.

14 Herz, *Scent of Desire*, pp. 33, 149–51; David Le Breton, *Sensing the World: An Anthropology of the Senses*, tr. Carmen Ruschiensky. London: Bloomsbury, 2017, pp. 134 (olfactory bubble), 140 (excrement and urine).

15 Gesualdo M. Zucco, Benoist Schaal, Mats Olsson and Ilona Croy, *Applied Olfactory Cognition*, foreword by Richard J. Stevenson. Frontiers Media, 2014, eBook, p. 15.

16 See Danielle Malmberg's article in Pascal Lardellier (ed.), *À fleur de peau: corps, odeurs et parfums.* Paris: Belin, 2003.

17 Joël Candau, *Mémoires et expériences olfactives: anthropologie d'un savoir-faire sensoriel.* Paris: PUF, 2000, p. 85.

18 Richard L. Doty and E. Leslie Cameron, 'Sex Differences and Reproductive Hormone Influences on Human Odor Perception', *Physiology and Behavior* 97, 25 May 2009, pp. 213–28.

19 Herz, *Scent of Desire*, pp. 149–51.

20 Le Guérer, *Pouvoirs de l'odeur*, pp. 254–60.
21 Corbin, *Foul and the Fragrant*, pp. 249–50, quoting research by the ethnologist Yvonne Verdier on foresters in the Châtillon region of central-eastern France in the twentieth century. Modern research would certainly seek to apply Freud's theories to female sexuality. Mauss's theory is quoted in Lucienne A. Roubin, *Le Monde des odeurs: dynamique et fonctions du champ odorant*. Paris: Méridiens Klincksieck, 1989, p. 237.
22 Herz, *Scent of Desire*, pp. 135–6.
23 Antonio R. Damasio, *Le Sentiment même de soi: corps, émotion, conscience*. Paris: Odile Jacob, 1999, pp. 60, 83–5, 283.
24 Roubin, *Monde des odeurs*, pp. 186, 206, 210–11, 241, 257, 262, 269.
25 Lydie Bodiou and Véronique Mehl (eds.), *Odeurs antiques*. Paris: Les Belles Lettres, 2011, pp. 80, 173, 223, 228–9, 232–3.
26 Lardellier, *À fleur de peau*, pp. 99, 137.
27 Jean de Renou, *Le Grand dispensaire médicinal. Contenant cinq livres des institutions pharmaceutiques. Ensemble trois livres de la Matière Médicinale. Avec une pharmacopée, ou Antidotaire fort accompli*, tr. Louys de Serres. Lyon: Pierre Rigaud, 1624, pp. 32–3. Unless otherwise stated, all quotations are translated by the translator.
28 Jason B. Castro, Arvind Ramanathan and Chakra S. Chennubhotla, 'Categorical Dimensions of Human Odor Descriptor Space Revealed by Non-Negative Matrix Factorization', *Plos One* 18 September 2013, http://dx.doi.org/10.1371/journal.pone.0073289
29 'Les 10 catégories d'odeurs les plus répandues', *Huffington Post* 20 September 2013: http://www.huffingtonpost.fr/2013/09/20/dix-catego ries-odeur-les-plus-repandues_n_3960728.html

Chapter 2 A pervasive stench

1 Dominique Laporte, *History of Shit*, tr. Nadia Benabid and Rodolphe El-Khoury. Cambridge, MA: MIT Press, 2002, p. 86.
2 'Hommes, parfums et dieux', *Le Courrier du musée de l'Homme* 6, November 1980.
3 Quoted by Augustin Galopin, *Le Parfum de la femme et le sens olfactif dans l'amour: étude psycho-physiologique*. Paris: Dentu, 1886, pp. 19–20.
4 Laporte, *History of Shit*, p. 4 and *passim*, wrongly fixes the date in 1539, when a French royal edict sought to solve the problem.
5 Jean-Pierre Leguay, 'La laideur de la rue polluée à la fin du Moyen Âge: "*immondicités, fiens et bouillons*" accumulés sur les chaussées des villes du royaume de France et des grands fiefs au XVe siècle', in *Le Beau et le Laid au Moyen Âge*. Aix-en-Provence: Presses Universitaires de Provence, 2000, pp. 301–17. See also by the same author *La Rue au Moyen Âge*. Rennes: Ouest France, 1984, and *La Pollution au Moyen*

Âge dans le royaume de France et dans les grands fiefs. Paris: Gisserot, 1999.

6 Nathalie Poiret, 'Odeurs impures: du corps humain à la Cité (Grenoble, XVIIIe–XIXe siècle)', *Terrain* 31, September 1998, pp. 89–102.

7 Jean Liébault, *Trois livres de l'embellissement et ornement du corps humain*. Paris: Jacques du Puys, 1582, p. 507.

8 See Alfred Franklin, *La Vie privée d'autrefois: l'hygiène*. Paris: Plon, 1890, for the full text of the edict, pp. 232–41.

9 Ouarda Aït Medjane, *Des maisons parisiennes: le Marais de 1502 à 1552. L'apport des inventaires après décès*. Master's dissertation, supervisor Robert Muchembled, Université de Paris-Nord, 2007, pp. 139–41.

10 Alain Croix, *L'Âge d'or de la Bretagne, 1532–1675*. Rennes: Ouest France, 1993, p. 306.

11 Quoted by Biniek, *Odeurs et parfums*, pp. 45–6.

12 Franklin, *Vie privée d'autrefois: l'hygiène*, pp. 71–2.

13 Ibid., pp. 132–3.

14 French national archives (henceforth AN), Y 12 830, police decree of 26 July 1777.

15 Roger-Louis Guerrand, *Les Lieux: histoire des commodités*. Paris: La Découverte, 1997, pp. 57–9; Franklin, *Vie privée d'autrefois: l'hygiène*, appendix, pp. 34–5.

16 Gustave Brunet, *Correspondance complète de Madame, duchesse d'Orléans, née Princesse Palatine, mère du régent*. . . . Paris: Charpentier, 1857, vol. 2, pp. 385–6.

17 De Renou, *Grand dispensaire médicinal*, p. 572.

18 Nicolas de Blégny, *Secrets concernant la beauté et la santé, pour la guérison de toutes les maladies et l'embellissement du corps humain*. Paris: Laurent d'Houry and Veuve Denis Nion, vol. 2, 1689.

19 Marie Meurdrac, *La Chymie charitable et facile en faveur des dames*. 3rd edn. Paris: Laurent d'Houry, 1687, p. 309 (1st edn 1666).

20 L. Kauffeisen, 'Au temps de la Marquise de Sévigné: l'eau d'émeraude, l'essence d'urine et l'eau de millefleurs', *Bulletin de la Société d'histoire de la pharmacie* 16, 1928, pp. 162–5.

21 Polycarpe Poncelet, *Chimie du goût et de l'odorat*. Paris: Le Mercier, 1755, p. 295 (pp. xix–xxi, on musical theory).

22 Pierre-Denis Boudriot, 'Essai sur l'ordure en milieu urbain à l'époque préindustrielle: boues, immondices et gadoue à Paris au XVIIIe siècle', *Histoire, économies et sociétés* 5, 1985, p. 524.

23 Ibid., pp. 515–28; Franklin, *Vie privée d'autrefois: l'hygiène*, pp. 156–7 and appendix, pp. 34–9.

24 Bernardino Ramazzini, *Essai sur les maladies des artisans*, tr. from the Latin [1700], with notes and additions, Antoine-François de Fourcroy. Paris: Moutard, 1777, pp. 84, 113, 122, 133, 144–50, 161, 167, 171, 175, 182, 202, 270, 308–9, 448.

25 Ibid., note 1, pp. 144–6.

26 Paul Brouardel, *La Mort et la mort subite*. Paris: J.-B. Baillière et fils, 1895, cites two cases, pp. 182–3.

27 The quote, referring to the eighteenth century, is from Poiret, 'Odeurs impures', 'S'enfuir à la campagne'. The article's clichéd view of rural life – single-roomed dwellings were rare and rubbish was generally added to the dung heap – contrasts with the excellent study of urban life.

28 Archives for the Nord *département* (henceforth ADN), B 1820, 208 v, 17 December 1651, Flers.

29 See Roubin, *Monde des odeurs*, on the Haut-Verdon region, quoted in chapter 1.

30 Franklin, *Vie privée d'autrefois: l'hygiène*, appendix, pp. 18–19.

31 ADN, B 1794, f. 245 v–246 v, 8 April 1602, at the inn in La Gorgue; B 1771, f. 13 v–14 r, c.1550–1, Éperlecques; B 1818, f. 31 r–v, 25 June 1638, place unknown.

32 Ibid., B 1800, f. 71 v–72 r, c.1594, Montigny-en-Ostrevent; B 1799, f. 71 v–72 r, 1 September 1612, Gonnehem; B 1820, f. 94v–95 r, 6 May 1644, Annœullin.

33 Ibid., B 1741, f. 184 v–185 v, 1529, place unknown, near the border between the county of Artois and France.

34 See Robert Muchembled, Hervé Bennezon and Marie-José Michel, *Histoire du grand Paris, de la Renaissance à la Révolution*. Paris: Perrin, 2009.

Chapter 3 Joyous matter

1 Erik Erikson, *Childhood and Society*. London: Vintage, 1995 (1st edn 1950), p. 365.

2 Georges Vigarello, *Concepts of Cleanliness: Changing attitudes in France since the Middle Ages*. tr. Jean Birrell. Cambridge: Cambridge University Press, 1988.

3 Robert Soussignan, Fayez Kontar and Richard E. Tremblay, 'Variabilité et universaux au sein de l'espace perçu des odeurs: approches inter-culturelles de l'hédonisme affectif', in Robert Dulau and Jean-Robert Pitte (eds.), *Géographie des odeurs*. Paris: L'Harmattan, 1998, p. 43.

4 H. Arthur Klein, *Graphic Worlds of Peter Bruegel the Elder*. New York: Dover Publications, 1963, pp. 103–5.

5 Mikhail Bakhtin, *Rabelais and His World*, tr. Hélène Iswolsky. Bloomington: Indiana University Press, 1984.

6 The extent of his readership is unknown but must be considerably lower than the eight to ten thousand potential readers in around 1660 cited by Alain Viala, *Naissance de l'écrivain: sociologie de la littérature à l'âge classique*. Paris: Minuit, 1985, pp. 132–3.

7 Klein, *Graphic Worlds*, pp. 84–5, *The Sleeping Peddler Robbed by the Apes*. On the stronger smell of human excrement, see above, chapter 2,

note 7, and the bourgeois storyteller Guillaume Bouchet, *Les Serées*, ed. C. E. Roybet. Paris: A. Lemerre, 1873–82, vol. 3, p. 162.

8 Ambroise Paré, *Traicté de la peste, de la petite verolle et rougeole*. Paris: Gabriel Buon, 1580, pp. 30–1 (1st edn 1568).

9 Roubin, *Monde des odeurs*, p. 205 (ethnographic study in the Haut-Verdon region).

10 Pierre de Ronsard, *Les Amours*, ed. Albert-Marie Schmidt. Paris: Le Livre de Poche, 1964, pp. 8, 48, 98, 154, 165, 181, 395.

11 Pierre de Ronsard, *Le Livret de folastries à Janot parisien*. Paris: Veuve Maurice de la Porte, 1553, p. 15 (repr. with additional material from the 1584 edn, Paris: Jules Gay, 1862).

12 Clément Marot, *Les Blasons anatomiques du corps féminin*. Paris: Charles L'Angelier, 1543. Available online in Les Bibliothèques Virtuelles Humanistes, www.bvh.univ-tours.fr. The following quotations are taken from the online edition: the breast, pp. 66–7, the nose, B 7 v–B 8 v, the twat, 27 v–28 v, the arse, 28 v–33 v, the fart, 37 r–38 r.

13 Bakhtin, *Rabelais and His World*, p. 34; Jean-Baptiste Porta [Giambattista della Porta], *La Physionomie humaine*. Rouen: Jean et David Berthelin, 1655 (original edn 1586), pp. 154, 334.

14 Both examples are taken from Jori Finkel, 'An Artist's Intentions (and Subjects) Exposed', *The New York Times*, 23 December 2015, p. C2.

15 ADN, B 1813, f. 114 v, January 1635, unknown location in the Spanish Netherlands.

16 Lucien Febvre, *Autour de l'*Heptaméron: *amour sacré, amour profane*. Paris: Gallimard, 1944.

17 Marguerite de Navarre, *L'Heptaméron*, ed. Michel François, based on the 1560 edn. Paris: Garnier, 1996, pp. 334–6 and appendix p. 443. English translation adapted slightly from *The Heptameron, Or The Tales of Margaret, Queen of Navarre*, tr. George Saintsbury. London: Society of English Bibliophiles, 1894, p. 19.

18 Gabriel A. Pérouse, *Nouvelles françaises du XVIe siècle: images de la vie du temps*. Geneva: Droz, 1977, pp. 163–8.

19 Ibid., pp. 29, 44–7, 63; Philippe de Vigneulles, *Les Cent Nouvelles nouvelles*, ed., intro. and notes Charles H. Livingston, assisted by R. Livingston and Robert H. Ivy Jr. Geneva: Droz, 1972, pp. 91–5 (no. 15), 124–5.

20 Erving Goffman, *Relations in Public: Microstudies of the Public Order*. New Brunswick: Transaction, 2010, pp. 44ff.

21 Bonaventure Des Périers, *Les Nouvelles récréations et joyeux devis de feu Bonaventure Des Périers, valet de chambre de la royne de Navarre*. Lyon: R. Granjon, 1558.

22 Pérouse, *Nouvelles françaises*, pp. 146, 161, 176; *Les Comptes du monde aventureux*, ed. Félix Frank. Geneva: Slatkine, 1969, vol. 2, pp. 30–6.

23 Pérouse, *Nouvelles françaises*, pp. 324, 413–14, 443.

24 [Étienne Tabourot, sieur des Accords], *Les Escraignes dijonnoises, composées par le feu sieur du Buisson*, 2nd edn. Lyon: Thomas Soubron, 1592, pp. 87–91.

25 Noël du Fail, *Contes et discours d'Eutrapel*, repr. D. Jouaust, intro., notes and glossary C. Hippeau. Paris: Librairie des Bibliophiles, 1875, vol. 1, pp. 135–6, 145; vol. 2, pp. 14–16, 35–6, 240.

26 Pérouse, *Nouvelles françaises*, pp. 284–6.

27 Ibid., pp. 381–5; Muchembled, *Invention de l'homme moderne*, pp. 112–34.

28 See chapter 7, where I try to apply this curious theory of imperial decline to the olfactory revolution in eighteenth-century France. Could it also be used to understand the political disasters of our own era?

29 Verdun L. Saulnier, 'Étude sur Béroalde de Verville: introduction à la lecture du *Moyen de Parvenir*', *Bibliothèque d'Humanisme et Renaissance* 5, 1944, pp. 209–326.

30 François Béroalde de Verville, *Le Moyen de parvenir*. Paris: Anne Sauvage, 1616. Edited by Les Bibliothèques Virtuelles Humanistes, www.bvh.univ-tours. fr, pp. 83, 196–7, 430–1, 492. The word count is based on this electronic edition. English edn: *The Way to Succeed: An Amalgam of All That Was, Is, and Will Be*, tr. Su Rathgeber. Munich: Bengelmann, 2013.

31 Ibid., pp. 134, 180, 188, 357, 433. References to English edn: pp. 149, 366, 62, 149, 317, 137–8, 320, 142, 432.

32 Barbara C. Bowen, *Humour and Humanism in the Renaissance*. Farnham: Ashgate, 2004, ch. XXI, 'Il faut donner dedans . . .', pp. 107–15. Bowen estimates that some 20 per cent of pages are free from scandalous vocabulary.

33 Translator's note: the English translation offers 'A donkey may mount you', 'caressed and fondled', 'ditch without a pick', 'sustains and rewards', 'indulged in carnal lust', 'affairs of the intestines', 'shaking that plum tree', 'a sweet death caused by his natural sword', 'caressing and playing with each other', 'to put flesh to flesh', 'tied a strap so tightly around the other man's thingy', 'administered the chaste girls' needs', 'creating poverty', 'the reason why'.

34 Béroalde de Verville, *Moyen de parvenir*, p. 317 (p. 236 in the English edn, translation modified). Does 'protype of an anagogic mob' mean 'prototype of the divine species', i.e. man? *Décoché* means having his penis removed: *cocher* is the verb used for a cockerel mounting a hen. In using the last two expressions as complements, Béroalde may be poking fun at the humanist notion of the androgyne, which was split in two to create men and women. Both halves thus seek to recreate their original fused oneness, which would only be possible in another life.

35 Ibid., p. 420: 'petite éminence de clitoris' (small mound of the clitoris).

36 Ibid., pp. 164–5, 367, 541. References in the English edn: pp. 126, 271, 405–7. The English edn keeps the French terms playing on the root word *con*.

37 Only the noun form *faguenas* is attested in the first edition of the French Academy's dictionary (1694), meaning a weak, unpleasant smell emanating from an unclean body in poor health.

38 Ibid., pp. 343, 405–6, 501. References in the English edn: pp. 370–1, 300, 150.

39 Ibid., pp. 22–4, 198–9. References in the English edn: pp. 19–20, translation modified, p. 150. An eighteenth-century variant of the tale of the two farts features in note 43 below.

40 Ibid., pp. 83, 414, 445, 591. References in the English edn: pp. 305, 328, 446.

41 Brunet, *Correspondance complète*, vol. 2, pp. 385–6, reproduces the two letters (the start of the first is quoted above, chapter 2, note 16).

42 See the section entitled 'Fountains of youth' in chapter 6 below for some examples.

43 Roger-Louis Guerrand, 'Prolégomènes à une géographie des flatulences', in Dulau and Pitte, *Géographie des odeurs*, pp. 73–7.

44 *Contes immoraux du XVIIIe siècle*, ed. Nicolas Veysman, pref. Michel Delon. Paris: Robert Laffont, 2010, pp. 153–7, 1253–4.

45 John G. Bourke, *Scatologic Rites of All Nations*. Washington, DC: W. H. Lowdermilk, 1891.

46 Pierre-Thomas Hurtault, *L'Art de péter*. En Westphalie [Paris]: Chez Florent-Q, rue Pet-en-Gueule, au Soufflet, 1775, pp. 81–2, 100, 111–20.

47 *Contes immoraux*, p. 1254.

48 Marc-André Bigard, Interview dated 18 August 2011, in 'La chasse aux pets? Mission impossible . . .', *L'Information santé au quotidien*, destinationsante.com

Chapter 4 Scent of a woman

1 Pliny the Elder, *Natural History*, tr. H. Rackham. Cambridge, MA: Loeb Classical Library, 1961, p. 549.

2 Sándor Ferenczi, *Thalassa: A Theory of Genitality*, tr. Henry Bunker. New York: Psychoanalytic Quarterly, 1938. Quoted by Diane Ackerman, *A Natural History of the Senses*. New York: Random House, 1990, p. 21.

3 Levinus Lemnius, *Les Occultes Merveilles et secretz de nature*. Paris: Galiot du Pré, 1574, f. 155 r., 166 v.

4 Ibid., f. 33 r.

5 Sara Matthews-Grieco. *Ange ou diablesse: la représentation de la femme au XVIe siècle*. Paris: Flammarion, 1991.

6 Nicolas de Cholières, *Les Neuf matinées du seigneur de Cholières*. Paris: Jean Richer, 1585, pp. 118–19, 168, 180, 195, 240, 242, 245.

7 Nicolas de Cholières, *Les Après Disnées du seigneur de Cholières*. Paris: Jean Richer, 1587, p. 203.

8 Jean Liébault, *Thrésor des remèdes secrets pour les maladies des femmes*. Paris: Jacques du Puys, 1585, p. 548.

9 Jean de Renou, *Les Œuvres pharmaceutiques du sr Jean de Renou ... augmentées d'un tiers en cette seconde édition par l'auteur; puis traduites, embellies de plusieurs figures nécessaires à la cognoissance de la médecine et pharmacie, et mises en lumière par M. Louys de Serres*. Lyon: N. Gay, 1637, pp. 113, 191.

10 Loys Guyon, *Le Miroir de la beauté et santé corporelle*. Lyon: Claude Prost, 1643, vol. 1, pp. 725–6.

11 BNF, Estampes, OA 22, 'Mœurs' reel M 142 280, 'Les plaisirs de la vie'.

12 BNF, Prints, engraving by Jeremias Falck, 'The sense of smell', seventeenth century, Reserve QB-201 (46)-FOL. See also the works by Jan Pieterszoon Saenredam, Crispin van de Passe (a different version from that discussed above) and an anonymous early sixteenth-century artist discussed by Biniek, *Odeurs et parfums*, pp. 194–8.

13 Sylvia Ferino-Pagden (ed.), *I cinque sensi nell'arte: immagini del sentire*. Centro culturale 'Città di Cremona' in San Maria della Pietà, Leonardo Arte, 1996, pp. 220–1. The work also contains other depictions of the sense of smell, including Ripa's. The man with the pipe comes from Holland.

14 Sébastien Locatelli, *Voyage de France: mœurs et coutumes françaises (1664–1665)*, tr. Adolphe Vautier. Paris: Alphonse Picard et fils, 1905, pp. 19, 240.

15 Muchembled, *Invention de l'homme moderne*, pp. 242–8.

16 Patricia Nagnan-Le Meillour, 'Les phéromones: vertébrés et invertébrés', in Roland Salesse and Rémi Gervais (eds.), *Odorat et goût: de la neurobiologie des sens chimiques aux applications*. Versailles: Quæ, 2012, p. 39.

17 Cholières, *Après Disnées*, p. 73.

18 Quoted in Fernand Fleuret and Louis Perceau, *Les Satires françaises du XVIe siècle*. Paris: Garnier frères, 1922, vol. 1, p. 246ff.

19 Montaigne, *Essais*, Book I, chapter 55, 'Des senteurs'.

20 Robert Muchembled, 'Fils de Caïn, enfants de Médée: homicide et infanticide devant le parlement de Paris, 1575–1604', *Annales Histoire, Sciences sociales* 62, 2007, pp. 1063–94.

21 Robert Muchembled, *Passions de femmes au temps de la reine Margot, 1553–1615*. Paris: Seuil, 2003, pp. 221–34.

22 F. A. E. [Frère Antoine Estienne], *Remonstrance charitable aux dames et damoyselles de France sur leurs ornemens dissolus*. Paris: Sébastien Nivelle, 4th edn, 1585, pp. 5, 8, 11, 14, 20–1 (the printing privilege is dated 1570). English translation: *A Charitable Remonstrance Addressed to the Wives and Maidens of France Touching Their Dissolute Adornments*, tr. William Rooke. Edinburgh: privately printed, 1887, p. 29.

23 Philippe Bosquier, *Tragoedie nouvelle dicte Le Petit Razoir des ornemens mondains, en laquelle toutes les misères de nostre temps sont*

attribuées tant aux hérésies qu'aux ornemens superflus du corps. Mons: Charles Michel, 1589 (repr. Geneva: Slatkine, 1970, pp. 50–2).

24 [Lambert Daneau], *Traité des danses.* [Geneva: François Estienne], 1579.

25 Paré, *Traicté de la peste*, p. 48.

26 Loys Guyon, *Les Diverses leçons.* Lyon: Claude Morillon, 1604, p. 138.

27 Jean Polman, *Le Chancre, ou couvre-sein féminin, ensemble le voile, ou couvre-chef féminin.* Douai: Gérard Patté, 1635.

28 Pierre Juvernay, *Discours particulier contre la vanité des femmes de ce temps.* Paris: J. Mestais, 1635; 3rd edn as *Discours particulier contre les femmes débraillées de ce temps* [*Particular discourse against the dishev-elled women of our time*]. Paris: Pierre Le Mur, 1637, pp. 56–7, 65–6, 86–7; then as *Discours particulier contre les filles et femmes mondaines découvrans leur sein et portant des moustaches* [*Particular discourse against girls and worldly women baring the breasts and wearing locks of hair loose over their cheeks*]. Paris: Jérémie Bouillerot, 1640, p. 87.

29 Claude Fleury, *Mœurs des chrétiens.* Paris: Veuve Gervais Clouzier, 1682.

30 Odet de Turnèbe, *Les Contents*, ed. Norman B. Spector. Paris: Nizet, 1984, pp. 33–5. English translation: *Satisfaction All Around*, tr. Donald Beecher. Ottawa: Carleton University Renaissance Centre, 1979, pp. 32–3.

31 Renou, *Œuvres pharmaceutiques*, p. 190.

32 Liébault, *Trois livres*, pp. 409, 516.

33 Pierre de Bourdeilles, seigneur de Brantôme. *Vie des dames galantes*, based on the 1740 edn. Paris: Garnier frères, 1864. Available online at Project Gutenberg, unpaginated.

34 Louis Gaufridy, *Confession faicte par messire Louys Gaufridi, prestre en l'église des Accoules à Marseille . . . à deux Pères capucins du couvent d'Aix, la veille de Pâques, le onziesme avril mil six cens onze.* Aix: Jean Tholozan, 1611.

35 Nicolas Barbelane, *Les Canards surnaturels, 1598–1630.* Master's dis-sertation, supervisor Robert Muchembled. Université de Paris-Nord, 2000, p. 64 (original news-sheets in the BNF collection).

36 Ibid., pp. 60–2. *Histoire prodigieuse d'un gentilhomme auquel le Diable s'est apparu, et avec lequel il a conversé sous le corps d'une femme morte.* BNF, Y2 42 478 (1613).

37 François de Rosset, *Les Histoires mémorables et tragiques de ce temps*, ed. Anne de Vaucher Gravili, based on the 1619 edn. Paris: Le Livre de Poche, 1994.

38 Jean-Pierre Camus, *L'Amphithéâtre sanglant*, ed. Stéphan Ferrari. Paris: Honoré Champion, 2001, pp. 237–8.

39 Brantôme, *Vie des dames galantes.*

40 Jacques Bailbé, 'Le thème de la vieille femme dans la poésie satirique du XVIe et du début du XVIIe siècle', *Bibliothèque d'Humanisme et Renaissance* 26 (1964), pp. 98–119. This is the source for the quotations in the following paragraph.

41 Robert Muchembled, *A History of the Devil: From the Middle Ages to the Present*, tr. Jean Birrell. Cambridge: Polity, 2003, pp. 49–50. Deutsch's engraving is held at the Kupferstichkabinett in Berlin.
42 Agrippa d'Aubigné, *Œuvres*, ed. Henri Weber. Paris: Gallimard, 1969, Ode XXIII of *Printemps*, pp. 311–15.
43 Marianne Closson, *L'Imaginaire démoniaque en France (1550–1650): genèse de la littérature fantastique*. Geneva: Droz, 2000, pp. 126–7, 338–41, 344, for the quotations. Many other texts, particularly by Régnier and Saint-Amant, develop the same theme.
44 Molière, *L'Étourdi*, act V, scene 9.

Chapter 5 The Devil's breath

 1 Paré, *Traicté de la peste*, pp. 3–9, 14, 21.
 2 Antoine Mizauld, *Singuliers secrets et secours contre la peste*. Paris: Mathurin Breuille, 1562, pp. 6–14.
 3 Arras municipal library (Pas-de-Calais), police decrees, BB 38, f. 126 r–v, 130 v, 146 r; BB 39, f. 48 v; BB 40, f. 5r–v, 94 v, 105 r–106 r, 113 v–114 r, 119 r, 150 r–153 v, 206 r, 359 v–360 r, 380 v.
 4 Paré, *Traicté de la peste*, pp. 51–4, 60.
 5 Jean de Lampérière, *Traité de la peste, de ses causes et de la cure. . . .* Rouen: David du Petit Val, 1620, pp. 57, 127–9, 132–3.
 6 Arnaud Baric, *Les Rares secrets, ou remèdes incomparables, universels et particuliers, préservatifs et curatifs contre la peste. . . .* Toulouse: F. Boude, 1646, pp. 15–17.
 7 Angélus Sala, *Traicté de la peste, concernant en bref les causes et accidents d'icelle, la description de plusieurs excellents remèdes, tant pour se préserver de son infection, que pour guérir les pestiferez*. Leiden: G. Basson, 1617, pp. 32–3.
 8 Mizauld, *Singuliers secrets*, pp. 27–32.
 9 Pierre Rainssant, *Advis pour se préserver et pour se guérir de la peste de cette année 1668*. Reims: Jean Multeau, 1668, pp. 30–1.
10 Renou, *Œuvres pharmaceutiques*, pp. 362, 764 (1st Latin edn, 1609).
11 Turnèbe, *Contents*, p. 12. (English translation p. 5).
12 Renou, *Œuvres pharmaceutiques*, p. 266.
13 Mizauld, *Singuliers secrets*, pp. 16–57. The rest of the book is devoted to patient care. See p. 139 on the use of urine in the Auvergne.
14 Guyon, *Diverses leçons*, p. 704.
15 Constance Classen, David Howes and Anthony Synnott. *Aroma: The Cultural History of Smell*. London: Routledge, 1994, pp. 59, 71–2.
16 Oger Ferrier, *Remèdes préservatifs et curatifs de peste*. Lyon: Jean de Tournes, 1548, pp. 49–52.
17 Lampérière, *Traité de la peste*, p. 152.
18 'Charles Delorme', in Louis-Gabriel Michaud, *Biographie universelle, ancienne et moderne*, new edn. Paris: A. Thoisnier Desplaces, 1852, vol.

10, p. 345; C. Salzmann, 'Masques portés par les médecins en temps de peste', *Æsculape* 1, January 1932, pp. 5–14.

19 Lampérière, *Traité de la peste*, pp. 409–11.

20 Classen et al., *Aroma*, p. 61.

21 Liébault, *Trois livres*, pp. 506, 513, 551.

22 Closson, *Imaginaire démoniaque*, p. 111.

23 M. Meurdrac, *Chymie charitable et facile*, pp. 75, 261.

24 Louyse Bourgeois, known as Boursier, *Recueil des secrets de Louyse Bourgeois*. Paris: Jean Dehoury, 1653, pp. 32–7 on the plague.

25 Paré, *Traicté de la peste*, pp. 44–7.

26 C. F. Bertrand, *Le Parfumeur impérial, ou l'art de préparer les odeurs. . . .* Paris: Brunot-Labbé, 1809, pp. 266, 275–6.

27 Kenelm Digby, *Remèdes souverains et secrets expérimentés de monsieur le chevalier Digby, chancelier de la reine d'Angleterre, avec plusieurs autres secrets et parfums curieux pour la conservation de la beauté des dames*. Paris: Cavelier, 1684, pp. 275–6; Simon Barbe, *Le Parfumeur françois*. Lyon: Thomas Amaulry, 1693, pp. 117, 124, 128, 130–1.

28 Renou, *Grand dispensaire médicinal*, pp. 16, 22, 147, 358, 361, 365, 495–6, 555, 581, 894.

29 Victor Gay and Henri Stein, *Glossaire archéologique du Moyen Âge et de la Renaissance*. Paris: Société Bibliographique, 1928, vol. 2, pp. 155, 205–6, 254.

30 Reindert L. Falkenburg, 'De duiven buiten beeld: over duivelafwerende krachten en motieven in de beeldende kunst rond 1500', in Gerard Rooijakkers, Lène Dresen-Coenders and Margreet Geerdes (eds.), *Duivelsbeelden: een cultuurhistorische speurtocht door de Lage Landen*. Barn: Ambo, 1994, pp. 107–22.

31 André Chauvière, *Parfums et senteurs du Grand Siècle*. Lausanne: Favre, 1999, p. 21.

32 François-L. Bruel, 'Deux inventaires de bagues, joyaux, pierreries et dorures de la reine Marie de Médicis (1609 ou 1610)', *Archives de l'art français, nouvelle période*, vol. 2, 1908, pp. 204, 214.

33 Madeleine Jurgens (ed.), *Ronsard et ses amis: documents du Minutier central des notaires de Paris*. Paris: Archives nationales, 1985, p. 234.

34 AN, ET VIII, 530, 27 April 1557, estate inventory for Jean Binet, glove merchant at the law court. See also Micheline Baulant, 'Prix et salaires à Paris au XVIe siècle: sources et résultats', *Annales ESC* 31, 1976, pp. 954–5.

35 Guyon, *Miroir*, vol. 2, pp. 63–4.

36 Blégny, *Secrets concernant la beauté*, vol. 1, pp. 100–1, 110, 112–16, and vol. 2, p. 16.

Chapter 6 Musky scents

1 Annick Le Guérer, *Le Parfum, des origines à nos jours*. Paris: Odile Jacob, 2005, p. 133.

2 Barbe, *Parfumeur françois*, 'Au lecteur' [To the reader], unpaginated.
3 Louis Lémery, *Traité des aliments*, 3rd edn. Paris: Durand, 1755. See particularly vol. 1, which includes the relevant comments, p. 481 on garlic and pp. 500–1 on angelica.
4 Quoted by Biniek, *Odeurs et parfums*, pp. 161–2.
5 Chauvière, *Parfums et senteurs*, p. 81; Blégny, *Secrets concernant la beauté*, vol. 2, pp. 404, 408.
6 Biniek, *Odeurs et parfums*, pp. 97–109 (works by Pierre Erresalde, Nicolas Lémery, Nicolas de Blégny and one anonymous work dating from 1698).
7 Guyon, *Miroir*, vol. 1, pp. 331–2.
8 Biniek, *Odeurs et parfums*, pp. 105–7, 110.
9 Paul Scarron, *L'Héritier ridicule ou la dame intéressée* [*The ridiculous heir, or, the self-interested lady*]. Paris: Toussaint Quinet, 1650, act V, scene 1.
10 Blégny, *Secrets concernant la beauté*, vol. 2, pp. 13, 386, 335–443, 470, 525, 531–4, 585, 621, 643.
11 Galopin, *Parfum de la femme*, pp. 208–9. Catherine-Henriette de Balzac d'Entragues, born in 1579, became Henri IV's favourite in 1599. They had two children who were subsequently given legitimate status and he gave her the title of Marquise de Verneuil.
12 Sylvie Clouzeau, *L'Art de paraître féminin au XVIIe siècle*. DEA dissertation, supervised by Robert Muchembled, Université de Paris-Nord, 2002, pp. 67, 73–4 and documents 7, 11 (women's garments).
13 [Marie de Romieu], *Instructions pour les jeunes dames*. Lyon: Jean Dieppi, 1573, pp. 28–9.
14 Barbe, *Parfumeur françois*, preface to the reader and opening remarks.
15 Liébault, *Thrésor des remèdes*, pp. 577–8.
16 Guyon, *Miroir*, vol. 1, p. 60. He claims the same of incense, myrrh, mint, sage, saffron and storax.
17 Ackerman, *Natural History*, pp. 12–14.
18 Biniek, *Odeurs et parfums*, pp. 133–47, gives an excellent overview of the subject and a thoughtful analysis of the 1656 statutes.
19 AN, ET XIII, 15, 19 April, 1632, records Annibal Basgapé. AN, O1 31, f. 9 v, 1686, Pierre Le Lièvre; O1 84, f. 172 r, 1740, Claude Le Lièvre; O1 94, f. 22 r, 1 February 1750, Élie-Louis Le Lièvre.
20 *Habit de parfumeur*, Paris, Musée Carnavalet. A coloured etching of the same work dates from around 1700 (figure 23), possibly the work of Nicolas Bonnart (1637?–1718).
21 Barbe, *Parfumeur françois*, pp. 76–87.
22 Biniek, *Odeurs et parfums*, pp. 149–61.
23 Vigarello, *Concepts of Cleanliness*.
24 AN, ET CXXII, 3, 7 March 1514 (new style calendar), estate inventory (henceforth EI) for Jean Eschars, spice merchant and apothecary; ET XXXIII, 6, 5 May 1522, EI for Robert Calier, merchant and apothecary.

25 The southern French town of Narbonne started producing an alcoholic extract of melissa and lavender in the mid-sixteenth century. By the early seventeenth century it was known as carmelite water or citronella water. Dejean, *Traité raisonné de la distillation*. Paris: Guillyn, 3rd edn, 1769, p. 143.

26 AN, ET VIII, 530, 27 April 1557, EI Jean Binet, glove merchant. One livre was worth 20 sous, one sou was worth 12 deniers. As seen in chapter 5 in the section on pomanders, a builder's mate earned 6 sous a day.

27 AN, ET C, 105, 10 April 1549 (new style calendar), EI Guillaume Degrain, glover and perfumer. 'Mollyet' may be a reference to the miraculous spring of Our Lady in Moliets in south-western France, whose sulphurous water was reputed to cure skin diseases.

28 AN, ET XXIV, 148, 5 November 1613, EI Dominique Prévost, perfume merchant.

29 Robert Muchembled, *La Société policée: politique et politesse en France du XVIe au XXe siècle*. Paris: Seuil, 1998, pp. 110–20.

30 AN, ET XXXV, 240, 20 June 1631, EI for the wife of Pierre Francœur, the king's perfumer and *valet de chambre*.

31 AN, ET VII, 25, 15 July 1636, EI for Antoine Godard, glover and perfumer.

32 Barbe, *Parfumeur françois*, pp. 93–113.

33 Philip Massinger, *The Plays*. Ed. W. Gifford. London: G. and W. Nicol, 1813, vol. 2, p. 46.

34 AN, ET CXIII, 13, 4 June 1641, EI Nicolas Rousselet, glover and perfumer; ET XXVI, 85, 5 September 1642, EI Charles Mersenne, perfume merchant; ET XXIV, 431, 14 April 1649, EI Pierre Courtan, merchant.

35 Charles Sorel, sieur de Souvigny, 'Les Loix de la galanterie', in *Recueil des pièces les plus agréables de ce temps*. Paris: Nicolas de Sercy, 1644.

36 P. S. Girard, 'Recherches sur les établissements de bains publics à Paris depuis le IVe siècle jusqu'à présent', *Annales d'hygiène publique et de médecine légale* 7, part 1, 1832, p. 34.

37 AN, ET LIV, 794, 21 June 1735, EI for Jean-Baptiste Douaire, glover and perfumer.

38 Stanis Pérez, 'L'eau de fleur d'oranger à la cour de Louis XIV', in *Artefact: techniques, histoire et sciences humaines* 1: *Corps parés, corps parfumés*. Paris: CNRS, 2013, pp. 107–25.

39 Chauvière, *Parfums et senteurs*, pp. 80, 96, 140, 148–50.

40 Renou, *Œuvres pharmaceutiques*.

41 Meurdrac, *Chymie charitable et facile*, pp. 327–8 for water of talc and p. 366 for orange flower water in hand pomade.

42 Nicolas Lémery, *Recueil de curiositez rares et nouvelles*. Lausanne: David Gentil, vol. 1, 1681; Lémery, *Recueil de curiositez rares et nouvelles . . . avec de beaux secrets gallans*. Paris: Pierre Trabouillet, 1686, pp. 156–9.

43 Barbe, *Parfumeur françois*, pp. 99–108.

44 J. D. B. [Jean de Bussières], *Les Descriptions poétiques*. Lyon: Jean-Baptiste Devenet, 1649, pp. 11–18.

Chapter 7 Civilizing floral essences

1 Wolfgang Schivelbusch, *Tastes of Paradise: A Social History of Spices, Stimulants, and Intoxicants*. Tr. David Jacobson. New York: Vintage, 1992.
2 Corbin, *Foul and the Fragrant*, pp. 65–70.
3 Bourke, *Scatologic Rites*, p. 341.
4 Dejean [Antoine Hornot], *Traité des odeurs*. Paris: Nyon, 1764, pp. 4–5, 26–8, 82–3, 91–2, 105, 108, 120–2, 424. Where exact references are not given, see the highly detailed final table in the treatise.
5 Classen et al., *Aroma*, p. 73, date the revolution in scents to the end of the eighteenth century.
6 Eugénie Briot, 'Jean-Louis Fargeon, fournisseur de la cour de France: art et techniques d'un parfumeur du XVIIIe siècle', in *Artefact: techniques, histoire et sciences humaines* 1: *Corps parés, corps parfumés*. Paris: CNRS, 2013, pp. 167–77.
7 See the section below on 'Sensual faces'.
8 Barbe, *Parfumeur françois*, pp. 87–9.
9 Dejean, *Traité des odeurs*, pp. 475, 485–505.
10 Louis Courajod (ed.), *Livre-journal de Lazare Duvaux, marchand bijoutier ordinaire du roi, 1748–1758*. Paris: Société des bibliophiles français, 1873, vol. 2, p. 120.
11 Dejean, *Traité des odeurs*, p. 16.
12 Ibid., pp. 138, 184, 190.
13 Ibid., pp. 246–55, 294–303.
14 *Vigée Le Brun*, exhibition catalogue, ed. Joseph Baillio, Katharine Baetjer and Paul Lang. New York: Metropolitan Museum of Art, 2016, p. 120. The 1784 painting *Madame Royale et le dauphin assis dans un jardin [Madame Royale and the Dauphin seated in a garden]* shows similar makeup, p. 100. On men, see p. 59 (the artist's brother in 1773), p. 104 and her 1784 portrait of Calonne (figure 21).
15 Dejean, *Traité des odeurs*, pp. 220–46, 445–6, 468–75.
16 Ibid., pp. 256–64, 336–423.
17 Barbe, *Parfumeur françois*, unpaginated note to the reader 'on flower-scented pomades', and pp. 39–41.
18 Dejean, *Traité des odeurs*, pp. 423–44.
19 Quoted by Alfred Franklin, *La Vie privée d'autrefois: les magasins de nouveautés*. Paris: Plon, 1895, pp. 96–9.
20 Dejean, *Traité des odeurs*, pp. 457–8.
21 Denis Diderot, 'Letter on the Deaf and Dumb', in *Diderot's Early Philosophical Works*. Tr. Margaret Jourdain. Chicago and London: Open Court, 1916, p. 165.

22 Ferino-Pagden, *Cinque sensi*, pp. 258–9.
23 *Corps parés, corps parfumés*, pp. 225–6, with pictures.
24 *Le jeune homme instruit en amour*. Paphos [Paris], 1764.
25 *Vigée Le Brun*, p. 89.
26 Dejean, *Traité des odeurs*, pp. 303–31.
27 Süskind, *Perfume*.
28 AN, ET XXVIII, 594, 25 Pluviôse an. VIII (14 February 1800), EI for André-Michel-Roch Briard, perfumer.
29 *Vigée Le Brun*, pp. 236–7.
30 Bertrand, *Parfumeur impérial*, detailed table and a useful list of ingredients in alphabetical order. On toilet vinegars, see pp. 266, 275–6.
31 Ibid., pp. 46–9.
32 Ibid., pp. 137, 190, 198, 202–4, 230–2.
33 Ibid., p. 319 and index entry for 'civette'.
34 Ibid., pp. 119–20 on eau de cologne.
35 AN, ET XLI, 795, 23 November 1807, EI for Jean-François Houbigant, perfumer. To the best of my knowledge, the inventory has not yet been fully studied by researchers. The following is just a general outline.
36 AN, ET XXVIII, 656, 5 May 1810, EI for Jean-Baptiste-Alexandre Briard, perfume merchant in bulk.
37 Bertrand, *Parfumeur impérial*, list of substances, 'civet'.

Conclusion

1 This is not specific to the present day, contrary to what Pascal Lardellier seems to suggest. See Lardellier, *À fleur de peau*, p. 12.
2 See chapter 3, note 13.
3 Bertrand, *Parfumeur impérial*, pp. 279–80, on waxing.
4 https://www.zoologistperfumes.com/
5 Rachel Syme, 'Do I Smell a Bat? Oh, It's You', *The New York Times*, 27 October 2016, p. D5.

Sources and bibliography

A note on quotations

Works are given with their original title. However, to make them easier to read, I have harmonized and modernized spelling, punctuation and capitalization without modifying the style. Words whose meaning might be misleading are defined in square brackets where necessary.

Principal manuscript sources

Archives nationales, Paris (AN)

Estate inventories (EI) from the central records of Paris notaries.
   (ET followed by a Roman numeral indicates the number of the notary's office, followed by the file number.)

ET CXXII, 3, 7 March 1514 (new style calendar), Jean Eschars, spice merchant and apothecary.
ET XXXIII, 6, 5 May 1522, Robert Calier, merchant and apothecary.
ET XXXIII, 2, 10 July 1528, Geoffroy Cocheu, apothecary.
ET VIII, 530, 27 April 1557, Jean Binet, glove merchant.
ET C, 105, 10 April 1549 (new style calendar), Guillaume Degrain, glover and perfumer.
ET VIII, 426, 18 September 1581, Nicolas Lefebvre, glover.
ET XXIV, 148, 5 November 1613, Dominique Prévost, perfume merchant.
ET XXXV, 240, 20 June 1631, wife of Pierre Francœur, perfumer and the king's *valet de chambre*.
ET XIII, 15, 19 April, 1632, Annibal Basgapé, perfumer.

ET VII, 25, 15 July 1636, Antoine Godard, glover and perfumer.
ET XLIX, 304, 12 February 1637, David Nerbert, perfumer and glover.
ET CXIII, 13, 4 June 1641, Nicolas Rousselet, glover and perfumer.
ET XXVI, 85, 5 September 1642, Charles Mersenne, perfume merchant.
ET XXVI, 85, 19 February 1644, Pierre Berger, apothecary.
ET XXIV, 431, 14 April 1649, Pierre Courtan, trader 'at the sign of the Cross of Lorraine'.
ET I, 133, 14 June 1659, Louis Le Clerc.
ET XV, 383, 3 April 1702, Nicolas Delaporte, glover and perfumer.
ET LIV, 794, 21 June 1735, Jean-Baptiste Douaire, glover and perfumer.
ET XXXVIII, 317, 6 July 1750, wife of Jean Poittevin, glover.
ET XXVIII, 594, 25 Pluviôse an. VIII (14 February 1800), André-Michel-Roch Briard, perfumer.
ET XLI, 795, 23 November 1807, Jean-François Houbigant, perfumer.
ET XXVIII, 656, 5 May 1810, Jean-Baptiste-Alexandre Briard, perfume merchant in bulk.

Bibliothèque municipale d'Arras, Pas-de-Calais (BM Arras)

Registers of police decrees for the city of Arras
BB 38 and 39 (late fourteenth–fifteenth centuries).
BB 40 (sixteenth and seventeenth centuries).

Primary sources

Aubigné, Agrippa d', *Œuvres*, ed. Henri Weber, Paris, Gallimard, 1969.
Barbe, Simon, *Le Parfumeur françois*, Lyon, Thomas Amaulry, 1693.
Baric, Arnaud, *Les Rares secrets, ou remèdes incomparables, universels et particuliers, préservatifs et curatifs contre la peste . . .*, Toulouse, F. Boude, 1646.
Bastiment des receptes, contenant trois petites parties de receptaires. La première traicte de diverses vertus et proprietez des choses. La seconde de diverses sortes d'odeurs et composition d'icelles. La tierce comprend aucuns secrets médicinaux propres à conserver la santé . . ., Poitiers, Jacques Bouchet, 1544.
Béroalde de Verville, François, *Le Moyen de parvenir*, Paris, Anne Sauvage, 1616. With corrections by Les Bibliothèques Virtuelles Humanistes, www.bvh.univ-tours.fr
Béroalde de Verville, François, *Le Moyen de parvenir (1616)*, ed. Michel Jeanneret and Michel Renaud, Paris, Gallimard, 2006.
Béroalde de Verville, François, *The Way to Succeed: An Amalgam of All That Was, Is and Will Be*, tr. Su Rathgeber, Munich, Bengelmann, 2013.
Bertrand, C. F., *Le Parfumeur impérial, ou l'art de préparer les odeurs . . .*, Paris, Brunot-Labbé, 1809.

Blégny, Nicolas de, *Secrets concernant la beauté et la santé, pour la guérison de toutes les maladies et l'embellissement du corps humain*, Paris, Laurent d'Houry and Veuve Denis Nion, 1688–9, 2 vols.

Bonnaffé, Edmond, *Inventaire des meubles de Catherine de Médicis en 1589*, Paris, Auguste Aubry, 1874.

Bosquier, Philippe, *Tragoedie nouvelle dicte Le Petit Razoir des ornemens mondains, en laquelle toutes les misères de nostre temps sont attribuées tant aux hérésies qu'aux ornemens superflus du corps*, Mons, Charles Michel, 1589 (repr. Geneva, Slatkine, 1970).

Bourgeois, Louyse, known as Boursier, *Recueil des secrets de Louyse Bourgeois*, Paris, Jean Dehoury, 1653.

Brantôme, Pierre de Bourdeilles, seigneur de, *Vie des dames galantes*, based on the 1740 edn, Paris, Garnier frères, 1864 (digital edn, Project Gutenberg, unpaginated).

Bruel, François-L., 'Deux inventaires de bagues, joyaux, pierreries et dorures de la reine Marie de Médicis (1609 ou 1610)', *Archives de l'art français, nouvelle période*, vol. 2, 1908, pp. 186–215.

Brunet, Gustave, *Correspondance complète de Madame, duchesse d'Orléans, née Princesse Palatine, mère du régent . . .*, Paris, Charpentier, 1857, 2 vols.

Camus, Jean-Pierre, *L'Amphithéâtre sanglant*, ed. Stéphan Ferrari, Paris, Honoré Champion, 2001.

Cholières, Nicolas de, *Les Neuf matinées du seigneur de Cholières*, Paris, Jean Richer, 1585.

Cholières, Nicolas de, *Les Après Disnées du seigneur de Cholières*, Paris, Jean Richer, 1587.

Comptes du monde aventureux (Les), ed. Félix Frank, Geneva, Slatkine, 1969, 2 vols.

Contes immoraux du XVIIIe siècle, ed. Nicolas Veysman, pref. Michel Delon, Paris, Robert Laffont, 2010.

Courajod, Louis (ed.), *Livre-journal de Lazare Duvaux, marchand bijoutier ordinaire du roi, 1748–1758*, Paris, Société des bibliophiles français, 1873.

Courtin, Antoine de, *Nouveau traité de la civilité qui se pratique en France parmi les honnestes gens*, Paris, H. Josset, 1671.

[Daneau, Lambert], *Traité des danses*, [Geneva, François Estienne], 1579.

Dejean [Hornot, Antoine, known as], *Traité raisonné de la distillation*, Paris, Guillyn, 3rd edn, 1769 (1st edn 1753).

Dejean [Hornot, Antoine, known as], *Traité des odeurs*, Paris, Nyon, 1764.

Diderot, Denis, *Œuvres complètes*, ed. Jules Assézat, Paris, Garnier, 1875, vol. 1.

Diderot, Denis, 'Letter on the Deaf and Dumb', in *Diderot's Early Philosophical Works*, tr. Margaret Jourdain, Chicago and London, Open Court, 1916.

Digby, Kenelm, *Remèdes souverains et secrets expérimentés de monsieur le chevalier Digby, chancelier de la reine d'Angleterre, avec plusieurs autres secrets et parfums curieux pour la conservation de la beauté des dames*, Paris, Cavelier, 1684.

Du Fail, Noël, *Contes et discours d'Eutrapel*, repr. D. Jouaust, intro., notes and glossary C. Hippeau, Paris, Librairie des Bibliophiles, 1875, 2 vols.

Duret, Jean, *Advis sur la maladie*, Paris, Claude Morel, 1619.

Erresalde, Pierre, *Nouveaux remèdes éprouvés, utiles et profitables pour toutes sortes de maladies; comme aussi pour se garantir de la peste*, Paris, Jean-Baptiste Loyson, 1660.

F. A. E. [Frère Antoine Estienne], *Remonstrance charitable aux dames et damoyselles de France sur leurs ornemens dissolus*, Paris, Sébastien Nivelle, 4th edn, 1585 (the printing privilege is dated 1570).

F. A. E. [Frère Antoine Estienne], *A Charitable Remonstrance Addressed to the Wives and Maidens of France Touching Their Dissolute Adornments*, tr. William Rooke, Edinburgh, privately printed, 1887.

Faret, Nicolas, *L'Honnête homme ou l'art de plaire à la Cour*, Paris, T. du Bray, 1630.

Ferrier, Oger, *Remèdes préservatifs et curatifs de peste*, Lyon, Jean de Tournes, 1548.

Firenzuola, Agnolo, *Discours sur la beauté des dames*, Paris, Abel L'Angelier, 1578 (Italian edn 1548).

Fitelieu, Antoine de, *La Contre-Mode*, Paris, Louis de Heuqueville, 1642.

Fleuret, Fernand, and Louis Perceau, *Les Satires françaises du XVIe siècle*, Paris, Garnier frères, 1922, 2 vols.

Fleury, Claude, *Mœurs des chrétiens*, Paris, Veuve Gervais Clouzier, 1682.

Franklin, Alfred, *La Vie privée d'autrefois: l'hygiène*, Paris, Plon, 1890.

Franklin, Alfred, *La Vie privée d'autrefois: les magasins de nouveautés*, Paris, Plon, 1895.

Gaufridy, Louis, *Confession faicte par messire Louys Gaufridi, prestre en l'église des Accoules à Marseille ... à deux Pères capucins du couvent d'Aix, la veille de Pâques, le onziesme avril mil six cens onze*, Aix, Jean Tholozan, 1611.

Guyon, Loys, *Les Diverses leçons*, Lyon, Claude Morillon, 1604.

Guyon, Loys, *Le Miroir de la beauté et santé corporelle*, Lyon, Claude Prost, 1643, 2 vols.

Hurtault, Pierre-Thomas, *L'Art de péter*, En Westphalie [Paris], Chez Florent-Q, rue Pet-en-Gueule, au Soufflet, 1775 [1st anonymous edn 1751].

J. D. B. [Jean de Bussières], *Les Descriptions poétiques*, Lyon, Jean-Baptiste Devenet, 1649.

Jeune homme instruit en amour (Le), Paphos [Paris], 1764.

Jurgens, Madeleine (ed.), *Ronsard et ses amis: documents du Minutier central des notaires de Paris*, Paris, Archives nationales, 1985.

Juvernay, Pierre, *Discours particulier contre la vanité des femmes de ce temps*, Paris, J. Mestais, 1635; 3rd edn as *Discours particulier contre les femmes débraillées de ce temps*, Paris, Pierre Le Mur, 1637; then as *Discours particulier contre les filles et femmes mondaines découvrans leur sein et portant des moustaches*, Paris, Jérémie Bouillerot, 1640 (repr. Geneva, Gay et fils, 1867).

Lampérière, Jean de, *Traité de la peste, de ses causes et de la cure ...*, Rouen, David du Petit Val, 1620.

Lémery, Louis, *Traité des aliments*, 3rd edn, Paris, Durand, 1755, 2 vols.

Lémery, Nicolas, *Recueil de curiositez rares et nouvelles*, Lausanne, David Gentil, 1681, vol. 1.

Lémery, Nicolas, *Recueil de curiositez rares et nouvelles ... avec de beaux secrets gallans*, Paris, Pierre Trabouillet, 1686.

Lemnius, Levinus, *Les Occultes Merveilles et secretz de nature*, Paris, Galiot du Pré, 1574 (1st Latin edn 1559; 1st French edn 1566).

Liébault, Jean, *Trois livres de l'embellissement et ornement du corps humain*, Paris, Jacques du Puys, 1582.

Liébault, Jean, *Thrésor des remèdes secrets pour les maladies des femmes*, Paris, Jacques du Puys, 1585.

Locatelli, Sébastien, *Voyage de France: mœurs et coutumes françaises (1664–1665)*, tr. Adolphe Vautier, Paris, Alphonse Picard et fils, 1905.

Marot, Clément, *Les Blasons anatomiques du corps féminin*, Paris, Charles L'Angelier, 1543.

Massinger, Philip, *The Plays*, ed. W. Gifford, London, G. and W. Nicol, 1813, vol. 2.

Meurdrac, Marie, *La Chymie charitable et facile en faveur des dames*, 3rd edn, Paris, Laurent d'Houry, 1687 (1st edn 1666; modern edn Paris, CNRS, 1999).

Mizauld, Antoine, *Singuliers secrets et secours contre la peste*, Paris, Mathurin Breuille, 1562.

Navarre, Marguerite de, *L'Heptaméron*, ed. Michel François, based on the 1560 edn, Paris, Garnier, 1996.

Navarre, Marguerite de, *The Heptameron, Or The Tales of Margaret, Queen of Navarre*, tr. George Saintsbury, London, Society of English Bibliophiles, 1894.

Nostredame, Michel de, *Excellent et moult utile opuscule à touts nécessaire qui désirent avoir cognoissance de plusieurs exquises receptes, divisé en deux parties. La première traicte de diverses façons de fardemens et senteurs pour illustrer et embellir la face ...*, Lyon, Antoine Volant, 1555.

Paré, Ambroise, *Traicté de la peste, de la petite verolle et rougeole*, Paris, Gabriel Buon, 1580 (1st edn 1568).

Périers, Bonaventure Des, *Les Nouvelles récréations et joyeux devis de feu Bonaventure Des Périers, valet de chambre de la royne de Navarre*, Lyon, R. Granjon, 1558.

Pliny the Elder, *Natural History*, tr. H. Rackham, Cambridge, MA, Loeb Classical Library, 1961.

Polman, Jean, *Le Chancre, ou couvre-sein féminin, ensemble le voile, ou couvre-chef féminin*, Douai, Gérard Patté, 1635.

Poncelet, Polycarpe, *Chimie du goût et de l'odorat*, Paris, Le Mercier, 1755.

Porta, Jean-Baptiste [Giambattista della Porta], *La Physionomie humaine*, Rouen, Jean et David Berthelin, 1655 (original edn 1586).

Quignard, Pierre, *Blasons anatomiques du corps féminin*, Paris, Gallimard, 1982.

Rainssant, Pierre, *Advis pour se préserver et pour se guérir de la peste de cette année 1668*, Reims, Jean Multeau, 1668.

Ramazzini, Bernardino, *Essai sur les maladies des artisans*, tr. from the Latin [1700], with notes and additions, Antoine- François de Fourcroy, Paris, Moutard, 1777.

Regulation (EC) No. 1334/2008 of the European Parliament and of the Council of 16 December 2008 on flavourings and certain food ingredients with flavouring properties for use in and on foods.

René, François [Étienne Binet], *Essai des merveilles de la nature*, Paris, 1621.

Renou, Jean de, *Le Grand dispensaire médicinal. Contenant cinq livres des institutions pharmaceutiques. Ensemble trois livres de la Matière Médicinale. Avec une pharmacopée, ou Antidotaire fort accompli*, tr. Louys de Serres, Lyon, Pierre Rigaud, 1624.

Renou, Jean de, *Les Œuvres pharmaceutiques du sr Jean de Renou ... augmentées d'un tiers en cette seconde édition par l'auteur; puis traduites, embellies de plusieurs figures nécessaires à la cognoissance de la médecine et pharmacie, et mises en lumière par M. Louys de Serres*, Lyon, N. Gay, 1637 (1st Latin edn 1609).

Rivault, David, *L'Art d'embellir*, Paris, Julien Bertault, 1608.

[Romieu, Marie de, attributed to], *Instructions pour les jeunes dames*, Lyon, Jean Dieppi, 1573.

Ronsard, Pierre de, *Le Livret de folastries à Janot parisien*, Paris, Veuve Maurice de la Porte, 1553 (repr. with additional material from the 1584 edn, Paris, Jules Gay, 1862).

Ronsard, Pierre de, *Les Amours*, ed. Albert-Marie Schmidt, Paris, Le Livre de Poche, 1964.

Rosset, François de, *Les Histoires mémorables et tragiques de ce temps*, ed. Anne de Vaucher Gravili, based on the 1619 edn, Paris, Le Livre de Poche, 1994.

Sala, Angélus, *Traicté de la peste, concernant en bref les causes et accidents d'icelle, la description de plusieurs excellents remèdes, tant pour se préserver de son infection, que pour guérir les pestiferez*, Leiden, G. Basson, 1617.

Scarron, Paul, *L'Héritier ridicule ou la dame intéressée*, Paris, Toussaint Quinet, 1650.

Sorel, Charles, sieur de Souvigny, 'Les Loix de la galanterie', in *Recueil des pièces les plus agréables de ce temps*, Paris, Nicolas de Sercy, 1644.

[Tabourot, Étienne, sieur des Accords], *Les Escraignes dijonnoises, composées par le feu sieur du Buisson*, 2nd edn, Lyon, Thomas Soubron, 1592.

Turnèbe, Odet de, *Les Contents*, ed. Norman B. Spector, Paris, Nizet, 1984.

Turnèbe, Odet de, *Satisfaction All Around*, tr. Donald Beecher, Ottawa, Carleton University Renaissance Centre, 1979.

Vigneulles, Philippe de, *Les Cent Nouvelles nouvelles*, ed., intro. and notes Charles H. Livingston, assisted by R. Livingston and Robert H. Ivy Jr, Geneva, Droz, 1972.

Select bibliography

'Les 10 catégories d'odeurs les plus répandues', *Huffington Post* 20 September 2013, http://www.huffingtonpost.fr/2013/09/20/dix-categories-odeur-les-plus-repandues_n_3960728.html

Ackerman, Diane, *A Natural History of the Senses*, New York, Random House, 1990.

Aït Medjane, Ouarda, *Des maisons parisiennes: le Marais de 1502 à 1552. L'apport des inventaires après décès*, Master's dissertation, supervisor Robert Muchembled, Université de Paris-Nord, 2007.

Albert, Jean-Pierre, *Odeurs de sainteté: la mythologie chrétienne des aromates*, Paris, Éditions de l'EHESS, 1990.

Bailbé, Jacques, 'Le thème de la vieille femme dans la poésie satirique du XVIe et du début du XVIIe siècle', *Bibliothèque d'Humanisme et Renaissance* 26, 1964, pp. 98–119.

Bakhtin, Mikhail, *Rabelais and His World*, tr. Hélène Iswolsky, Bloomington, Indiana University Press, 1984.

Barbelane, Nicolas, *Les Canards surnaturels, 1598–1630*, Master's dissertation, supervisor Robert Muchembled, Université de Paris-Nord, 2000.

Barthes, Roland, *Système de la mode*, Paris, Seuil, 1967.

Barwich, Anne-Sophie, 'What Is So Special about Smell? Olfaction as a Model System in Neurobiology', *Postgraduate Medical Journal*, November 2015, http://dx.doi.org/10.1136/postgradmedj-2015-133249

Baulant, Micheline, 'Prix et salaires à Paris au XVIe siècle: sources et résultats', *Annales ESC* 31, 1976, pp. 954–5.

Berriot-Salvadore, Évelyne, *Un corps, un destin: la femme dans la médecine de la Renaissance*, Paris, Champion, 1993.

Bigard, Marc-André, Interview dated 18 August 2011, in 'La chasse aux pets? Mission impossible . . .', *L'Information santé au quotidien*, destinationsante.com

Biniek, Aurélie, *Odeurs et parfums aux XVIe et XVIIe siècles*, Master's dissertation, supervisor Robert Muchembled, Université de Paris-Nord, 1998.

Blanc-Mouchet, Jacqueline, with Martyne Perrot, *Odeurs: l'essence d'un sens*, Paris, Autrement, 1987.

Bodiou, Lydie, and Véronique Mehl (eds.), *Odeurs antiques*, Paris, Les Belles Lettres, 2011.

Boillot, Francine, Marie-Christine Grasse and André Holley, *Olfaction et patrimoine: quelle transmission?*, Aix-en-Provence, Edisud, 2004.

Bologne, Jean-Claude, *Histoire de la pudeur*, Paris, Olivier Orban, 1986.

Boudriot, Pierre-Denis, 'Essai sur l'ordure en milieu urbain à l'époque préindustrielle: boues, immondices et gadoue à Paris au XVIIIe siècle', *Histoire, économies et sociétés* 5, 1985, pp. 515–28.

Bourke, John G., *Scatologic Rites of All Nations*, Washington, DC, W. H. Lowdermilk, 1891.

Bowen, Barbara C., *Humour and Humanism in the Renaissance*, Farnham, Ashgate, 2004.

Briot, Eugénie, 'Jean-Louis Fargeon, fournisseur de la cour de France: art et techniques d'un parfumeur du XVIIIe siècle', in *Artefact: techniques, histoire et sciences humaines* 1: *Corps parés, corps parfumés*, Paris, CNRS, 2013, pp. 167–77.

Brouardel, Paul, *La Mort et la mort subite*, Paris, J.-B. Baillière et fils, 1895.

Bushdid, Caroline, Marcelo O. Magnasco, Leslie B. Vosshall and Andreas Keller, 'Humans Can Discriminate More Than 1 Trillion Olfactory Stimuli', *Science* 343, 2014, pp. 1370–2.

Cabré, Monique, Marina Sebbag and Vincent Vidal, *Femmes de papier: une histoire du geste parfumé*, Toulouse, Éditions Milan, 1998.

Camporesi, Piero, *Les Effluves du temps jadis*, Paris, Plon, 1995.

Candau, Joël, *Mémoires et expériences olfactives: anthropologie d'un savoir-faire sensoriel*, Paris, PUF, 2000.

Castro, Jason B., Arvind Ramanathan and Chakra S. Chennubhotla, 'Categorical Dimensions of Human Odor Descriptor Space Revealed by Non-Negative Matrix Factorization', *Plos One* 18 September 2013, http://dx.doi.org/10.1371/journal.pone.0073289

Chauvière, André, *Parfums et senteurs du Grand Siècle*, Lausanne, Favre, 1999.

Classen, Constance, David Howes and Anthony Synnott, *Aroma: The Cultural History of Smell*, London, Routledge, 1994.

Closson, Marianne, *L'Imaginaire démoniaque en France (1550–1650): genèse de la littérature fantastique*, Geneva, Droz, 2000.

Clouzeau, Sylvie, *L'Art de paraître féminin au XVIIe siècle*, DEA dissertation, supervisor Robert Muchembled, Université de Paris-Nord, 2002.

Condorcet, Jean-Antoine-Nicolas de Caritat, Marquis de, *Condorcet: Political Writings*, ed. Steven Lukes and Nadia Urbinati, Cambridge, Cambridge University Press, 2012.

Corbin, Alain, *The Foul and the Fragrant: Odor and the French Social Imagination*, tr. Miriam Kochan, Cambridge, MA, Harvard University Press, 1986.

Corps parés, corps parfumés: *Artefact: techniques, histoire et sciences humaines* 1, Paris, CNRS, 2013.

Coulmas, Corinna, *Métaphores des cinq sens dans l'imaginaire occidental*, vol. 3: *L'odorat*, Paris, Les Éditions La Métamorphose, undated.

Croix, Alain, *L'Âge d'or de la Bretagne, 1532–1675*, Rennes, Ouest France, 1993.

Damasio, Antonio R., *Le Sentiment même de soi: corps, émotion, conscience*, Paris, Odile Jacob, 1999 (edn Poche, 2002).

Dauphin, Cécile, and Arlette Farge (eds.), *Séduction et sociétés: approches historiques*, Paris, Seuil, 2001.

Delaveau, Pierre, *Histoire et renouveau des plantes médicinales*, Paris, Albin Michel, 1982.

Dobson, Mary, *Smelly Old History: Tudor Odours*, Oxford, Oxford University Press, 1997 (for children).

Donzel, Catherine, *Le Parfum*, Paris, Éditions du Chêne, 2000.

Doty, Richard L., and E. Leslie Cameron, 'Sex Differences and Reproductive Hormone Influences on Human Odor Perception', *Physiology and Behavior* 97, 25 May 2009, pp. 213–28.

Doucet, Sébastien, Robert Soussignan, Paul Sagot and Benoist Schaal, 'The Secretion of Areolar (Montgomery's) Glands from Lactating Women Elicits Selective, Unconditional Responses in Neonates', *Plos One* 23 October 2009, http://dx.doi.org/10.1371/journal.pone.0007579

Dulau, Robert, and Jean-Robert Pitte (eds.), *Géographie des odeurs*, Paris, L'Harmattan, 1998.

Duperey, Anny, *Essences et parfums*, Paris, Ramsay, 2004 (anthology).

Elias, Norbert, *The Civilizing Process*, Oxford, Blackwell, 1969, 1982 (1st German edn 1939).

Erikson, Erik, *Childhood and Society*, London, Vintage, 1995 (1st edn 1950).

Falkenburg, Reindert L., 'De duiven buiten beeld: over duivelafwerende krachten en motieven in de beeldende kunst rond 1500', in Gerard Rooijakkers, Lène Dresen-Coenders and Margreet Geerdes (eds.), *Duivelsbeelden: een cultuurhistorische speurtocht door de Lage Landen*, Barn, Ambo, 1994, pp. 107–22.

Faure, Paul, *Parfums et aromates de l'Antiquité*, Paris, Fayard, 1987.

Febvre, Lucien, *Autour de l'Heptaméron: amour sacré, amour profane*, Paris, Gallimard, 1944.

Ferenczi, Sándor, *Thalassa: A Theory of Genitality*, tr. H. Bunker, New York, Psychoanalytic Quarterly, 1938.

Ferino-Pagden, Sylvia (ed.), *I cinque sensi nell'arte: immagini del sentire*, Centro culturale 'Città di Cremona' in San Maria della Pietà, Leonardo Arte, 1996.

Finkel, Jori, 'An Artist's Intentions (and Subjects) Exposed' [on Isaac van Ostade], *The New York Times*, 23 December 2015, p. C2.

Galopin, Augustin, *Le Parfum de la femme et le sens olfactif dans l'amour: étude psycho-physiologique*, Paris, Dentu, 1886.

Gay, Victor, and Henri Stein, *Glossaire archéologique du Moyen Âge et de la Renaissance*, Paris, Société Bibliographique, 1928, vol. 2.

Gerkin, Richard C., and Jason B. Castro, 'The Number of Olfactory Stimuli that Humans Can Discriminate Is Still Unknown', *eLIFE*, 7 July 2015, http://dx.doi.org/10.7554/eLife.08127

Girard, P. S., 'Recherches sur les établissements de bains publics à Paris depuis le IVe siècle jusqu'à présent', *Annales d'hygiène publique et de médecine légale* 7, part 1, 1832, pp. 5–59.

Godard de Donville, Louise, *Signification de la mode sous Louis XIII*, Aix-en-Provence, Edisud, 1978.

Goffman, Erving, *Relations in Public: Microstudies of the Public Order*, New Brunswick, Transaction, 2010.

Guerrand, Roger-Louis, *Les Lieux: histoire des commodités*, Paris, La Découverte, 1997.

Guerrand, Roger-Louis, 'Prolégomènes à une géographie des flatulences', in Robert Dulau and Jean-Robert Pitte (eds.), *Géographie des odeurs*, Paris, L'Harmattan, 1998, pp. 73–7.

Hatt, Hanns, and Regine Dee, *La Chimie de l'amour: quand les sentiments ont une odeur*, Paris, CNRS Éditions, 2009.

Herz, Rachel, *The Scent of Desire: Discovering Our Enigmatic Sense of Smell*, New York, William Morrow, 2007.

Holley, André, *Éloge de l'odorat*, Paris, Odile Jacob, 1999.

'Hommes, parfums et dieux', *Le Courrier du musée de l'Homme* 6, November 1980 (exhibition newsletter).

Kassel, Dominique, 'La pharmacie au Grand Siècle: image et rôle du pharmacien au travers de la littérature', IVe rencontres d'histoire de la médecine et des représentations médicales dans les sociétés anciennes, université de Reims-Champagne-Ardennes, Troyes, 20–1 January 2006, http://artet patrimoinepharmaceutique.fr/Publications/p63/La-pharmacie-au-Grand-siecle-image-et- role-du-pharmacien-au-travers-de-la-litterature

Kauffeisen, L., 'Au temps de la Marquise de Sévigné: l'eau d'émeraude, l'essence d'urine et l'eau de millefleurs', *Bulletin de la Société d'histoire de la pharmacie* 16, 1928, pp. 162–5.

Klein, H. Arthur, *Graphic Worlds of Peter Bruegel the Elder*, New York, Dover Publications, 1963.

Laget, Mireille, 'Les livrets de santé pour les pauvres aux XVIIe et XVIIIe siècles', *Histoire, économies et sociétés* 4, 1984, pp. 567–82.

Laporte, Dominique, *History of Shit*, tr. Nadia Benabid and Rodolphe El-Khoury, Cambridge, MA, MIT Press, 2000.

Lardellier, Pascal (ed.), *À fleur de peau: corps, odeurs et parfums*, Paris, Belin, 2003.

Le Breton, David, *Sensing the World: An Anthropology of the Senses*, tr. Carmen Ruschiensky, London, Bloomsbury, 2017.

Le Guérer, Annick, *Les Pouvoirs de l'odeur*, Paris, François Bourin, 1998.

Le Guérer, Annick, *Le Parfum, des origines à nos jours*, Paris, Odile Jacob, 2005.

Leguay, Jean-Pierre, *La Rue au Moyen Âge*, Rennes, Ouest France, 1984.

Leguay, Jean-Pierre, *La Pollution au Moyen Âge dans le royaume de France et dans les grands fiefs*, Paris, Gisserot, 1999.

Leguay, Jean-Pierre, 'La laideur de la rue polluée à la fin du Moyen Âge: "immondicités, fiens et bouillons" accumulés sur les chaussées des villes du royaume de France et des grands fiefs au XVe siècle', in *Le Beau et le Laid au Moyen Âge*, Aix-en-Provence, Presses Universitaires de Provence, 2000, pp. 301–17.

Liebel, Silvia, *Les Médées modernes: la cruauté féminine d'après les canards imprimés (1574–1651)*, Rennes, PUR, 2013.

Mandrou, Robert, *Introduction à la France moderne: essai de psychologie historique, 1500–1640*, Paris, Albin Michel, 1961; new edition, 1998.

Matthews-Grieco, Sara, *Ange ou diablesse: la représentation de la femme au XVIe siècle*, Paris, Flammarion, 1991.

Meister, Markus, 'On the Dimensionality of Odor Space', *eLife*, 7 July 2015, http://dx.doi.org/10.7554/eLife.07865

Menjot, Denis (ed.), *Les Soins de beauté au Moyen-Âge et début des Temps modernes*, actes du IIIe colloque international de Grasse, 26–8 April 1985, Nice, Université de Nice, 1987.

Michaud, Louis-Gabriel, *Biographie universelle, ancienne et moderne*, new edn, Paris, A. Thoisnier Desplaces, 1852, vol. 10.

Muchembled, Robert, *L'Invention de l'homme moderne: culture et sensibilités en France du XVe au XVIIIe siècle*, Paris, Hachette, 1994.

Muchembled, Robert, *La Société policée: politique et politesse en France du XVIe au XXe siècle*, Paris, Seuil, 1998.

Muchembled, Robert, *A History of the Devil: From the Middle Ages to the Present*, tr. Jean Birrell, Cambridge, Polity, 2003.

Muchembled, Robert, *Passions de femmes au temps de la reine Margot, 1553–1615*, Paris, Seuil, 2003.

Muchembled, Robert, 'Fils de Caïn, enfants de Médée: homicide et infanticide devant le parlement de Paris, 1575–1604', *Annales Histoire, Sciences sociales* 62, 2007, pp. 1063–94.

Muchembled, Robert, Hervé Bennezon and Marie-José Michel, *Histoire du grand Paris, de la Renaissance à la Révolution*, Paris, Perrin, 2009.

Musset, Didier, Claudine Fabre-Vassas (eds.), *Odeurs et parfums*, Paris, Comité des travaux historiques et scientifiques, 1999.

Nagnan-Le Meillour, Patricia, 'Les phéromones: vertébrés et invertébrés', in Roland Salesse and Rémi Gervais (eds.), *Odorat et goût: de la neurobiologie des sens chimiques aux applications*, Versailles, Éditions Quæ, 2012, pp. 39–46.

Pérez, Stanis, 'L'eau de fleur d'oranger à la cour de Louis XIV', in *Artefact: techniques, histoire et sciences humaines* 1: *Corps parés, corps parfumés*, Paris, CNRS, 2013, pp. 107–25.

Pérouse, Gabriel A., *Nouvelles françaises du XVIe siècle: images de la vie du temps*, Geneva, Droz, 1977.

Poiret, Nathalie, 'Odeurs impures: du corps humain à la Cité (Grenoble, XVIIIe–XIXe siècle)', *Terrain* 31, September 1998, pp. 89–102.

Renaud, Michel, *Pour une lecture du Moyen de parvenir de Béroalde de Verville*, 2nd rev. edn, Paris, Champion, 1997.

Roubin, Lucienne A., *Le Monde des odeurs: dynamique et fonctions du champ odorant*, Paris, Méridiens Klincksieck, 1989.

Roudnitska, Edmond, *Le Parfum*, Paris, PUF, 1990.

Salesse, Roland, and Rémi Gervais (eds.), *Odorat et goût: de la neurobiologie des sens chimiques aux applications*, Versailles, Éditions Quæ, 2012.

Salmon, Xavier (ed.), *De soie et de poudre: portraits de cour dans l'Europe des Lumières*, Arles, Actes Sud, 2004.

Salzmann, C., 'Masques portés par les médecins en temps de peste', *Æsculape* 1, January 1932, pp. 5–14.

Saulnier, Verdun L., 'Étude sur Béroalde de Verville: introduction à la lecture du *Moyen de parvenir*', *Bibliothèque d'Humanisme et Renaissance* 5, 1944, pp. 209–326.

Schivelbusch, Wolfgang, *Tastes of Paradise: A Social History of Spices, Stimulants, and Intoxicants*, tr. David Jacobson, New York, Pantheon, 1992.

Secundo, Lavi, et al., 'Individual Olfactory Perception Reveals Meaningful Nonolfactory Genetic Information', *Proceedings of the National Academy of Sciences of the United States of America* 112(28), 14 July 2015, pp. 8750–55.

Sennett, Richard, *The Fall of Public Man*, New York, Vintage, 1974.

Soussignan, Robert, Fayez Kontar and Richard E. Tremblay, 'Variabilité et universaux au sein de l'espace perçu des odeurs: approches inter-culturelles de l'hédonisme affectif', in Robert Dulau and Jean-Robert Pitte (eds.), *Géographie des odeurs*, Paris, L'Harmattan, 1998, pp. 25–48.

Sulmont-Rossé, Claire, and Isabel Urdapilletta, 'De la mise en mots des odeurs', in Roland Salesse and Rémi Gervais (eds.), *Odorat et goût: de la neurobiologie des sens chimiques aux applications*, Versailles, Éditions Quæ, 2012, pp. 373–9.

Süskind, Patrick, *Perfume: The Story of a Murderer*, tr. John E. Woods, New York, Vintage, 1986.

Syme, Rachel, 'Do I Smell a Bat? Oh, It's You', *The New York Times*, 27 October 2016, p. D5.

Tran Ba Huy, Patrice, 'Odorat et histoire sociale', *Communications et langages* 126, 2000, pp. 84–107.

Viala, Alain, *Naissance de l'écrivain: sociologie de la littérature à l'âge classique*, Paris, Minuit, 1985.

Vigarello, Georges, *Concepts of Cleanliness: Changing Attitudes in France since the Middle Ages*, tr. Jean Birrell, Cambridge, Cambridge University Press, 1988.

Vigée Le Brun, exhibition catalogue, ed. Joseph Baillio, Katharine Baetjer and Paul Lang, New York, Metropolitan Museum of Art, 2016.

Winter, Ruth, *The Smell Book: Scents, Sex, and Society*, Philadelphia, Lippincott, 1976.

Zoologist perfumes, https://www.zoologistperfumes.com

Zucco, Gesualdo M., Rachel S. Herz and Benoist Schaal (eds.), *Olfactory Cognition: From Perception and Memory to Environmental Odours and Neuroscience*, Amsterdam and Philadelphia, John Benjamins, 2012.

Zucco, Gesualdo M., Benoist Schaal, Mats Olsson and Ilona Croy, *Applied Olfactory Cognition*, foreword Richard J. Stevenson, Frontiers Media, 2014, eBook.

Index

Note: illustrations are indicated by references in italics.